TRACING YOUR
EAST END ANCESTORS

FAMILY HISTORY FROM PEN & SWORD

Tracing Your Yorkshire Ancestors
Rachel Bellerby

Tracing Your Royal Marine Ancestors
Richard Brooks and Matthew Little

Tracing Your Pauper Ancestors
Robert Burlison

Tracing Your Labour Movement Ancestors
Mark Crail

Tracing Your Army Ancestors
Simon Fowler

A Guide to Military History on the Internet
Simon Fowler

Tracing Your Northern Ancestors
Keith Gregson

Your Irish Ancestors
Ian Maxwell

Tracing Your Scottish Ancestors
Ian Maxwell

Tracing Your London Ancestors
Jonathan Oates

Tracing Your Air Force Ancestors
Phil Tomaselli

Tracing Your Secret Service Ancestors
Phil Tomaselli

Tracing Your Criminal Ancestors
Stephen Wade

Tracing Your Police Ancestors
Stephen Wade

Tracing Your Jewish Ancestors
Rosemary Wenzerul

Fishing and Fishermen
Martin Wilcox

TRACING YOUR
EAST END ANCESTORS

A guide to tracing ancestry from what is now the London Borough of Tower Hamlets, including: Aldgate, Artillery Liberty, Bethnal Green, Bishopsgate, Blackwall, Bow (Stratford le Bow), Bromley, East Smithfield, Limehouse, Mile End, Mile End New Town, Millwall, Norton Folgate, Old Ford, Portsoken, Poplar, Ratcliff, St Katharine's, Spitalfields, Stepney, The Isle of Dogs, Tower Liberty, Wapping and Whitechapel

J A N E   C O X

Pen & Sword
FAMILY HISTORY

First published in Great Britain in 2011 by
PEN & SWORD FAMILY HISTORY

an imprint of
Pen & Sword Books Ltd
47 Church Street
Barnsley
South Yorkshire
S70 2AS

ISBN 978-1-84884-160-4

A CIP catalogue record for this book
is available from the British Library

Typeset in 10/12pt Palatino by Concept, Huddersfield
Printed and bound in Great Britain by
CPI Antony Rowe, Chippenham, Wiltshire

Pen & Sword Books Ltd incorporates the Imprints of Pen & Sword
Aviation, Pen & Sword Maritime, Pen & Sword Military,
Wharncliffe Local History, Pen & Sword Select, Pen & Sword
Military Classics, Leo Cooper, Remember When, Seaforth Publishing
and Frontline Publishing.

For a complete list of Pen & Sword titles please contact
PEN & SWORD BOOKS LIMITED
47 Church Street, Barnsley, South Yorkshire, S70 2AS, England
E-mail: enquiries@pen-and-sword.co.uk
Website: www.pen-and-sword.co.uk

CONTENTS

Dedication

This book is dedicated to my family, especially Lil Daniels, my nan, wood chopper of Old Ford; Henry Daniels, my Great-Uncle who exposed a scam for providing fresh air for sick Bethnal Green children and died in Poplar Workhouse; his brother, who worked in the Whitechapel Bell Foundry; his sister, Esther, who died of phossyjaw contracted in the match factory; my granddad, Sid Short, oil and colourman of Roman Road, attender at Old Ford Wesleyan; his brother, Sam, Baptist butcher of Bethnal Green; Lil Short, my mum, who won the gold medal for the best soprano at the Bow and Bromley musical festival (c. 1930); Vi Short, my aunt, twice head girl of Coborn School; my first husband, Jim, with whom I lived in Stepney and drank in the Brown Bear (see p. 167); my son, Charles, born in the London Hospital; my son, Oliver, who works in the Isle of Dogs; his daughter, Georgia, who, in the best traditions of East Enders (although she is not one), has a mix of blood, mainly Irish; his sons, Joseph and James, descended from a good old East End line on their mother's side.

PREFACE

East Enders are a very special breed and tracing your East End ancestry is going to be tremendous fun. Everyone has got some East End ancestors – and if they haven't they invent them, rollicking chaps, larky and resourceful, talking a funny language to keep 'them' guessing, eating at eel and pie shops, shouting out their wares in clattering, colourful markets. Their wives and masters (' 'er in doors') are brazen lassies, smart as paint, tough as their men folk, presiding over an undoubted matriarchal society where Mum rules OK? The good tales are of bright little kids, unshod and street wise, rising above their origins and making a mint. The bad ones are of indescribable horror – children dying in diseased heaps, infant sex for sale and gangs of armed bandits terrorising the neighbourhood.

The East End of our great grandparents' days was another world. Let us see just what we can find out.

ACKNOWLEDGEMENTS

M y thanks to the staff of Tower Hamlets Local History Library, the old Guildhall Library, the London Metropolitan Archives and The National Archives.

I am grateful to Jane Seal for splendid maps, to Yvonne Hughes for photographs, to Geoff Mann for access to his research on the Short family, to Charles Hoare for IT help, to Katharine Hoare for advice and encouragement, to Jan Hoare for telling me what questions I should address, and to Patsy Douglas for proofreading.

All websites listed were correct at the time of going to press. Please be aware that some LMA records transferred from Guildhall have now been returned – notably the Livery Company records – and therefore it is advisable to check before visiting.

ABBREVIATIONS

A2A	Access to Archives at: www.nationalarchives.gov.uk/a2a
Admons	Letters of administration (made in cases of intestacy)
AGFHS	Anglo German Family History Society
AIM25	Archives in the London and M25 area at: www.aim25.ac.uk/
Ancestry	Ancestry website at: www.ancestry.co.uk
Baps	Baptisms
BG	Bethnal Green
BL	British Library
BHOL	British History Online
CLRO	Corporation of London Record Office
EoLFHS	East of London Family History Society
FFHS	Federation of Family History Societies
The Genealogist	Website at: www.thegenealogist.co.uk
GRO	General Register Office (referring to the central registration of births, marriages and deaths)
IGI	International Genealogical Index – Mormon index of parish register entries and other material
IHGS	Institute of Heraldic and Genealogical Studies
IOL	India Office Library (collection now at BL)
JGSGB	Jewish Genealogical Society of Great Britain
LDS	Church of Jesus Christ of Latter-Day Saints (Mormons)
LMA	London Metropolitan Archive (now incorporating most of the archives formerly held at Guildhall Library and Corporation of London Record Office)

MEOT	Mile End Old Town
MENT	Mile End New Town
MI	Monumental inscription
MID	Museum in Docklands
MS	Manuscript
NRA	National Register of Archives (at TNA)
Origins	British Origins website at: www.originsnetwork.com
PCC	Prerogative Court of Canterbury
PPR	Principal Probate Registry
RD	Registration District
SOG	Society of Genealogists
THAOL	Tower Hamlets Archives On Line
THHOL	Tower Hamlets History On Line
THLHLA	Tower Hamlets Local History Library and Archives
TLMAS	*Transactions of the London & Middlesex Archaeologica Society*
TNA	The National Archives
VCH	*Victoria County History* online at: www.british.history.ac.uk
WDA	Westminster Diocesan Archives

INTRODUCTION:
LONDON'S EAST END,
A PLACE OF COMING AND GOING

The slum that developed on London's eastern flank was christened the 'East End' in the late nineteenth century. This is a vague term, possibly embracing what are now the London Boroughs of Newham, Hackney and parts of Islington, as well as Tower Hamlets. Some people even seem to think that it includes the ancient suburb of Southwark, south of the River Thames! The true East End, however, is the area to the immediate east of the City of London, and this is the area covered within this book. When reference is made to 'East Enders' this refers exclusively to the inhabitants of what is now the London Borough of Tower Hamlets, an area of 7.6 square miles to the east of the City, most of it formerly in the county of Middlesex. The Index of Multiple Deprivation ranks it as England's most deprived borough, in spite of the huge financial development at Canary Wharf. For hundreds of years it has been a place of coming and going.

On a genealogical lecture tour of Australia and New Zealand some years ago, I got into the habit of asking my audience (which often numbered several hundred) to raise their hands if any of them had ancestry from Stepney or Bethnal Green. There was always a forest of hands. Conversation with them afterwards revealed that the names Mile End, Limehouse and the rest were as familiar to them as they are to me. It was the same when I visited Salt Lake City in the USA.

New World families with some East End ancestry are legion. From Stepney's riverside hamlets some 400 years ago, explorers set off in search of America, recruiting local lads, many of whom settled there. As the group of little towns and villages on London's eastern flank swelled and merged together to become the notorious Victorian slum, its trademarks became crime and poverty. Numerous East Enders were deported to the Australian colonies and later went as voluntary emigrants to start a new life.

Here in the UK, too, it is a rare family that does not at some point in its history have some East End connections. For hundreds of years 'London's backyard' offered work and cheap accommodation to 'Dick Whittingtons' from the countryside. From the days of Henry VIII young people from all over England and Wales, from Scotland and from Ireland, would leave the land, partly driven out by the enclosure of common land and partly drawn to the 'Great Wen' to make their fortune. Perhaps their family stayed put for a couple of generations. By the late nineteenth century, as many people lived in the eastern suburbs of London as did in the whole of Berlin or Philadelphia. This new East End even claimed the outlying villages of East and West Ham, which had hitherto retained their rural aspect. A vast city of the poor lay on London's side, where no gentry were to be found, except the clergy, a place feared and abhorred by the 'better sort'. 'Poverty,' wrote the father of Sir William Beveridge, architect of the welfare state, 'wore a

Tower Hamlets as part of Greater London.

15

worse face in the East End than it did in Calcutta'. Anyone who did well for themselves moved away, many of them to the sunnier climes of north London or rural Essex, others further a field.

As the river access point to London from the Continent, offering employment in the servicing of the capital, free from the City's trade restrictions, with numerous lodging houses and inexpensive properties, the East End has been the traditional place of initial settlement for religious exiles and traders from abroad. In the Middle Ages came the Flemings, then the Irish, Jews from Spain and then Eastern Europe, followed by West Indians and, these days, immigrants from India, Pakistan and Bangladesh.

For the period that primarily concerns today's family historian, namely the last 200 years, East End ancestry can be a challenge. Trying to trace people in this huge shifting, unruly society has its particular problems. Many of these are the issues encountered in any search for poor individuals; these ancestors of ours tended to leave less account of themselves than their 'betters'. A tiny proportion of Victorian or Edwardian East Enders left wills, for instance, and you are unlikely to find any collections of private family papers. Hardly anybody owned

London boroughs, 1900–65.

the house they lived in, or were even the chief tenants, so deeds are unlikely to help much. Often they did not bother with formal marriage; according to Henry Mayhew, writing in the 1850s, costers rarely married. East Enders resisted the registration of births and, according to Alexander Heriot Mackonochie, ritualist vicar at St Peter's London Docks, reporting in 1883, displayed a 'positive hostility to the sacrament of baptism'. The fear of authority common among 'the submerged' made them more likely than most to avoid the census enumerator or to be economical with the truth. Just to add to the confusion, many

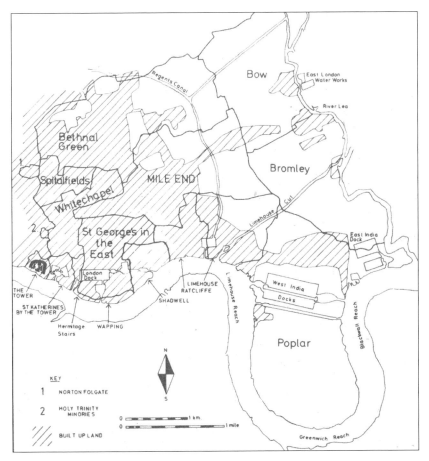

The East End in 1832. Map by Robert Higgins, copied from Colm Kerrigan's *History of Tower Hamlets* (Tower Hamlets, 1982)

foreigners settling here changed their names, often without going through any legal formality. It was always easy to hide in the over-crowded lodging houses and multi-occupation dwellings of a great conurbation and it comes as no surprise that many of our East End forbears have covered their tracks.

Another set of problems arise from the rapid growth of the area, the proliferation of parishes and other administrative units and boundary changes. Should you look for your ancestors in the records of London or Middlesex, for instance? It is a good idea when consulting indexes or searching websites for places in Tower Hamlets to look at both London and Middlesex entries. Stepney is especially confusing; it starts as one great Middlesex parish encompassing most of modern Tower Hamlets, shrinks almost to nothing and then becomes a London borough, larger in size than the old parish.

This guide in designed to help the stranger through the maze of courts and alleys that was the home of his ancestors and to bring to life that vibrant, polyglot society, which was a nursery for great endeavour, the cradle of the architects of a New World and the school room of socialism. It will take him back though the Blitz, the Depression, the Edwardian music halls, the Victorian workhouses, past the shifty costers in Petticoat Lane, the desperate men clamouring for work at the dock gates, to the days when sailors whistled along Wapping High Street, the Great Windmill whirred in Whitechapel, Bethnal Green and Spitalfields hummed with the clack of looms and cattle lowed in the lush pastures of the Isle of Dogs.

Chapter 1

OUR ANCESTORS IN CONTEXT: A SUMMARY HISTORY OF TOWER HAMLETS

I hate to see how this vast area is popularly regarded as a mere aggregate of dull and commonplace poverty, interesting only as an object of philanthropic effort or social research, or as a show-place to gratify a morbid curiosity to learn 'how the poor live'.

Sir Hubert Llewellyn Smith,
historian of East London, 1939

Was it Always a Poor, Deprived Area?

We are all familiar with the East End's reputation: the swirling smogs of Dickens' Limehouse, the grey monotony of the streets of two-up two-downs, families of ten living in a single room in Bethnal Green, the horrors of the Poplar Workhouse, the 'ghetto' in Whitechapel, Jack the Ripper and all his works. In virtually any history of London, the east side is noticeably absent until the issue of poverty is addressed.

There is another tradition, held by some East Enders themselves, that not so long ago it was a splendid place with pretty squares, fine houses and idyllic villages beyond.

The truth lies somewhere between the two. The collection of towns and villages to the City's east were most diverse in character, some similar to slums of long ago. The suburbs that grew up near the Tower were rough in medieval times, outside Aldgate there was industrial activity in Chaucer's day, bread for the City was baked on a large scale in Bow and by the seventeenth century the riverside hamlets were full of sailors' lodging houses. Bethnal Green and Spitalfields became poor weaving towns in the eighteenth century, while Mile End Old Town and Stepney village were up-market, residential districts. It was not until the late nineteenth century that a combination of factors saw the East End as we know it come into being as a 'city of terrible night' and the 'working end of town'.

Before then London's industrial quarters were distributed all over the place, with 'rookeries', as the slums were known, snuggling close up to some of the wealthiest areas. In the eighteenth and nineteenth centuries the worst part of London was Seven Dials and Drury Lane, followed by Saffron Hill and the Fleet Ditch area between Clerkenwell Green and Smithfield, where Fagin had his kitchen. By the time the County of London came into being at the very end of the nineteenth century, however, no middle-class person would venture east of Aldgate Pump, except do-gooders and the clergy.

The Middle Ages

This period will not be examined in too much detail as the chances of researching a family back to medieval times in Tower Hamlets or anywhere else is rather remote. However, it is feasible; descent has been traced from Richard Etgoose, who ran the lime kilns in fifteenth-century Limehouse. In any case, if you are going to be truly proud of your East End heritage, you should know a little about how it all started.

To start at the very beginning, recent archaeological discoveries have revealed Old Ford is probably older than London itself and that the Romans built a port at Ratcliff.

Stepney is the first East End place name to appear in the records, as Stybbanhythe (in 1000 AD), although its hamlets have Saxon names and are almost certainly of great antiquity. Perhaps from early Saxon times, the Lord of Stepney Manor was the Bishop of London, holding sway over all Tower Hamlets and most of Hackney. He certainly was by the time William the Conqueror arrived, as the Domesday Book shows, and he continued to be the major landholder until the Reformation, when the Wentworth family took over. Medieval Shadwell belonged to the canons of St Paul's, the Portsoken (East Smithfield and Aldgate) to Holy Trinity Priory.

Stepney village (where the church still stands and, according to tradition, has done since the seventh century) stood on fertile flood-plain gravel, half a mile or so from the river bank. To the north (Bethnal Green area, where the Bishop's palace was) lay an immense forest, where stags, bucks, boars and bulls flourished. Wapping, Shadwell and Stepney Marsh were soggy places that had to be drained to be of any use. By the opening of the fourteenth century, Bow (the baking centre at the bridgehead over the Lea) and Whitechapel were busy enough to have their own chapels. Whitechapel and Aldgate were becoming centres for gun smiths and allied trades, because of their proximity to the armouries at the Tower. Stepney Marsh was quite a lively farming area, with its own little chapel of St Mary, until the Great Flood of 1448 put the peninsula and much of the rest of Stepney parish under water for sixteen years.

Most medieval East Enders were, of course, engaged in farming and fishing. Hay was cultivated for the metropolitan horses, corn for the City's bread and the low-lying wetlands were pasture or fisheries. There must have been a number of millers around to man the water mills on the Lea and the Thames and the windmills in the area; Dickens noticed the stump of an old windmill still standing in Limehouse in his day. A good deal of corn had to be ground to supply loaves for the City; Bow was already London's 'bread basket'. Lime for use as mortar for building work was made at the kilns and bricks were produced in Whitechapel. Limehouse acquired its name in the fourteenth century and Brick Lane was so-named within a hundred years. In the late fifteenth century, Richard Etgoose was the chief limeman, although he had started out in life as a fisherman. By the time of his death in 1503, he owned the local kilns and also kilns in Greenwich, two wharves, had built some thirteen houses, owned a brewery and 50 acres in the Marsh.

At Ratcliff (now the Limehouse Link area) there was some ship building and everywhere there were breweries. It was a brewer who paid for Stepney church's fifteenth-century belfry, just as Charrington's supported the church 400 years later. There was a brewery where the Prospect of Whitby pub now stands, in Wapping Wall; it belonged to the City monastery of St Thomas of Acon, and was sold by Henry VIII for an astronomical sum when he closed the monasteries down.

Already by this time there were a number of foreign immigrants in the area. In the 1440s the rector of Stepney employed Flemings in his brewery and in the 1480s the great Ratcliff brewery was run by a Fleming called William Harman. In the fifteenth century Flemish,

Dutch and German immigrants were a strong presence in the East End, known collectively as 'Dochemen'. Brought in originally by Edward III to improve the cloth trade, they continued to come and settled in St Katharine's, East Smithfield, Aldgate, Whitechapel and Bow. The main concentration of foreigners in London was not, as is often claimed, in St Clement Danes and Southwark. As the alien-tax lists clearly show, there were as many, if not more 'Dutch' on the east side of the city. In the unruly parts near the Tower poor Flemish girls plied their trade as prostitutes and rich madams ran brothels and gaming houses, paying a fine to the Abbot of St Mary Graces for breaking the law, year after year.

This medieval East End was a watery place and this is reflected in many of the personal names that feature in the records at a time when ordinary people were beginning to be known by their address (or trade). Our first Limehouse limeman was called Dyk (dyke); the atte Ferry family presumably lived down at the tip of the Marsh where a ferry crossed to Greenwich; there were families called Langdych (longditch), Othordych (of the ditch?), Attewall (living by the river wall), Etgoose (at the marsh), Conewall (rabbit wall), Attewater and Bythestronde (by

Bell cast at Whitechapel Bell Foundry in 2004 for Christ Church, Hampstead, in memory of Susan Staines, sister of the author. Bells have been made at Whitechapel since the Middle Ages. Author's Collection

the beach). Occupational names appear but nothing of any particular significance: Smith, Brewer, Carter and Baker. Families evidently moved into the area from other parts of London and the shires. When Solomon Waleys collected the Bishop's rents in 1361 among the tenants were families from Croyden, Staines, Shoreditch, Holywell, Tottenham and Waltham.

As time passed, servile farm hands and artisans freed themselves sooner than most from their feudal ties, presumably because of their proximity to the great market of London. Peasants became small holders and, in some cases, small holders acquired considerable property for themselves, setting up industrial enterprises, running fishing fleets, building and fitting out ships, buying wharves and engaging in trade.

So, the medieval East End was a farming, fishing place, with a little industrial activity, famous for the beauty of its countryside. The Black Prince himself had a palace in Poplar and City merchants, like the fabulously wealthy John Philpot (remembered in Whitechapel's Philpot Street), had mansions around Mile End Green.

Tudor Times: Sea Dogs and the 'Country East Enders'

At the advent of the Tudors most of the East End was a rural place with swathes of hay fields, its pretty villages, scattered farmsteads, woods and parklands providing a retreat from the City and its evils, the plague and the pox. Early in the sixteenth century the boys from Dean Colet's school at St Paul's were sent to Stepney for safety during plague times. A hundred years later, as will be seen, the plague hit hardest here, an indication of the overcrowded, poor living conditions.

It was against a background of religious revolution and bloodshed, the closure of its monasteries and hospitals, the torture of its priests, the smell of Smithfield faggots that the countryside east of the Tower would be changed beyond recognition.

In the Reformation, Stepney and its hamlets played a vital role. Our Tudor ancestors, in these parts, were a very radical bunch, both in religion and politics. Historians of late have made much of the resistance to the Church revolution in the countryside, but in Whitechapel and Aldgate, Stepney and Limehouse it was very different.

John Colet, briefly vicar of Stepney and then Dean of St Paul's, made vitriolic attacks on the luxury and hypocrisy of the clergy in the early years of the century, and made his mother's Great Place in Stepney a safe house during the Reformation. Very soon after his death, the new Lutheran ideas about the worship of God started to filter into the East End, brought by the sailors on German ships docking at Ratcliff and Limehouse. Flemish and Dutch refugees, joining the local community of 'Doche' brewers and bakers, brought radical Anabaptist notions with them. The very first cause célèbre (in 1513) involved William Marshall, parson of Whitechapel, and one Richard Hunne, a tailor of Lollard (the old English-bred version of Protestantism) sympathies, who refused to pay his 'mortuary gift', a sort of death duty.

In the mid-century, Thomas Cromwell, the organising genius behind Henry's church coup and his Vicar General, dissolved the monasteries from his base at Stepney's Great Place. He installed there as vicar one Richard Layton, who was to produce some of the most damning reports of goings-on in monasteries. The area was a hot bed of reformist zeal, except Bow, which was said to be rather conservative. John Harrydance, a bricklayer, declaimed the forbidden doctrines from the window of his house in the Whitechapel Road in 1537. During the re-instatement of Catholicism in Mary's reign the parishioners of St Dunstan's gave their 'stout Popish prelate' (Henry More, rector 1545–54, former Abbot of St Mary Graces) a very rough ride, led by the Limehouse 'Hot Gospeller', William Underhill. At St Botolph's Aldgate it was with undoubted glee that the locals fell upon the treasures horded in their churches and attacked what a local Gospeller called their 'old mum-symnissis', ignorant old conservative priests.

While all this turmoil was going on, London's population was expanding. Between 1530 and 1600 the population of the capital rose from about 50,000 to about 200,000, with the eastern suburbs taking the heaviest load. Shoreditch grew six-fold; Aldgate and Southwark swelled, but Stepney increased the most. In 1568 there were seven marriages in Stepney church; in 1619 there were ninety. In 1580, 'because of many houses builded in the parish', they put up a gallery in the church. The hamlets of Limehouse, Poplar, Bethnal Green, Ratcliff and Mile End had their own chapels in St Dunstan's by 1532. Bow was the most populous of the hamlets and had its own church, although was not made a parish until the eighteenth century. Ratcliff and Limehouse ranked next in terms of population.

Lads and lassies poured in from the shires in search of the streets paved with gold, driven from their home villages by enclosure and a series of bad harvests. There grew up a large shanty town population of newcomers – country East Enders, living, for the most part, in old houses divided up by rapacious landlords. Young men arrived Dick-Whittington style; their sisters came to go into service, join the burgeoning 'rag trade', to work as bar maids, prostitutes, midwives and wet nurses. City people commonly put their babies to wet nurses in the suburbs (like Richard Hunne), and Stepney's burial registers are full of little mites who died in Hog Lane (Petticoat Lane) and Spitalfields. Wages were higher than in the country; a builder, for instance, picked up perhaps 1s 6d a day as opposed to a shilling in the country. There was work available in the Ratcliff sugar house, in the lime kilns in Limehouse, the brick kilns in Spitalfields, the breweries, cooperages and the Bow bakehouses.

But what changed the East End most in these years was the seafaring connection. The 'Armada Map' of 1588 shows a built-up area stretching along the river from Wapping to Blackwall, in size half the area of the whole conurbation of London and Westminster. Henry VIII built up his navy and royal dockyards were opened at Woolwich and Chatham. There was some ship building on the north bank of the Thames, but it was for ships' chandlery and marine crafts that Wapping, Ratcliff and Limehouse would become renowned, for their anchor smiths, rope makers, carpenters, mast makers, sail makers and allied trades. Ships were fitted here and got ready for sail, food and men were taken on board. Hence the growth of the local seafaring community and all the other associated traders: the slop sellers, physicians, apothecaries and midwives to deliver the bastards, barmaids and victuallers, pimps and prostitutes.

During Elizabeth's forty-five-year reign the trade and shipping of London took on worldwide importance and English merchants and sailors seized their share of the new trade with America and the Indies, which the Pope had appropriated for Spain and Portugal. In this explosion of seafaring endeavour, mariners took over in Stepney's riverside hamlets and the City's eastern overspill. Great sea captains and wealthy shipwrights ran Stepney vestry and Sir Walter Raleigh was a frequent visitor to his brother-in-law's house in Mile End. Local lads, perhaps trained up by their fishermen fathers, and hopefuls from all over the country came to make their fortune riding the seven seas; sailors in the royal service got 2s 6d a day and those in the merchant service more, with prize money when privateering went on. Huge wealth came into the area, and the will archive is full of sailors who made good. William Borgine, who set off for Norway in the autumn of 1599, left his Limehouse property to his 'dearest love', Christian Jarves, and in his cedar sea chest he had gold earrings, two 'Barbary duckets' (ducats), which he had brought back for his mother, and a purse of Spanish gold.

Men made rich by New World gold had fine 'stout' houses in Mile End, Poplar and Limehouse, but the sudden influx of country folk brought its problems for parish administrators. Sailors and soldiers were all around, the latter because of the proximity of the Tower, and many a bastard was spawned in the fields around or in the dingey alleys along by the river bank. The illegitimacy rate, according to Stepney's baptismal registers, was something above 10 per cent, and was probably much higher than this in actual fact.

Vagrancy and the problem of the poor were increasingly matters of urgency for the Elizabethan government and a new system of Poor Law was introduced at the very beginning of the seventeenth century; a poor rate was levied and workhouses set up. The situation in the East End was severe. Aldgate church presided over a rough 45 acres which included the Minories and East Smithfield. Just before Christmas 1583, they distributed to eighty paupers 'all the collection gathered at the communion service and put into the poor box'. On New Year's Day 1587 the curate held 3 communion services specifically to raise money for the poor, at which just 306 people consumed 6 gallons of wine and a 'pottell of malmsy'. At Stepney an embryonic workhouse was established in the parsonage barn in the 1580s and the old leper hospital at Mile End was taken over by the parish. The old and the sick, old soldiers and single mums, destitute sailors and beggars from all over the country huddled together in the great tithe barn, once stacked high with sheaves of corn. Many girls claimed to have been seduced by gentlemen; the mother of William, born in Hog Lane in Armada Year, said she was married to a gentleman with the unlikely name of Sweetser.

Although the aristocracy, gentry, mercantile and seafaring men had elegant houses in the still-rural peace of Bethnal Green and around the green at Mile End, part of the East End was already getting a reputation. In *The Devil is an Ass*, Ben Jonson has the Vice 'Iniquity' fly around the roughest parts of London:

> Let us survey the suburbs, and make forth our sallies
> Down Petticoat Lane, and up the Smock allies
> To Shoreditch, Whitechapel and St Kather'n's
> To drink with the Dutch there ...

St Katharine's (where the marina is now) was notorious. It was a liberty, free from the jurisdiction of the Bishop, being attached to the Royal Hospital of St Katharine. As such it attracted a number of immigrants, mainly from the Low Countries. They crowded into an enclosed precinct of squalid alleys and courts (Pottlepot and Maidenhead alley among them) foul with the acrid smoke of tallow burning and stiff with little Dutch breweries.

When John Stow wrote his famous *A Survey of London* at the end of the century the river banks between St Katharine's and Limehouse were lined with houses and wharves. Ratcliff was the heart of the seafaring East End and the Cross was the place where East Enders gathered to exchange news and gossip. Meanwhile, to the north, the fields that had belonged to the Priory of St Mary, the 'Spital', closed at the Reformation, were dug to make bricks for the jerry built properties which were being flung up for the newcomers. The pretty country Hog Lane, where pigs were driven from Hoxton to Whitechapel, was quite changed and, as is evident from the Stepney parish registers, had become a place of gaming houses, bowling alleys, alehouses, lodging houses and brothels.

It was a vibrant mix in Spitalfields, Aldgate and Whitechapel, with religious refugees coming in: French, Dutch, Walloons and Flemings. A significant number arrived following the massacre of St Batholomew's Day in France in 1572 and others after the sack of Antwerp in 1585. Many joined the already established silk-weaving industry or went into the drink trade; the Coopers' Company authorised the apprenticing of Dutch barrel makers.

Puritans, Sailors and French Weavers, 1600–1700

In 1614 the most successful and prestigious of trading companies, the East India Company, moved its operation from south of the river and built a great dockyard at Blackwall. From this point onwards, for over 200 years, the company's presence in the East End (especially Poplar) was overwhelming. It gave direct or indirect and lucrative employment to numbers of men and its officers, merchants and ship builders had houses built for themselves in Limehouse, Blackwall and Poplar, while old sailors and their widows were accommodated in Poplar almshouses. The company established an almshouse for old seamen and their widows (1628) and a chapel in its grounds (1652–4, now St Matthias's Church).

Likewise, the Corporation of Trinity House had moved its head-quarters to Stepney from Deptford by 1621. The Corporation regulated pilotage, was responsible for ballast and lighthouses and provided relief for old salts and their families.

Grandees of the East India Company and officials of Trinity House, along with members of the ship-building families of Limehouse, ran Stepney vestry. Theirs was no easy task.

Dissent from the established Church continued to flourish and in the forty years leading up to the Civil War the East End became a very troubled place. A total of three bouts of plague in 1603, 1625 and 1635 decimated 'sailortown' and bankrupted Stepney parish; church-wardens were having to pay out of their own pockets for plague and poor relief. The vestry appealed for help to the Mercers' Company, one of the chief local landowners, and East India Company director Robert Salmon spoke, in 1641, of 'common beggars up and down the streets of Limehouse'. The wardens made a desperate plea to the local magistracy: 'The poor of the parish are so numerous and their necessities so great . . . that they were like to perish for want of relief'.

Parish organisation in all of London's large suburban parishes was collapsing under the strain of steep population growth and high turnover, combined with the effects of the plague, and Stepney's case was the most extreme. Still immigrants came pouring in from the shires; in December 1640 the wardens complained to the Sessions that a Shadwell shipwright and an East Smithfield cooper had 'created tenements for the poor in several Shadwell houses' and were refusing to pay plague expenses.

Meanwhile, William Laud, as Bishop of London, then Archbishop of Canterbury, introduced High Church reforms that smacked of popery to the puritanically inclined East Enders, as to many others. Probably more upsetting for the locals was the purge on morals, Sunday trading, selling tobacco during service time, selling calves on holy days and much more. Between 1632 and 1639 literally hundreds of local victuallers, other traders, sailors and their women, millers and 'costers' were hauled before the Church courts to be fined and humiliated. When an alehouse kept by a Dutch couple was raided in November 1638, the landlady let out a stream of abuse and accused the officer of being an 'incense promoter'.

The Puritan group known as Independents (later Congregationalists), to which Oliver Cromwell himself and most of the Army subscribed, was establishing itself firmly in Stepney. The populace, groaning under the strain of their poverty, smarting from Laud's lash and, as a last straw, forced to pay a swingeing church rate to shore up a crumbling St Dunstan's, turned their face against Church and King. The local leading lights, accounted 'the sailors' favourites', were the most celebrated Independent preachers of the age, Jeremiah Burroughs and William Greenhill, known as the 'Morning and Evening Stars'.

So, in the great seventeenth-century conflict, our East End ancestors were overwhelmingly Roundhead, led as they were by a Trinity House, which had no love for the Stuarts, and 'godly mariners' of the East India Company, who had fought popery in the flesh in the form of Portuguese sailors. The very first Puritan Lectureship authorised by the revolutionary Long Parliament in September 1641 was at Stepney. Later the Lord Protector's close friend Maurice Thomson moved into the mansion near the church known as Worcester House and effectively ran the parish from there.

Before the East End of Good King Charles's Golden Days is considered, the records known as the Protestation Returns should be examined. During 1641 Parliament organised a sort of referendum, a national protest against 'an arbitrary and tyrannical government'. All males over 18 were required to take an oath of loyalty to the Protestant religion and Crown and in support of the rights and privileges of Parliament. The returns, which came in the following year, provide a partial census of the country just before civil war broke out. Although the population figures available from them are far from reliable (the returns show that Stepney's population was something in the region of 15,500, when it was considerably more), the documents give a firm indication of the relative size of the hamlets and, for genealogists, lists of names (see pp. 113–14).

Of Stepney's hamlets, the riverside places of Limehouse and Ratcliff had by far the greatest number of inhabitants (the busiest part of Wapping belonging to Whitechapel, so was not in the Stepney list), Poplar had half as many. The growing immigrant area of Spitalfields was next, having nearly as many people as Poplar and about one-third of the names were French or Dutch; the names ascribed to some of the newcomers were clearly plucked out of the air and give an idea of how the locals felt about them, Charles Lepoxon and Jaques Monsieur, for instance (see p. 150). Mile End and Bethnal Green were still select residential places. The ancient bread-making village of Bow, still notionally part of the parish, was flourishing, and the tiny village of Old

Stepney village in the days of Samuel Pepys, 1681.

Ford, a place for bathing in the River Lea, makes an appearance, with just thirty-six names listed.

When, in 1660, Charles II re-established the monarchy and the Church of England with it, many East Enders still adhered to their old sects. Puritan congregations, or 'conventicles', as they were now known, continued to meet, although subject to periodic bouts of prosecution, until the Dutch king, William III, arrived in 1689 and toleration was proclaimed. In 1669 there were as many as fourteen 'fixed conventicles' in Stepney, as well as many others at private houses, meeting 'sometimes at one house, sometimes at another'. There were significant Presbyterian, Baptist and Quaker congregations, but the foremost was the Independent chapel, Stepney Meeting, which, in the 1690s, was said to draw the biggest crowds in London. This strong association between the East End and protestant Nonconformity was to last at least another 250 years.

The years following the Restoration saw the Great Plague wreaking terrible havoc; at its peak a hundred corpses a day were buried in Stepney churchyard. There were sailors' riots in the streets of Wapping following the threatened Dutch invasion of 1667 and weavers' riots in Spitalfields in 1675. The issue of poverty continued to concern the authorities, with collection boxes put in all taverns, alehouses and public places in 1680. A series of harsh taxes was imposed; disastrous for our ancestors, but helpful to those wishing to trace individuals. The records of these taxes, the hearth tax, poll tax and others, provide an excellent source for the late seventeenth-century East End.

By this time the eastern suburbs contained about a third of the whole (growing) population of the London area and, as can be seen from a glance at the 1677 *Directory of Merchants and Traders of the City of London*, it was a thriving business place, not just some green open spaces with colonies of sailors and weavers. Still the young were coming in from the countryside and, following the Great Fire of 1666, a number of City dwellers moved out east. Among them were the Michells, parents of one of diarist Samuel Pepys's many wenches, shopkeepers in Westminster Hall, who lost their house in the Fire and moved out to Shadwell.

Shadwell, which had been riverside meadows belonging to St Paul's in the sixteenth century, with a line of wharves and a few scattered cottages, had become an industrial 'new town', a dense estate of small houses for the workers. The topographer, historian and silk merchant's son from Petticoat Lane John Strype described it as 'one of the great nurseries of navigation and breeders of seamen'. 'Without Shadwell', he declared, 'England would not be England'. Stepney's other new town, which was actually called that – Mile End New Town (MENT), was built for the weavers, whose numbers greatly increased from 1685 onwards with the arrival of Huguenot weavers, French Protestants, fleeing persecution for their faith. Mile End New Town was a small estate of houses, slightly larger than the Shadwell dwellings, jerry built, lying to the east of Brick Lane. Thus came the first really famous band of East End immigrants; one hopes their reception was not too hostile, the rector of Whitechapel describing them as the 'very offal of the earth'.

Jack Tars, Silk Weavers and Nabobs, 1700–1800

At the beginning of the eighteenth century Stepney was at its peak, and our East End ancestors, who are reasonably accessible to us, may well have enjoyed a good lifestyle.

According to John Strype, Stepney was 'one of the greatest towns in England' with 'Populousness, Traffick, Commerce, Havens, Shipping, Manufacture, Plenty and Wealth the crown of all'. The population of this vast parish alone was 86,000 and if to this was added the 'inner East

End' areas of Whitechapel, Aldgate, Bishopsgate and East Smithfield it would be considerably over 100,000. This huge 'province', as Strype called it, was well over four times the size of the great port of Bristol.

These were golden years for the East End, with a flourishing silk industry, naval victories and booming foreign trade. Daniel Defoe found between the Pool of London and Blackwall in the 1720s 3 wet docks for laying up ships, 22 dry docks for repairing them and 33 shipyards for building merchantmen. There were warehouses stuffed with velvets and spices from the East, with sugar, rum, tobacco and coffee from the West Indies and a myriad alehouses and taverns.

The elderly and indigent were well provided for; all the hamlets set up their own workhouses and, in 1766, there were no less than eleven almshouses in Stepney parish belonging to various livery and trading companies.

Joel Gascoyne's 1701 map of Stepney, the first proper survey of the East End, ornamented with a drawing of cattle, presents a country place. In all this talk of trade and industry it is easy to forget that farming was still the occupation of many. The nine towns of Stepney still lay in open country, set amid hay and corn fields, orchards, pasture and market gardens. In Bow and Mile End there were big dairy herds and farms of 80–100 acres, while the cattle fattened on the lush pastures of the Isle

St Dunstan's, Stepney, c. 1792, when its parish was one of the 'most ample' in England.
Author's Collection

of Dogs produced the best beef in Europe, or so they said at Smithfield Market. To the north was the weaving town concentration of Spitalfields and Mile End New Town, spreading into Bethnal Green. To the south was the riverside development, the 'sailor town' of Wapping, Ratcliff, Limehouse, Poplar and Blackwall.

Whitechapel was 'all town', and had been since Chaucer's day, but was a very far cry from the 'Ripper Land' of the next century; 'good inns for the reception of travellers' and substantial houses lined its 'spacious fair street'. The age-old industry of bell making flourished (as it still does); Philadelphia's famous 'Liberty Bell' was made here in 1752. The 'rag trade' predominated, as it did for many years, and second-hand clothes and stolen goods of one sort and another changed hands at the notorious Rag Fair, down in East Smithfield. Jews were present, but they were not the poor exiles that would transform Whitechapel in the 1880s, but comfortable merchants who made their homes in and around Goodmans' Fields.

Of Stepney's hamlets, Ratcliff was the most built-up and populous at the start of the century; there was said to be a 'great multiplying of houses'. Here were breweries, glass works, cooperages, anchor smiths, the great dock and the sugar house, which had been there for 150 years. In 1794 there were 1,150 houses and 36 warehouses. There was little open ground and when Ratcliff was assessed for tithes there were numerous folk classified as 'poor' in Ratcliff Square, Periwinkle Street, Vinegar Yard, Bell Yard, Love Lane and Glasshouse Fields.

Shadwell, very much a town unto itself, with its own church, water-works, charity school and almshouses (in Elbow Lane) was, likewise, a working place, inhabited by ballast men, ships' chandlers, biscuit bakers, wholesale butchers, mast makers, sail makers, anchor smiths, coopers, tallow chandlers, distillers and brewers. There were also some excise men and attorneys, and a smattering of gentlemen.

Bow was still the bread-baking centre, and also produced fine china, although it remained predominantly a farming community and would take longer than the rest of Tower Hamlets to sink into poverty. By this time, Mile End Old Town is probably the most superior of East End locations. It was a fine little town, with a magnificent twenty-two-bedroomed hostelry in the White Horse (see p. 87). Wealthy merchants and naval officers were local residents; when he married in 1763, Captain Cook moved here from Wapping to a house in Assembly Row. By the end of the century, according to Daniel Lysons, the character of the hamlet was changing; in its northern part were three large breweries, 'Mr Minish's hartshorn manufacture', Cooke's workshops making patent sponges for ships, two major rope walks and the West Ham waterworks.

Wapping, half belonging to Stepney and half to Whitechapel, buzzed with maritime life. Wellclose Square was leafy and elegant; there were two Scandinavian churches, the much-painted Danish church, dating from 1696, and the Swedish church built in 1727. Virginia Street and Broad Street, where 'Bligh of the Bounty' lodged, boasted expensive houses. But, it was a mix of a place; wherever sailors congregate it will be rackety and Dr Johnson told Boswell 'Go down to Wapping and see life'. Here were brothel keepers and slave masters, prostitutes and press-gang men and everywhere 'jack tars' in their 'bum-freezer' jackets, their pockets jingling with cash.

As the century progressed, increasing numbers of German sugar bakers came into Wapping and poor Irishmen to work as ballast men or at coal heaving, unloading the cargoes from the collier boats from Newcastle. In Shadwell there was an alehouse called the North Country Pint. Wapping-Stepney had a population twice the size of Spitalfields or Limehouse and was separated from Stepney parish in 1727, acquiring its own church, St George-in-the-East. In the next century the new parish would descend swiftly into the worst slum area of all, nicknamed 'St George-in-the-Dirt'.

The division of Stepney's enormous parish had been a likely prospect since the Interregnum and when, in 1711, Parliament voted money for the building of churches to celebrate Marlborough's victory at Blenheim, it was the top of the list. It was hoped that this injection of cash might stem the rising tide of Nonconformity, which will be discussed in more detail later.

Limehouse and Spitalfields would join St George-in-the-East as independent parishes, with Limehouse, which was much given over to dairy farms and market gardening, taking part of the very populous Ratcliff. The new parish of Christ Church, Spitalfields, would include the 'industrial north' of the parish, weaver town, although the poor Mile End New Town would stay as part of the mother parish until 1841.

The three Hawksmoor churches, St George's, St Anne's and Christ Church, were all consecrated in 1729. All belonged to Brasenose College, Oxford, which had purchased the patronage of Stepney, Whitechapel and Wapping churches in 1708. The new monster churches dwarfed the ancient parish church of St Dunstan and removed a good part of its income from marriage and burial fees, much to the sexton's disgust.

Fifteen years later Bethnal Green would also break free and have its own church; Bow (made parochial in 1719) and Poplar chapels were repaired. Poplar would not become a parish until 1817.

For family researchers the break up of Stepney parish in the mid-eighteenth century is of great significance. From this point what had been one parish became four; Stepney lost half its domain and well as over half its households.

Although the rectors and vestry of Stepney deplored the diminishing of their great empire, they were eager to offload Bethnal Green. With the severe fluctuations to which the weaving industry was notoriously subject, the poor weavers that lived there became an increasing burden on Stepney parish and an irritant to the people of Whitechapel.

Blethenhale (Bethnal Green) had been a village since early medieval times, having grown up around the Bishop's palace. In the opening years of the seventeeth century only about 4 per cent of the population of Stepney parish lived there, and it was a most desirable spot when Pepys enjoyed the sunshine and a vast quantity of strawberries there in Sir William Ryder's beautiful garden (see p. 115) The arrival of the French and the expansion of the weaving industry would change it radically.

In 1685, because of the 'great increase of inhabitants and great charge of the poor', Stepney vestry had given Bethnal Green its own church-warden. The village grew and grew and became an embarrassment and a nuisance to the worthies of Mile End who now ran Stepney parish. The 'Increase of Dissoluteness of Morals and a Disregard for Religion, too apparent in the younger and poorer sort ... hath ... been the occasion that many of the better sort of people have removed from their Habitations in the said hamlet to the great Impoverishment thereof'. In 1743 the hamlet had 1,800 houses and a population of 15,000; by 1901 there would be 129,680 people. Most of the inhabitants were poor weavers; master weavers were more likely to be found in the vicinity of Spital Square. Sunday in Bethnal Green was a day for fun in the tea gardens, all the riotous savagery of bull and bear baiting and the cockpit. It was claimed that the hamlet was too poor to sustain its own church, but the scheme went ahead and St Matthew's Church, a squat brick building, designed by George Dance the Elder, was consecrated on 15 July 1746.

Some thirty years later John Wesley went to Bethnal Green: 'I began visiting those of our Society who live in Bethnal Green hamlet. Many of them I found in such poverty as few can conceive without seeing it.'

Wesley's new creed, Methodism as it was nicknamed, found favour with the artisans and craftsmen here and in Ratcliff, Wapping and Spitalfields, the latter one of his strongholds. He would take over the French Huguenot chapel in Brick Lane, l'Eglise Neuve (which later became a synagogue and then a mosque).

Dock Hands and Manufacturers, 1800–50

The creation of the enclosed docks in Wapping, St George-in-the-East, Blackwall and St Katharine's changed the character of the East End for good. In the first fifteen years of the nineteenth century the London Dock, the East and West India Docks were built and the cargoes once loaded and unloaded on the river at the 'legal quays' in the Pool of London were now brought into the great new docks, the wonder of the world. In 1828, St Katharine's Dock opened; in the clearing of the precinct 11,300 inhabitants lost their homes.

Men of all sorts and conditions flooded in to service the docks and the medieval porterage brotherhood lost its old monopoly for unloading. Originally, there had been about 900 fellowship porters, by the 1850s there were over 10,000 dockers.

Newcomers arrived from the countryside in search of dock and factory work, with Irishmen fleeing the Great Famine. The silk-weaving industry began to collapse, unable to cope with competition from France and from the new cotton manufacturers of the north; in the 1830s, 30,000 silkmen were unemployed in Spitalfields, Bethnal Green and Mile End New Town. In 1834, no less than a thousand houses stood empty in Mile End New Town. The weavers, in the main, resorted to casual labour in the docks, which, according to Mayhew, 'constitute as it were a house colony to Spitalfields'.

The arrival of the docks did not, however, immediately reduce the entire place to a slum; initially it was rather the reverse. With money coming in, shops were filled with luxury goods and squares of 'Cockney Corinthian' were laid out in imitation of the West End in Stepney and Bow: Trafalgar, Beaumont, Arbour and Tredegar, with their magnificent 'South Kensington' houses, offered elegant homes to professional and merchant families. The new Commercial Road was lined with substantial properties, some of which are still there. The docks brought in excise men and customs officers, well-paid stevedores and dock foremen. In Stepney Green, north side, in 1851 lived: a ships' insurance broker, 6 customs officers, 2 merchants, a ship master, a wool ware-houseman, a ships' broker, a landowner, a rich Jamaica merchant and his family and a superintendent of the Commercial Gas Company. Mrs Riddell, a local novelist, writing in the 1860s, remembered the mansions of her youth, one 'with a staircase so wide you could drive a coach and four down it and a hall so large you could turn the horses round'.

Cross's New Plan of London, drawn in 1847, although strikingly different from the Cruchley map of 1829, shows that there was still quite a lot of open ground north of the Mile End Road at this time; Bromley and Bow were still very rural in aspect, with wide expanses of pasture, corn fields and open marsh land. As relentless rows of houses began to march across the fields and the land was criss-crossed and scarred by railways (the North London, Blackwall and Great Eastern), the air thickened with smoke and chemicals, while sheep still grazed on Stepney Green and windmills whirred in Whitechapel and around the Isle of Dogs.

'The People of the Abyss', 1850–1900

'Hardly a man or woman above 5ft 4″ among them' noted Charles Booth's researcher while watching the crowd at a Bethnal Green funeral in 1898 (http://booth.lse.ac.uk/, B 350, p. 15). William C. Preston wrote, in 1883, of the 'pestilential human rookeries' in Ratcliff and Shadwell, inhabited by 'stunted, misshapen, and often loathsome objects'.

By the second half of the nineteenth century the 'air of aldermanic gentility', which Mrs Riddell remembered from the days of her youth, was quite lost and the East End proper came into being, a seething boil of poverty and overcrowding on the side of the richest city in the world. Stepney's old hamlets and the out parishes of Aldgate and Bishopsgate were now one monotonous agglomeration; 'a Great Joyless City of two million people without a gentlemen among them', according to Walter Besant. A population explosion bringing many thousands into the East End in search of work, mass immigration of poor Jewish refugees from Eastern Europe, the collapse of local industries were the factors that combined to transform Tower Hamlets and make it into what Beatrice Webb called a 'bottomless pit of decaying life'.

The final death blow to the silk weavers came in 1860 when a treaty with France allowed the import of French silk. Many redundant silk workers went to the docks; a good number of the women became part of the notorious Whitechapel sweated industry, the 'rag trade'. East London would become a finishing centre for the new, cheap, ready-made clothes, with needlewomen working for a pittance at home or in small workshops.

The sugar-baking industry that had dominated in St George-in-the-East collapsed because of the introduction of sugar bounties; the workforce dropped from 1,437 to 616 in the 20 years after 1861. Many Poplar shipyards closed following the financial crash of 1866 and the industry moved to the Clyde, near to the source of iron. In January 1867 there were 30,000 people on relief in Poplar. The rope makers of Ratcliff and Shadwell had their livelihoods threatened by the introduction of wire rope and factory-made rope from the north of England. The boom in building and railway construction came to an end, sending more men to look for work in the docks. During the bitter winter of 1866–7 the river froze over; 10,000 of the 40,000 population of St George-in-the-East (all dockers) were out of work.

Work, when you could get it, was irregular, casual and seasonal, notoriously at the docks, where conditions and pay were scandalous and would eventually result in the great strike of 1889. Many thousands, thrown out of their usual trades, resorted to jobs that had no restrictions on entry and businesses that were cheap to set up; they became sweeps, firewood choppers (my grandmother, Lil Daniels of Bow, was one such, as listed in the 1901 census), cobblers, costers, hawkers, touters, messengers, cabmen, sandwichmen and theatrical extras. Children might fix the bristles in scrubbing brushes at the rate of one penny for filling a hundred holes. Girls risked developing the terrible disease of 'phossyjaw' for the relatively high wages offered by Bryant and May at their match factory in Bow (opened in 1861). Men queued up at the dock gates in the hope of getting a day's work. In the autumn there was a lull in dock work, and dockers, match girls and female 'home workers' and others went 'hopping'. In the mid-1870s as many as 35,000 Londoners, most of them East Enders, decamped to the hop fields of Kent. 'Hopping is hell', one hopper told the rector of Stepney.

There was no adequate structure for dealing with such poverty and unemployment; middle-class do-gooders went 'East Ending' and charitable endeavours operated on an unprecedented scale. As conditions worsened into the darkest days of all, in the 1880s, thousands were forced into the workhouses and many were on out relief. Alexander Heriot Mackonockie, vicar of St Peter's London Docks, reported in 1883 that all his parishioners were on poor relief. In 1888, Poplar Workhouse had nearly 2,192 inmates, as well as 'casuals' who went in for 'a night's kip on the spike'.

Houses built in the earlier boom times for family occupation were let out as single rooms, as is detailed in the census returns. Developers took advantage of the demand for housing and covered the East End in terraces of tiny cheap, two-storey houses, which were then, themselves, subdivided. Families crammed into cellars where cess pools over-flowed. There were lodging houses of unbelievable squalor where you could have a bed for tuppence a night; if you couldn't afford the tuppence, you could sleep on the stairs.

Slum-clearance projects did little to improve matters; the poor had to live near their work so they just huddled up together somewhere else. The 5s a week rent charged for accommodation in the new 'Model Dwellings', like the Peabody Estates, proved much too expensive for East Enders; in 1891 only 2 per cent of the people of Tower Hamlets lived in them.

The Bitter Cry of Outcast London, a pamphlet published in 1883, had the most enormous impact on the country at large; from this point society and government would really take the problem of the East End seriously. The pamphlet was written by a Congregational minister called William C. Preston, and researched by another called Andrew Mearns. They took a close look at three of the worst areas: Shadwell, Ratcliff and Bermondsey, at the 'courts reeking with poisonous and malodorous gases arising from accumulation of sewage and refuse ... where the sun never penetrates'. Windows were broken, there was no furniture and the inhabitants just huddled together and slept on the floor. Corpses of dead children were left to rot and toddlers were placed in charge of babies. Incest was rife and no body ever married or went near a church or chapel. What price our 'lost ancestors'? No wonder they cannot be found in the records!

With the advent of cheap travel by omnibus, tram or train, things started to look up and numbers of our East End ancestors no longer needed to live near their work, and moved out to more salubrious parts. The new London County Council (1899) not only built public housing in the old slums, it put up blocks of flats in Tooting, Hammersmith, Croydon and Tottenham. Only the very poor were left behind in the 'Jewish East End'.

There were, actually, always more indigenous British people in the East End than foreign immigrants, something that should not be forgotten in all this discussion of the vibrant melting pot of cultures. But the suddenness and size of the Jewish influx in the 1880s, and the concentration in Whitechapel, Spitalfields and Stepney, later spreading out east to Bow, made a huge impact on East End life. Between 1870 and 1914, 120,000 Poles, Lithuanians and Russians came to England, fleeing from the pogroms. By the end of the 1880s there were about 30,000 in the East End. They landed at Irongate Stairs, just near the Tower of London, hordes of them, strange bearded men with homburg hats and women with dark curly wigs, gabbling away in a foreign tongue. If they were lucky enough to have relations, they stayed with them, if not, they went to the Poor Jews Temporary Shelter in Leman Street and thence to whatever cheap lodgings were available. Most settled in Whitechapel and Spitalfields, crammed into what was soon called 'the Ghetto', 3,000 to the acre. The vast majority was absorbed into the tailoring trades and Jewish sweat shops would become notorious. Soon enough the culture and customs of this immigrant group would impress themselves firmly on this part of London.

In fact, the Jewish East End was a fairly short-lived phenomenon, lasting less than a hundred years. By the time the twenty-first century dawned about one-third of inhabitants were South Asian, mainly Bangladeshi, and overwhelmingly Muslim; less than 0.1 per cent were Jewish.

'A Great Family Party', From 1900

The Edwardian East End is, for some of us, remembered in family tales told, long ago, by our grandparents. It was not so bad. Food was cheaper than it had been for years, the trade unions were flexing their muscles, radicals, Liberals and foreign revolutionaries, fleeing the oppression of the Tsar and the Kaiser, engaged in the fight to rescue the East End. Socialists among the caring intelligentsia combined with union men to form a Labour Party. Working men were elected to Parliament, albeit in small numbers, among them Will Crooks of Poplar. In 1910, Lloyd George brought in the first state old-age pension. There were still ragged children and some pretty terrible living conditions, but, in the sunshine days, before the First World War, even in London's backyard there was something of an atmosphere of gaiety.

There were music halls, the Wonderland in the Whitechapel Road, the Paragon in Mile End, Foresters' Music Hall in Cambridge Heath Road, the Marlow in Bow, the Queens and the Hippodrome in Poplar.

'A great family party'. An outing from St Stephen's Church, Bow, 1930. Author's Collection

Sundays might be spent on Hampstead Heath (you could get there by train) or in the pub. The poor rarely went to church or chapel; the *Daily News* survey of 1903 showed that only about 5 per cent of all East Enders went near a place of worship. They more often than not sent their children off to Sunday school, especially if there was the chance of getting a handout. As a very little girl, my nan was despatched to the East London Tabernacle in Burdett Road for this very reason, and ran home crying because she was ashamed to take the free orange that was on offer. In the lively markets, Petticoat Lane, Roman Road, Chrisp Street and the rest, 'rollicking Cockney girls' in their ostrich feathers and sham fur coats jostled with costers selling jellied eels, hot chestnuts and baked potatoes, crockery and cheap clothes. E.V. Lucas, writing in 1906, reckoned the West End was mistaken in its habit of pitying the East, where 'life goes quite as merrily ... There is a continental bustle ... People know each other here. Friends on buses whistle to friends on the pavements ... no where else in London, in England, is fruit so eaten. Sunday is here no day of gloom: to a large part of the population it is a shopping day, to a large part it is a holiday'. Inspector Pearce, reporting for Booth's survey in Bethnal Green, noted: 'Population increases but no-one leaves if he can help it. Inhabitants form a great family party.'

In the opening months of the First World War, the East End seemed to be infected by the atmosphere of excitement. 'Native patriotism has been thrilled', wrote a local journalist and a shopkeeper in the Commercial Road put up a notice: 'Business as usual during European alterations'.

The mood soon changed and the East End's response to recruitment drives was poor. Conscription was introduced early in 1916 and the Poor Law Guardians were, naturally, anxious to get as many unemployed men into the forces. Locals resisted and the Stepney Appeals Tribunal had its work cut out examining the numerous men who dredged up every excuse possible to avoid military service. One Spitalfields coster claimed his partner was a cripple and his numerous dependants included a widow who had fits and a blind brother-in-law. Sylvia Pankhurst and other socialists distributed pamphlets against conscription around the locality and the gentile East Enders fumed at their Jewish neighbours, who, until the Aliens' Military Service Bill of May 1917, were exempt from service if they had been born abroad.

By the 1920s suburban London stretched out eastwards; long lines of new houses marched through West and East Ham, Ilford, Forest Gate, Walthamstow and Romford. Industrial London would expand mainly to the west; in the interwar years factories sprang up in a vast 'industrial park' which stretched from Wembley and Park Royal to Twickenham. The only major new industry in the East End was the American firm Fords of Dagenham, which opened in 1921. East Enders who could afford it were leaving their old home and making for the new suburbs, where lines of mock Tudor houses spread out over the fields, with 'kitchenettes' instead of sculleries and wash houses.

For those left behind, the dockers, rag-trade workers and their families, it was a hard time, marked by anger, unemployment and distress. However, there was not the terrible destitution that there had been and people did not starve. The 1911 National Insurance Act introduced a limited health and unemployment insurance scheme, and tiny grants were to be had from the Poor Law Guardians; food, coal and clothing tickets might be distributed to the needy.

In 1921, one in five of the breadwinners in the borough of Poplar were out of work and the rate burden to pay benefits was overwhelming. The councillors, led by George Lansbury, took a stand and decided to refuse to levy the rates due to the LCC, the Metropolitan Police and the Asylums Board. Councillors were arrested and thousands turned out to protest. Five years later, for nine terrifying days in May, down at the docks, soldiers unloaded the ships while machine guns were trained

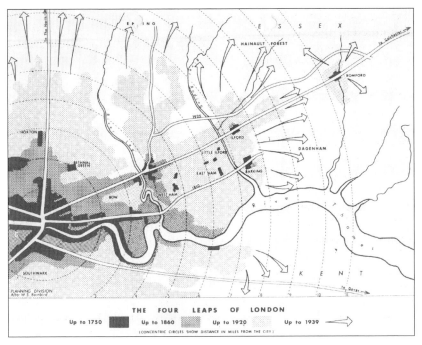

THE FOUR LEAPS OF LONDON

Up to 1750 ■ Up to 1860 ▨ Up to 1920 ░ Up to 1939 ⟹

(CONCENTRIC CIRCLES SHOW DISTANCE IN MILES FROM THE CITY)

London's eastward expansion. From *Newham, Background to the Borough* (London Borough of Newham, 1972)

on pickets. The workers of the whole country had gone on 'General Strike', notionally in sympathy with miners who refused to accept a cut in wages, but, actually, in an explosion of rage at the unfairness of it all.

The recession reached its lowest depth in Britain with the economic crisis of August 1931. Prime Minister Ramsay MacDonald earned the enduring hatred of East Enders, and many more besides, by imposing a 10 per cent cut on the national-insurance benefits for the unemployed. Llewellyn Smith's poverty survey of the previous year had shown that the worst areas of London were Stepney, Poplar, Bethnal Green, Bermondsey and North Kensington. Unemployment in Stepney and Poplar was between 15 and 20 per cent. Cuts in benefit would be felt most sorely here and Father Groser of Christ Church, Watney Street, took action: 'We ... started a campaign by leaflets and open air meetings in which we tried to point out that the causes of the present crisis lies at the root of the devilish and inhuman capitalist system under which we

43

live'. In 1934, Labour finally won the LCC elections and its new leader, Herbert Morrison, proclaimed: 'Let Labour build a new London'.

There was always the 'flicks'. East Enders took to the cinema with a passion. For a few pence you could find entertainment at the Majestic, a fleapit at the top of Whitehorse Lane, or, for special occasions, there was the huge, plush Troxy in Commercial Road, where the management sprayed you with scent to make you feel good. If you went to the Classic in the Mile End Road you could have a fish and chip supper afterwards at Isaac's, next door.

'Those brave people, hemmed in by poverty, and with almost a total lack of possessions', wrote a Stepney teacher, 'led more useful and far more gay lives than their counterparts in today's brick chasms could ever imagine'. The clergy performed 'miracles' for the poor and unemployed, rents were low and food inexpensive. Most families managed to eat well – you could buy twelve herrings for sixpence and butchers sold off meat cheaply on Saturday evenings. A proper 'Sunday roast with two veg' was the norm, with the joint cooked by the local baker. Edith Ramsay, 'friend of four generations of East Enders',

Aldgate, 1925. Hanslip Fletcher, Private Collection

remembered the children playing in the streets: 'Dark Man's Scenery', 'Hi Jimmy Nacker', 'Cracker Nut Boxes'. According to Bernard Marks, in *My East End Childhood*, 'It was a wonderful area, Christians and Jews lived together and everyone helped one another. There were no real troubles. We lived in harmony.'

Distance lending a little enchantment, perhaps, and there are some anti-Semitic tales to be told. But fascists Oswald Mosley and William Joyce ('Lord Haw-Haw') certainly came unstuck when they campaigned in the East End: 'Why are you out of work, why have you no proper homes. The Jews have your house, your job. The Jews are bribing your government. Why don't we turn them out as the Germans have done?' On 4 October 1936 a march of the fascist blackshirts started off from Gardiners' Corner, where the Whitechapel Road meets Commercial Road. Surrounded by a vast number of mounted policemen they started to move towards Cable Street. Whereupon some 300,000 people, Jews, Catholics, communists, dockers, trade unionists and housewives went on the attack. Barricades of paving stones were thrown up and lorries overturned. Children threw marbles under the horses' hooves and put bags of pepper under their noses. This was the famous Battle of Cable Street.

The legendary heroism of East Enders during the Blitz, which would soon follow, is too well documented to brook any dissent; it was the best of times and the worst of times. The continual horrific bombardment from the air of the docks and their hinterland rendered more than a third of the houses uninhabitable, with most of the others damaged. Whole streets disappeared and evacuation reduced the population by well over half. In Stepney Borough there were only 80,000 people left at the end of the war, as opposed to 200,000 in 1939.

The mass exodus continued in the postwar era. The Jewish community had all but gone by the 1970s, and between 1966 and 1975 the docks were run down and 20,000 jobs lost.

No more dockers, no more Jewish tailors, new sorts of immigrants arrived and Brick Lane became 'Banglatown'. The old East End was gone: Wapping is now desirable and the Isle of Dogs glitters.

This overview of the history of the Tower Hamlets concludes with some lines from *Family and Kinship in East London*, the hugely influential book that analysed society in Bethnal Green in the 1950s. The authors are describing the move to Debden in Essex (called 'Greenleigh' in the book):

Canal Road Bridge and Solebay Street, Stepney, 1959. Private Collection

Instead of the hundred fussy, fading little pubs, there are just the neon lights and armchairs of the Merchant Venturer and the Yeomans Arms. Instead of the barrel organ in Bethnal Green Road there is an electrically amplified musical box in a mechanical ice-cream van. In place of tiny workshops squeezed into a thousand back-yards rise the first few glass and concrete factories which will soon give work to Greenleigh's children. Instead of the sociable squash of people and houses, workshops and lorries, there are drawn-out roads and spacious open ground ...

'When I first came,' said Mrs Sandeman, 'I cried for weeks, it was so lonely'.

Michael Young and Peter Willmot, *Family and Kinship in East London* (first published Institute of Community Studies, 1957, this edn published 1975), p. 122.

This chapter is based on my MS history of Stepney parish (deposited at THLHLA). Other reference works include:

S. Inwood, *A History of London* (Macmillan, 1998)

W.J. Fishman, *East End 1888* (Five Leaves Publications, 1988)

G. Stedman Jones, *Outcast London* (OUP, 1971)

Booth Archives at London School of Economics (access at: www.booth. lse.ac.uk).

Chapter 2

RESEARCH

Start with yourself, your parents or your grandparents and work backwards, finding out first of all if any member of the family has done research before, and familiarising yourself with any family lore.

The Internet eases research immeasurably, but it is perfectly possible to do it without, as you will see.

Archives

The archives that are of prime use for locating East Enders are:

- The London Metropolitan Archive (LMA) in Clerkenwell, which now has, in addition to its own records, some from the old Guildhall Library Manuscripts Section and the Corporation of London Record Office. Records for the whole of the Metropolitan Area are at LMA. Other London boroughs have their own archives. Boroughs adjoining Tower Hamlets are Hackney (to the north) and Newham (to the east). On the west is the City (most records at LMA).
- The Tower Hamlets Local History Library and Archives (THLHLA) in Mile End. See Appendix 5 for a summary list of holdings. Records catalogued at Access to Archives (A2A).
- The National Archives (TNA) at Kew.

More details of these archives can be found in Appendix 8.

Websites

Do not imagine that the Internet is all. In fact, two of the most vital sources, GRO certificates of birth, marriage and death, and wills (from 1858), cannot be accessed online, in spite of the claims of some genealogical companies.

General genealogical commercial websites are legion, all offering many thousands of names. They are the most wonderful tool, and there is nothing to stop you starting research straight away. You might get your family back to the days of Bligh of the *Bounty* by dinner time! But be careful and always check the source of any piece of information.

- Most sites are fee paying. Avoid 'pay as you go' as it is really irritating to find your voucher (or whatever) has expired when you are in the middle of some fascinating research.
- Avoid boxes that say 'search all records' and sites that don't tell you what the sources are.
- If the records have been digitised, always look at the image of the original document; transcription errors are common.
- Most sites offer some way of finding out about what research has been done on your family name, or indeed your own family. This may be useful, but be circumspect about swallowing other people's research whole.

The foremost general genealogical websites (using a variety of sources for tracking down individuals) are:

- Ancestry at: www.ancestry.co.uk. One of the most useful for London; referred to in the text as Ancestry.
- The Origins Network, British Origins at: www.origins.net. Best for pre-census and registration records, linked to SOG; referred to in the text as Origins.
- The Genealogist at: www.thegenealogist.co.uk. The only site for TNA Nonconformist registers and Fleet marriages; very important for East End ancestry; referred to in the text as The Genealogist.
- Docklands Ancestors at: www.parishregister.com. For ancestors north and south of the river.
- Genes Reunited at: www.genesreunited.co.uk. For living relatives too.
- Findmypast at: www.findmypast.co.uk.
- GENUKI at: www.genuki.org.uk. London Genealogy section has useful topographical and source information; a free site.
- The Church of Jesus Christ of Latter-Day Saints' (LDS) website FamilySearch at: www.familysearch.org. Make sure you type this

address exactly. It has the 1881 census and the famed index to parish registers, the IGI (go to 'search records' and then 'International Genealogical Index'). It also provides a good guide to sources; go to 'library catalogue' and then 'place search'; a free site.

See FFHS website (below) for more about websites and buy Peter Christian's *The Genealogist's Internet*, 4th edn (TNA, 2007).

Websites for useful organisations and specific groups of records will be referred to in the text. Those of general use in terms of providing information and online catalogues are:

- London Metropolitan Archives (now also holding most Guildhall Manuscripts), LMA, at: www.cityoflondon.gov.uk/lma.
- The National Archives, TNA, at: www.nationalarchives.gov.uk.
- TNA's Access to Archives, A2A, at: www.nationalarchive.gov.uk/a2a.
- The Society of Genealogists, SOG, at: www.sog.org.uk.
- The Federation of Family History Societies, FFHS, at: www.ffhs.org.uk.
- East of London Family History Society, EoLFHS, at: www.eolfhs.org.uk. This is tremendously useful, especially its 'parish information' section. As well as the East of London registration district and Tower Hamlets, it covers Barking and Dagenham, Hackney, Havering, Newham and Redbridge.
- Guild of One Name Studies at: www.one-name.org.
- Tower Hamlets History On Line, THHOL, at: www.thhol.org.uk. A collection of fascinating articles about the East End.
- The East London History Society, ELHS, at: www.mernick.org.uk/elhs.
- Tower Hamlets Archives On Line, THAOL, at: www.ideastore.co.uk/en/articles/localhis. This features some useful indexes (which are noted in text).
- www.eastlondonhistory.com is a 'posting site' with contributions, history and reminiscences.

Assistance

Some genealogical websites provide access to specialists, and LMA offers a research service. The most useful information about the locality and local records is provided by the Tower Hamlets Local History Library and Archives. The best advice on using or interpreting specific groups of records is to be found in the archive where they are held, such as TNA, LMA etc.

It would be a good idea to join the East of London Family History Society. There are other specialist societies for people researching particular types of ancestors, and these will be referred to as we go along.

The Association of Genealogists and Researchers in Archives and TNA will supply you with contacts if you want someone to carry out research for you or someone to read or interpret a document. In addition, you could try the expertgenealogy website.

See Appendix 8 for contact details.

Understanding the Records

Reading the Writing

You are unlikely to have too much difficulty reading the records until you get back to the early seventeenth century. If you are stuck you can get help from experts (see above).

The exception to the above is the PCC (pre-1858) will archive at TNA (available through documents online at TNA's website) which can be quite tricky. Make a copy of the will and take it to a meeting of the EoLFHS or an expert. Alternatively, you can order the original will at TNA; this will have a PROB 10 reference. The wills you read online or on film at TNA are the registered copies of wills (ref. PROB 11); the original (written by a lawyer or even the deceased himself) is almost always much easier to read.

Handwriting samples for wills of various periods are provided by TNA online. Go to: www.nationalarchives.gov.uk>DocumentsOnline>wills and you can read and download samples.

Dates

Before 1752 the year started on 25 March, so any date between 1 January and 24 March is, by modern reckoning, a year later than it says it is. Thus, what appears in the records as 4 February 1733 is 4 February 1734.

Legal records may be dated by 'regnal year', for example, 12 George III, meaning the twelfth year of the reign of George III, calculated from his accession. Useful tables of regnal years can be found in C.R. Cheney (ed.), *The Handbook of Dates* (Royal Historical Society, 1970).

What's in a Name?

One of the most accommodating facets of our ancestors was their use of Christian names. Among ordinary families, until the twentieth century, it was very common, virtually the norm, for the first male child born to a family to be named after its father and the first girl after its mother.

It is not uncommon to find two (or more) children with the same first name in one family. This is especially common when one died and another child, born after the death, was given the same name.

Grandparents' names were regularly used and often the wife's maiden name was used as a son's Christian name, especially if the wife's family was better off than the husband's. Thomas Thirwall, curate of St Dunstan's, Stepney, married, in 1792, the widow of one William Connop, a wealthy Mile End apothecary. The curate's second son was, accordingly, given the Christian name of Connop, in gratitude to the deceased apothecary, whose riches had allowed the family to live in one of the finest houses in Stepney, Lord Morley's old residence on Mile End Green.

The vast majority of people born before the late nineteenth century were called either John, Thomas, William, Edward, Mary, Elizabeth, Jane or Ann or Mary-Ann. Anything else might be useful as a 'family name'; thus the name Francis or Frances repeats itself in the Short family tree (see pp. 56–7). Less usual names may be an indication of wealth or status – Salvidore Salmon of Shadwell, for instance, had a daughter Pollidocia (burial register 1721); Puritans favoured Old Testament names or names like Praisegod.

For the polyglot society in the East End names can be a vital clue to origins. Van (Dutch) names are quite common in the East End from the late Middle Ages. Le (French) names usually indicate Huguenot ancestry. Irish, German and Jewish names speak for themselves; Sephardic Jews (from the Iberian Peninsular) have names like Fernandez and Rodrigues, while Ashkenazi Jews from Central and Eastern Europe have names like Cohen and Levy. Immigrants often changed their names; there are some records of the formal procedure (see Chapter 5, 'Immigrants').

Foundlings, noted as 'dropt' in parish registers, were often called after the place where they were found – Christian Shadwell, for instance.

How Our East End Ancestors Lived

The following notes are useful to bear in mind when carrying out research:

- Co-habitors may not have married; this applies especially in the nineteenth century. They usually married, or got together, in their twenties.
- Re-marriage (or forming a new partnership) was very, very common and often took place soon after the death of the original partner.
- Illegitimacy rates were high. The fathers of bastards were chased up by the parish.
- Very large families are not apparent until the mid-nineteenth century.
- Infant mortality was very high, so it is important to check death and burial records. Grace Foakes of Wapping wrote in *My Part of the River* (Shepheard-Walwyn Publishers, 1972) about her mother: 'I think she had fourteen children altogether, but I am not sure of this, for some died at birth and some only lived a few weeks'.
- According to Beatrice Webb, writing in *My Apprenticeship* in 1926, women 'could chaff each other about having babies by their father and brother'.
- People tended to die young, especially in the poor East End.
- It was a shifting population in Tower Hamlets. People came in search of work or asylum and their families left after a few generations. While in the East End they were unlikely to live very long at one address, although they probably didn't go far – there was a good deal of 'moonlighting' when you couldn't pay the rent.
- A very high proportion of East Enders was Nonconformist, so a good number of baptisms were not recorded in the parish church registers. Marriages, however, were supposed to be documented in this way between 1754 and 1837.
- A good number of our East End ancestors belonged to criminal sub-classes and as such avoided any sort of authority, including the census enumerator.

- People coming into the East End from the countryside tended to come from Essex and East Anglia. People leaving the East End were likely to relocate to the east. Jewish families favoured Golders Green and Stamford Hill.
- Girls often went into service at quite a young age, sometimes in other parts of London or in Essex, where there were (from 'slum times') more likely to be households who could afford servants.
- Among poor East Enders, birth registration dodging was common; perhaps as many as 15 per cent of births may have gone unregistered, especially before 1875 when there was no penalty for non-registration. It may be prudent to look for baptisms instead, although many parents didn't bother with this either. Dodging went on until 1939 when evidence of registration was needed for the issue of ration books.

Chapter 3

THE PRIME SOURCES

These days, with a little nous, a modest outlay and a computer, you can do a good deal of family history research without moving from your chair, with no more initial information than your own birth. Even without your own computer this is a feasible exercise, if you can get yourself to one of the places that hold GRO indexes of births, marriages and deaths and census returns. You will save yourself a good deal of time and frustration if you collect what information (or tales) you can about your family from relatives, so long as you take it all with a pinch of salt.

The chief building blocks for starting a pedigree (following which ever line you fancy, of course) are birth, marriage and death certificates (from 1837 to present) and census returns. Do not be tempted to trace downwards from a supposed ancestor who fought at the Battle of Trafalgar as this is very difficult indeed.

General Register Office (GRO), 1837–Present

You will need GRO records for researching the following:

- The modern family post-census, i.e. from 1911 to present.
- Filling in census 'gaps'; finding out the maiden name of wives especially, finding out when people died, addresses they may have lived at between census years, children who 'escape' the census, either by being born and dying within a ten-year period or by being farmed out to relatives.

Birth, marriage and death certificates cannot be inspected online; you have to buy them from the Registrar General, although there are

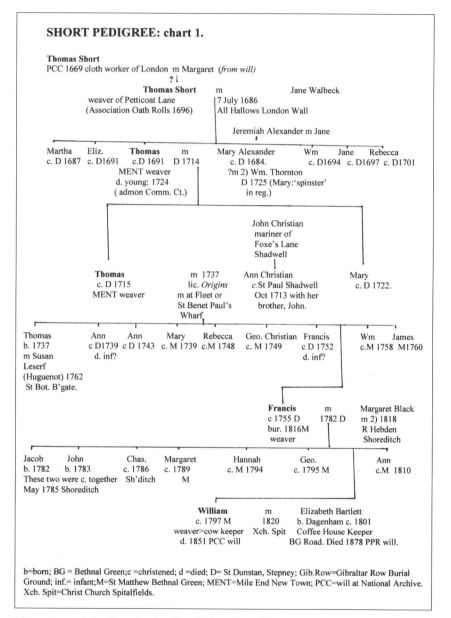

SHORT PEDIGREE: chart 1.

Thomas Short
PCC 1669 cloth worker of London m Margaret *(from will)*
? |

Thomas Short   m   Jane Walbeck
weaver of Petticoat Lane   7 July 1686
(Association Oath Rolls 1696)   All Hallows London Wall

Jeremiah Alexander m Jane

Martha	Eliz.	**Thomas**	m	Mary Alexander	Wm	Jane	Rebecca
c. D 1687	c. D1691	c.D 1691 D 1714		c. D 1684.	c. D1694	c. D1697	c. D1701
		MENT weaver		?m 2) Wm. Thornton			
		d. young: 1724		D 1725 (Mary:'spinster'			
		(admon Comm. Ct.)		in reg.)			

John Christian
mariner of
Foxe's Lane
Shadwell
|

Thomas   m 1737   Ann Christian   Mary
c. D 1715   lic. *Origins*   c.St Paul Shadwell   c. D 1722.
MENT weaver   m at Fleet or   Oct 1713 with her
                 St Benet Paul's brother, John.
                 Wharf

Thomas	Ann	Ann	Mary	Rebecca	Geo. Christian	Francis	Wm	James
b. 1737	c D1739	c D 1743	c. M 1739	c.M 1748	c. M 1749	c D 1752	c.M 1758	M1760
m Susan	d. inf?	d. inf?				d. inf?		
Leserf								
(Huguenot) 1762								
St Bot. B'gate.								

Francis   m   Margaret Black
c 1755 D   1782 D   m 2) 1818
bur. 1816M   R Hebden
weaver   Shoreditch

Jacob	John	Chas.	Margaret	Hannah	Geo.	Ann
b. 1782	b. 1783	c. 1786	c. 1789	c. M 1794	c. 1795 M	c.M 1810
These two were c. together		Sh'ditch	M			
May 1785 Shoreditch						

William   m   Elizabeth Bartlett
c. 1797 M   1820   b. Dagenham c. 1801
weaver>cow keeper Xch. Spit Coffee House Keeper
d. 1851 PCC will   BG Road. Died 1878 PPR will.

b=born; BG = Bethnal Green;c =christened; d =died; D= St Dunstan, Stepney; Gib.Row=Gibraltar Row Burial
Ground; inf.= infant;M=St Matthew Bethnal Green; MENT=Mile End New Town; PCC=will at National Archive.
Xch. Spit=Christ Church Spitalfields.

The pedigree of the Short family, East Enders since the seventeenth century. Much of the research was done via the Internet. Geoff Mann and the Author

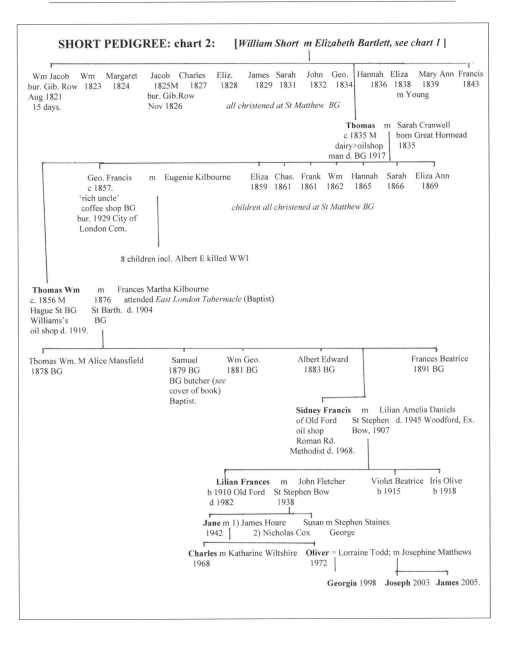

SHORT PEDIGREE: chart 2: *[William Short m Elizabeth Bartlett, see chart 1]*

| Wm Jacob bur. Gib. Row Aug 1821 15 days. | Wm 1823 | Margaret 1824 | Jacob 1825M bur. Gib.Row Nov 1826 | Charles 1827 | Eliz. 1828 | James 1829 | Sarah 1831 | John 1832 | Geo. 1834 | Hannah 1836 | Eliza 1838 | Mary Ann 1839 m Young | Francis 1843 |

all christened at St Matthew BG

Thomas m Sarah Cranwell
c 1835 M | born Great Hormead
dairy>oilshop | 1835
man d. BG 1917

Geo. Francis m Eugenie Kilbourne   Eliza 1859   Chas. 1861   Frank 1861   Wm 1862   Hannah 1865   Sarah 1866   Eliza Ann 1869
c 1857.
'rich uncle'
coffee shop BG
bur. 1929 City of
London Cem.

children all christened at St Matthew BG

8 children incl. Albert E killed WWI

Thomas Wm m Frances Martha Kilbourne
c. 1856 M   1876   attended *East London Tabernacle* (Baptist)
Hague St BG   St Barth. d. 1904
Williams's   BG
oil shop d. 1919.

| Thomas Wm. M Alice Mansfield 1878 BG | Samuel 1879 BG BG butcher (*see* cover of book) Baptist. | Wm Geo. 1881 BG | Albert Edward 1883 BG | Frances Beatrice 1891 BG |

Sidney Francis m Lilian Amelia Daniels
of Old Ford   St Stephen d. 1945 Woodford, Ex.
oil shop   Bow, 1907
Roman Rd.
Methodist d. 1968.

Lilian Frances m John Fletcher   Violet Beatrice   Iris Olive
b 1910 Old Ford   St Stephen Bow   b 1915   b 1918
d 1982   1938

Jane m 1) James Hoare   Susan m Stephen Staines
1942 | 2) Nicholas Cox   George

Charles m Katharine Wiltshire   **Oliver** = Lorraine Todd; m Josephine Matthews
1968   1972 |

Georgia 1998   **Joseph** 2003   **James** 2005.

websites where you can look at the indexes. The registration districts for Tower Hamlets are listed in Appendix 1 and see map on p. 59.

GRO Indexes

The indexes can be searched free at: www.freebmd.org.uk (complete for Tower Hamlets to 1965). Other genealogical sites also have the indexes and you can consult them at TNA, LMA, the City of Westminster Archives or your local LDS centre. To find your nearest LDS centre, consult the telephone book or go to: www.londonfhc.org.uk. The central London LDS library is the Family History Centre in Exhibition Road.

Tower Hamlets Register Office has the records of the present Tower Hamlets RD (1983–date), former RDs of Bethnal Green (1837–1965), Poplar (1837–1965), Poplar and Bethnal Green (1965–82), Whitechapel (1837–1926), Stepney (1837–1926), MEOT (1857–1926), St George-in-the-East (1837–1926) and Stepney (1926–1983); you can search the indexes on their website.

You will be at a loss if you do not know the approximate date and place of the event you are looking for, unless the name is particularly unusual. It is a good idea to start with someone whose details you know – or think you know. Index entries look like this one for my mother:

Births registered in April, May and June 1910
SHORT ... Lilian Frances Poplar 1a 484

1a is the volume number and 484 the page or folio. You will need these to order the certificate, as well as the name, quarter (April–June in this case) and registration district (Poplar here).

To find out who an individual's parents were, their address and the father's occupation, and exactly when the date of birth was, you will have to buy a certificate. To order certificates (c. £9.50 each) go to: www.gro.gov.uk/gro/content/certificates, telephone 0845 6037788 or write to GRO. You can also order certificates from Tower Hamlets Register Office at 020 7364 7880 for £9.25. Having done that, you can trace back, looking for a marriage and so on through the generations, buying certificates as you go. Alternatively, or additionally, you can look for the individual in the 1911 census and trace the family back through the other censuses. (See the Short pedigree on pp. 56–7.)

1 KENSINGTON	19 LONDON CITY
2 CHELSEA	20 SHOREDITCH
3 S¹ GEORGE-HANOVER-SQ¹	21 BETHNAL GREEN
4 WESTMINSTER	22 WHITECHAPEL
5 S¹ MARTIN-IN-THE-FIELDS	23 S¹ GEORGE-IN-THE-EAST
6 S¹ JAMES WEST-M¹	24 STEPNEY
7 MARYLEBONE	25 POPLAR
8 HAMPSTEAD	26 S¹ SAVIOUR SOUTHWARK
9 PANCRAS	27 S¹ OLAVE SOUTHWARK
10 ISLINGTON	28 BERMONDSEY
11 HACKNEY	29 S¹ GEORGE SOUTHWARK
12 S¹ GILES	30 NEWINGTON
13 STRAND	31 LAMBETH
14 HOLBORN	32 WANDSWORTH
15 CLERKENWELL	33 CAMBERWELL
16 S¹ LUKE	34 ROTHERHITHE
17 EAST LONDON	35 GREENWICH
18 WEST LONDON	36 LEWISHAM

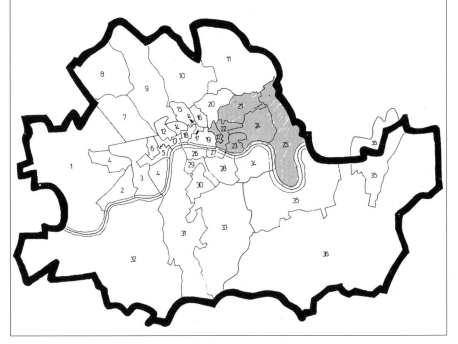

London registration districts. By Witney Lumas

GRO Certificates

Please be wary as the informant gave the registrar the information contained in the certificates and there was no automatic check on it. Refer to the examples shown on pp. 62–5.

Birth Certificates

Until the twentieth century, children were usually born at home (or in the workhouse). Very commonly the first child was born before the wedding (if there was one) and great numbers died in infancy.

Birth certificates supply the same information between 1837 and 1969: the child's name and sex, its father's name and occupation (left blank in cases of illegitimacy), mother's name and maiden name, signature (or mark) name, address and occupation of the informant. A time on the certificate indicates a multiple birth. If there is no Christian name for the child it may indicate that the child died soon after birth. Foundlings are listed after the letter Z. Illegitimate births appear under the mother's name, unless the couple are living 'as man and wife'.

Among poor East Enders, birth registration dodging was common; perhaps as many as 15 per cent of births may have gone unregistered, especially before 1875 when there was no penalty for non-registration. Baptism was free and a search for baptism records is an option; see Appendices 2 and 3. It seems to have taken some time for the costers, dockers and tailors and their wives to take on board the fact that baptism was no longer a necessity for claiming poor relief. There was, moreover, still a feeling that the little creatures, perhaps not long for this life, needed God's blessing. Walter Austin, in the 1880s, met a docker's wife who had lost three children in the space of a fortnight: 'Poor little souls', she said. 'Maybe they're happy now they're dead ... while they lived I know they hadn't much to make 'em happy'.

Marriage Certificates

Weddings tended to take place near the bride's home, although this is far from being the invariable rule in the East End. Marriage certificates show date and place of marriage, whether by banns or licence. Names and ages of the bride and groom are given; 'full age' means over 21 (until 1969). Ages on marriage certificates are not altogether reliable. The status of bride and groom is given ('spinster', 'widower' etc.) and the groom's occupation. There is unlikely to be an occupation listed for the bride until the twentieth century. The address given, for either party, may not mean much, as a residence qualification could be established by a short stay. Names and occupations of the couple's fathers should appear and the signatures of the couple may be revealing. Witnesses are often family members and this may be helpful as evidence that you have got the right family.

Marriages in church continued to be the norm for some years after the introduction of civil marriages in register offices in 1837, and a search of parish registers is an option (see below). You should, however, bear in mind that Protestant Nonconformity was strong in Tower Hamlets; the couple may have married in chapel, rather than church (see the lists of chapels in Appendix 3); also Nonconformists tended to favour civil marriage more than members of the established Church. The parish magazine of November 1906 for St Dunstan's, Stepney, once the great 'marrying church' for the area, dissenters and all, reports only two weddings, one in June and one in September.

If you fail to locate a marriage, it may well be that there wasn't one. According to Mayhew, writing in the 1850s, costers never married; it was often a case of 'I sticks to Sal, and Sal sticks to me'. Reluctance to marry was something that the East End clergy addressed by offering cheap, informal affairs. Arthur Morrison, in *A Child of the Jago* (1896) describes weddings 'Jago style' (1860s–85): 'There was a church in Bethnal Green [this was the 'Red Church', St James the Great] where you might be married for seven pence if you were fourteen years old and no questions asked ... You just came in, drunk if possible, with a batch of some scores, and rowdied about the church with your hat on, and the curate worked off the crowd at one go, calling the names one after another'.

Divorce, before 1858, was uncommon and expensive and only achieved by going to the House of Lords. It did not become accessible to the generality until legal aid was extended in the 1920s and was rare among the poor until the 1960s. Records are at TNA; download the research guide *Divorce Records After 1858*. For recent divorces (from 1938) contact the Principal Registry of the Family Division, Decree Absolute Section.

Death Certificates
Ignore these at your peril. It is all too easy to bang on with your research, assuming you have got the right ancestor from his birth certificate,

CERTIFIED COPY OF AN ENTRY OF BIRTH

GIVEN AT THE GENERAL REGISTER OFFICE

Application Number 7007078

REGISTRATION DISTRICT _Bethnal Green_

1878. BIRTH in the Sub-district of _Church_ in the _County of Middlesex_

Columns:	1	2	3	4	5	6	7	8	9	10*
No.	When and where born	Name, if any	Sex	Name and surname of father	Name, surname and maiden surname of mother	Occupation of father	Signature, description and residence of informant	When registered	Signature of registrar	Name entered after registration
300	First July 1878 60 New York Street	Thomas William	Boy	Thomas William Short	Frances Martha Short formerly Kilburn	Oilman Assistant	T. W. Short Father 60 New York Street Bethnal Green	Second August 1878	Thomas Earl Registrar	

CERTIFIED to be a true copy of an entry in the certified copy of a Register of Births in the District above mentioned.

Given at the GENERAL REGISTER OFFICE, under the Seal of the said Office, the 28th day of July 19 94.

*See note overleaf

BXBZ 631208

CAUTION:- It is an offence to falsify a certificate or to make or knowingly use a false certificate or a copy of a false certificate intending it to be accepted as genuine to the prejudice of any person or to possess a certificate knowing it to be false without lawful authority.

WARNING: THIS CERTIFICATE IS NOT EVIDENCE OF THE IDENTITY OF THE PERSON PRESENTING IT.

Dd 8384412 270165 100M 2/94 McC235370

62

Examples of birth, death and marriage certificates: birth of Thomas William Short, 7 August 1878, Bethnal Green.

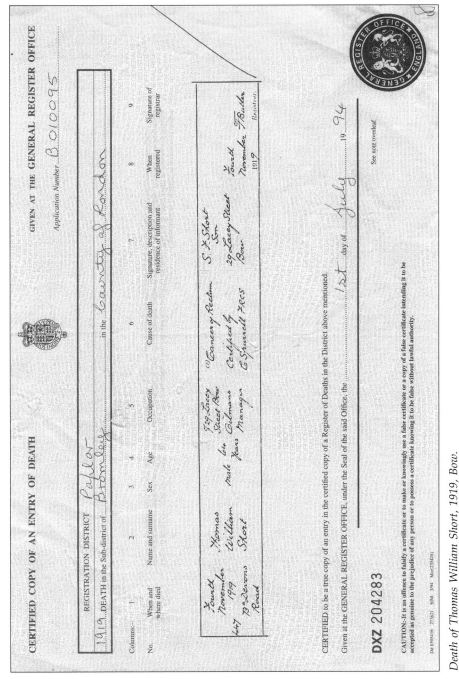

CERTIFIED COPY OF AN ENTRY OF DEATH

GIVEN AT THE GENERAL REGISTER OFFICE

Application Number B 010095

REGISTRATION DISTRICT Poplar

1919 DEATH in the Sub-district of Bromley in the County of London

Columns:—	1	2	3	4	5	6	7	8	9
No.	When and where died	Name and surname	Sex	Age	Occupation	Cause of death	Signature, description and residence of informant	When registered	Signature of registrar
447	Fourth November 1919 73 Devons Road	Thomas William Short	male	64 Years	79 Lacey Street Bow Gasman Manager	(1) Cancer of Rectum Certified by G Spurrell FRCS	S. F. Short Son 29 Lacey Street Bow	Fourth November 1919	T Butler Registrar

CERTIFIED to be a true copy of an entry in the certified copy of a Register of Deaths in the District above mentioned.

Given at the GENERAL REGISTER OFFICE, under the Seal of the said Office, the 1st day of July 19 94

DXZ 204283

See note overleaf

CAUTION:–It is an offence to falsify a certificate or to make or knowingly use a false certificate or a copy of a false certificate intending it to be accepted as genuine to the prejudice of any person or to possess a certificate knowing it to be false without lawful authority.

Dd 8905416 273621 50M 3/94 Mer(285428)

63

Death of Thomas William Short, 1919, Bow.

CERTIFIED COPY OF AN ENTRY OF MARRIAGE

GIVEN AT THE GENERAL REGISTER OFFICE, LONDON

Application Number R149267

18 — Marriage solemnized at St John's Church in the Parish of St John's .... in the County of Middlesex

No.	When Married.	Name and Surname.	Age.	Condition.	Rank or Profession.	Residence at the time of Marriage.	Father's Name and Surname.	Rank or Profession of Father.
59	June 9th 1869	Benjamin Young	full age	bachelor	Rilman	151 Bethnal green Road	Henry Young	Plumber
		Eliza Short	full age	spinster		149 Bethnal green Road	William Short	Cowkeeper

Married in the St John's Church according to the Rites and Ceremonies of the Established Church, by Banns or after Banns by me,

This Marriage was solemnized between us { Benjamin Young / Eliza Short } in the Presence of us, { George Short / Samuel Clifford }

William Loreen Officiating Minister

CERTIFIED to be a true copy of an entry in the certified copy of a register of Marriages in the Registration District of Bethnal Green
Given at the GENERAL REGISTER OFFICE, LONDON, under the Seal of the said Office, the 26th day of April 89

MX 255045

Dd 8098501   8640004   75M   5/88   Mcr(73966)

Form A513MX

Marriage of Eliza Short and Benjamin Young, 1867, St John's, Bethnal Green.

64

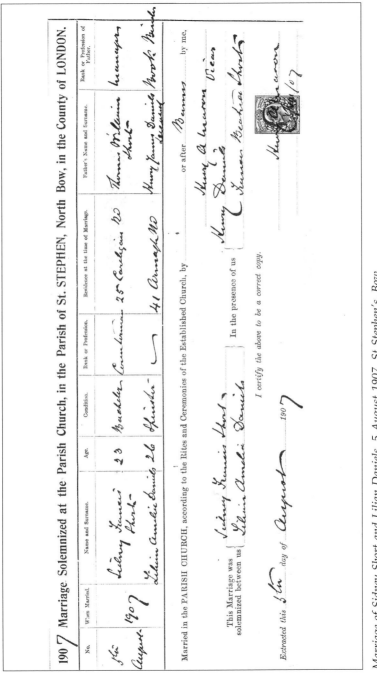

Marriage of Sidney Short and Lilian Daniels, 5 August 1907, St Stephen's, Bow.

when actually he died as a child and a sibling was born and given the same Christian name. This was a regular occurrence. In addition, you will need the date of death to do a will search (see p. 82).

Certificates show when and where a person died and give a cause of death; from 1866 their age at death is given in the indexes and from 1969 their birth date. These dates may be inspired guesses on the part of the informant.

If you can't find a death registered it may mean the individual left the country, changed their name or 'went underground'.

I have already noted reasons why you may fail to find a birth, marriage or death certificate. The most common reason for a failed search, however, is to do with names. You may have a different spelling for either surname or Christian name or the individual may have been known to the family by a nickname.

Census

Everyone in the country (in theory at least) can be found for the census years 1841, 1851, 1861, 1871, 1881, 1891, 1901 and 1911. You will find them listed with their families in household schedules, unless, of course, they were working or staying away from home, in the workhouse or infirmary, or in the armed services.

This, together with the fact that there are complete indexes and transcripts, make these records the prime tool for family history. There are no census returns available to the public after 1911 and few with names before 1841. Refer to Peter Christian and David Annal, *Census: The Expert Guide* (TNA, 2008).

You can search all census returns at home on the computer (1881 is free; for the rest you must pay), or go to TNA or LMA where you can access them online free of charge. THLHLA has censuses on film and some indexes, as well as census returns for Poplar registration district for 1821 and 1831. The 1831 can be bought on CD-ROM from EoLFHS. If you want to scroll through the returns to get an idea of the area where your ancestors lived, it is easy to do with the microfilms at TNA or THLHLA.

Access the 1911 census online at Findmypast and Genes Reunited (things change by the minute, so do a '1911 census' Internet search) or inspect it at TNA or LMA. There are name indexes and place indexes, choose between transcripts and digital copies.

The 1881 census is free at Familysearch, where you can view an abstract of the entries; the original images are available at The Genealogist. The 1841, 1851, 1861, 1871, 1891 and 1901 censuses are available at Ancestry, The Genealogist and Findmypast. The 1901 census is available at Findmypast and at Genesreunited. Origins only has censuses for the period 1841–71.

Information varies slightly from census to census; the 1841 is not so informative as the others as it rounds ages off to the nearest five and does not supply the place of birth, merely telling you whether or not your ancestor was born in the same county as he is now residing in. The others give names, places of birth, occupations and relationships within the household. The 1911 census is most informative as it tells you how many children have been born to the household members, even if they have died.

You can trace your family back through the censuses, starting in 1911, for seventy years. From the 1851 census you can take the place of birth and proceed to the various sources for parish records (see p. 72). Information in the census should be supplemented with birth, marriage and death certificates of the individuals concerned to build the full picture.

Warnings and Tips
The following notes are useful to bear in mind:

- There are many transcription errors. If you can't find who you are looking for, look for a sibling with a more easily recognisable name. Thus, John Smith is more likely to be correctly transcribed than his brother Caractacus Smith.
- If you search for 'place of birth' you can never be sure you've got it exactly right. Instead, ask for all the individuals of the same name born about the same date in London/Middlesex and browse through them to see which one is likely to be the one you are looking for.
- The man known to the family as Fred may really have been called something quite different; perhaps this was his second name, or it may not have been his proper name at all.
- People lied to the enumerator about their age quite often and for a variety of reasons, but generally because they were not sure themselves.

- Places of birth are not always to be trusted. Do you know exactly where you were born? Often family members' births are all stated to have been in the same place, regardless.
- Children, especially girls going into service, often left home in their early teens. Sometimes children were looked after by other family members, especially if the family was very poor and the wife had to work.

Supplementing the Census from GRO

From a census search you can sketch an outline tree, but you will not know any of the wives' maiden names and will not be sure if there were more children than those listed. From the GRO certificates you can fill in these gaps, check up on ages and find out when any individual died. For GRO indexes and certificates see pp. 55–66.

Using Parish Registers Instead of GRO Certificates, from 1837

Searching the GRO indexes and ordering certificates can be laborious and expensive, but at least there is one central index for all. An option is to search the parish registers for marriages, baptisms and burials. The entries in some of these have been digitised and indexed, but the source is far from being as comprehensive as the GRO indexes. You could try first in the records of the ecclesiastical parish given in the census for where the family lived. For more about parish registers, see p. 72 and the list in Appendix 2.

Finding the right parish can be a problem in an East End that was rapidly expanding, with new parishes being formed. Bethnal Green is the best example of this. Originally it was part of Stepney parish, then it became independent and St Matthew's Church was consecrated in 1746. From 1837, in rapid succession, no less than twelve new churches were built and maintained their own set of registers.

To find out which churches/chapels served your area, and what records are available, a most useful source is the 'parish information' section on the EoLFHS's website. Go to: www.eolfhs.org.uk>parish information.

If you have a street name a good way to find out which parish it was in is to consult the *Victorian London A–Z Street Index* at: homepage. ntlworld.com/hitch/gendocs/lon-str.html. It is free and easy to use. Thus, the entry for Hague Street in Bethnal Green will tell you that in 1862 it was in the parish of All Saints', Bethnal Green, in 1872 it

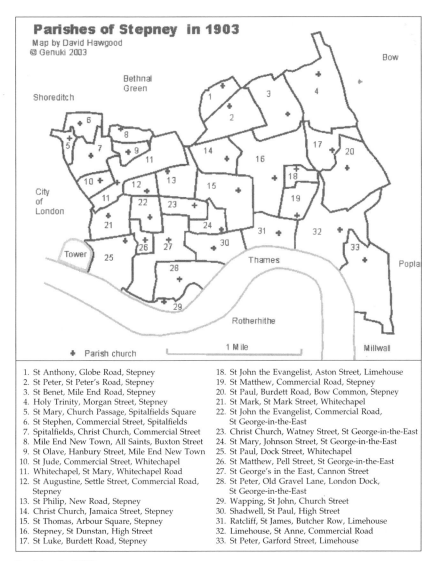

Parishes of Stepney in 1903
Map by David Hawgood
© Genuki 2003

Bow

Bethnal
Green

Shoreditch

City
of
London

Tower

Thames

Popla

Rotherhithe

1 Mile

Millwall

✛ Parish church

1. St Anthony, Globe Road, Stepney
2. St Peter, St Peter's Road, Stepney
3. St Benet, Mile End Road, Stepney
4. Holy Trinity, Morgan Street, Stepney
5. St Mary, Church Passage, Spitalfields Square
6. St Stephen, Commercial Street, Spitalfields
7. Spitalfields, Christ Church, Commercial Street
8. Mile End New Town, All Saints, Buxton Street
9. St Olave, Hanbury Street, Mile End New Town
10. St Jude, Commercial Street, Whitechapel
11. Whitechapel, St Mary, Whitechapel Road
12. St Augustine, Settle Street, Commercial Road, Stepney
13. St Philip, New Road, Stepney
14. Christ Church, Jamaica Street, Stepney
15. St Thomas, Arbour Square, Stepney
16. Stepney, St Dunstan, High Street
17. St Luke, Burdett Road, Stepney
18. St John the Evangelist, Aston Street, Limehouse
19. St Matthew, Commercial Road, Stepney
20. St Paul, Burdett Road, Bow Common, Stepney
21. St Mark, St Mark Street, Whitechapel
22. St John the Evangelist, Commercial Road, St George-in-the-East
23. Christ Church, Watney Street, St George-in-the-East
24. St Mary, Johnson Street, St George-in-the-East
25. St Paul, Dock Street, Whitechapel
26. St Matthew, Pell Street, St George-in-the-East
27. St George's in the East, Cannon Street
28. St Peter, Old Gravel Lane, London Dock, St George-in-the-East
29. Wapping, St John, Church Street
30. Shadwell, St Paul, High Street
31. Ratcliff, St James, Butcher Row, Limehouse
32. Limehouse, St Anne, Commercial Road
33. St Peter, Garford Street, Limehouse

Parishes in 1903. Sourced at GENUKI

was described as being off the Bethnal Green Road and in 1997 it was Bethnal Green E2.

Tower Hamlets' parish registers are, for the most part, at LMA; some recent registers are still at the churches concerned, if they are still functioning as churches. LMA registers are listed in Appendix 2; the majority of them have been digitised and indexed by Ancestry and are available online.

Remember the following:

- Online sources are not always comprehensive; you may have to go to the archive or church.
- Families, especially the very poor, are likely to have moved around and it is not always easy to locate the church where the children were baptised (if they were).
- Many East Enders were Nonconformists, so their babies, if they were baptised at all, would have been baptised in the appropriate chapel; a list of these is in Appendix 3. They have not been digitised or indexed. Nonconformist marriages may still be found in the parish registers, but increasingly they will be located in register offices and chapel registers.
- Marriages may have taken place in register offices from 1837, although this did not become usual for some time after its introduction.

Marriage records from parish registers for churches in Tower Hamlets have been digitised and indexed and can be accessed at Ancestry's database 'London England Marriages and Banns 1754–1921'. Just type in the name of groom or bride with a date and scroll down to find your marriage. Then read the original document.

Ancestry also has a database of London births and baptisms for the period 1813–1906 and deaths and burials for 1813–1980, taken from parish registers and Poor Law union records. These sources are quick and easy to use.

A search for the marriage of my grandparents, Sidney and Lil Short, at Ancestry was revealing. The couple were married in about 1907, according to the 1911 census. I typed in 'Sidney Short 1907' and the 'hit' shows:

Sidney Francis Short born *c.* 1884 marries 5 August 1907
Lilian Amelia Davids at St Stephen Poplar.

The digitisation of the original entry in the marriage register shows that the bride's maiden name has been wrongly transcribed. It is, in fact, 'Daniels'; the vicar's writing makes it look like Davids, but Lil's signature, at the bottom, is clearly Daniels.

The wedding took place on 5 August 1907, at the local church of St Stephen's Bow [Tredegar Road]. Sidney Francis Short, bachelor and counterman of 25 Cardigan Road, Bow, aged 23, marries Lilian Amelia Daniels, spinster 30 years old of 41 Armagh Road Bow. The bride's signature is appended in a shaky and uneducated hand! The groom's signature, however, is done with an educated flourish, as is that of his sister Frances Beatrice, one of the witnesses. The groom's father is named as Thomas William Short, 'manager' and the bride's as Henry Daniels, 'bookbinder deceased'.

Accessed at Ancestry's 'London Marriages': register of St Stephen, Bow, original at LMA. See the photograph of their wedding below.

For Nonconformist ancestors, see p. 119; for Roman Catholics, see p. 141.

Before GRO (1837) and Census (1841)

You've got back to about 1790 – there are no more censuses available and no birth, marriage or death certificates registered – now what?

For those who have got their families back to the days of periwigs and tricorn hats, when canaries sang from weavers' workshops in Bethnal

The wedding of Sidney Short and Lilian Daniels, Bow, 1907. Author's Collection

Green and sea captains swaggered in Wapping, research becomes more complicated. There are many online sources, but there is no one central block of contemporary data and you may, eventually, have to go off to the archives, if you haven't already. On the plus side, there were considerably fewer people around in the eighteenth-century East End and they were not so poor, so were more likely to have left wills or some other account of themselves.

Parish Registers

Your 'stock-in-trade' now is church (parish) registers, where you can search for the baptisms, marriages and burials of family members. If your ancestors were Nonconformists or Catholics their baptisms will not be here (see sections on Nonconformists and Irish/Roman Catholics in Chapter 5), but their marriages should be (except Quakers and Jews). In the East End there were seventeen parish churches for the period before 1837. They are listed in Appendix 2 and shown on the map on p. 73. To find out which churches/chapels served your area, go to: www.eolfhs.org.uk>parish information.

The chief source for searching for ancestors before central registration are the registers of baptisms, marriages and burials kept by the established Church from the mid-sixteenth century, and the transcripts of them kept by the diocese, where they exist. The survival of parish registers is very good, although there are some gaps. Almost all the early registers for Tower Hamlets are at LMA, where you can read them on film. They are being digitised by Ancestry (see below). Indexes and collections of data from the registers are many and varied (see Appendix 2).

The two main block sources for pre-GRO parish-register searching for this area are:

- The International Genealogical Index (IGI) (baptisms, but very few marriages).
- Ancestry London databases (before 1813 no indexes, except for marriages, which are indexed from 1754).

Marriage indexes are dealt with separately at pp. 75–81.

The IGI is available at: FamilySearch.org, LMA, TNA, LDS centres and a whole variety of archives and libraries.

The great LDS (Mormon) database of parish-register baptisms (and some marriages) remains the first port of call for pre-GRO researchers.

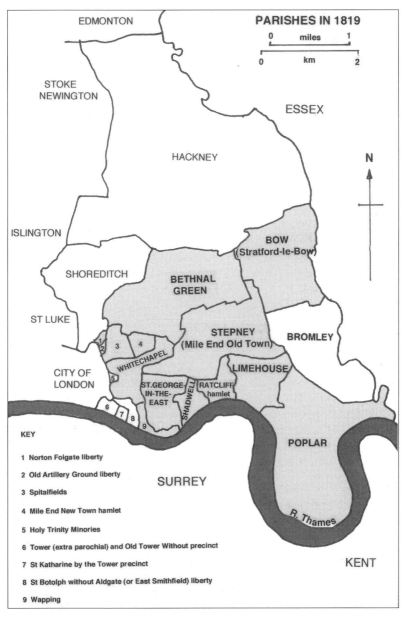

Parishes in 1819. The shaded area was originally all part of Stepney parish. Drawn by Jane Seal

Even though it is not comprehensive, it is the best available to date. To research online, go to: FamilySearch.org (make sure you have the LDS website and not any other similarly named), click on to 'search records' and then on to 'International Genealogical Index'. Always check entries for their source; only trust those that are from an accredited source, namely parish records; many of the IGI's entries have been submitted by members of the Mormon Church. To find out which parishes are in the IGI you could go to FamilySearch.org>library catalogue>place name search (enter Stepney, Bethnal Green, Poplar or wherever)>'church records and church records indexes'. This lists all the LDS film holdings, which can be ordered and read at any LDS Family History Centre.

The Ancestry London Databases

There are three very useful indexed Ancestry databases: 'London England Births and Baptisms 1813–1906', 'Marriages and Banns 1754–1921' and 'Deaths and Burials 1813–1980'. The Ancestry database 'London England baptisms, Marriages and Burials 1538–1812' has digitisation of parish registers but, as yet, is unindexed. See Appendix 2 for lists of parishes covered in these databases, and for indexes and other means of reference for individual parishes.

Baptisms

Living in times when having a baby christened is far from the usual practice, it may seem to the new researcher that relying on baptismal entries for evidence of the existence of ancestors is a rather haphazard way of proceeding. It is not so. Initiation into the religious fold was taken seriously and, that apart, baptism was far from being just a religious rite. Babies had to be registered as members of their local community for a variety of reasons, not least in case there was a need to claim poor relief. Parish registers (pre-1837) are probably as secure, comprehensive and reliable a source as the GRO.

Many East Enders were Protestant Nonconformists: Quakers, Methodists, Baptists or Independents/Congregationalists. Their marriages (except Quakers) had to be conducted in the parish (Church of England) church and many of them were buried in the parish churchyard, although there were some Nonconformist burial grounds. Baptisms or their equivalent were, however, performed in their own chapels and the records kept there. See the section on Nonconformists in Chapter 5 and Appendix 3 for lists of chapel registers.

For Catholics, see p. 141 and for Jews, p. 154.

The content of entries varies; sometimes the occupation of the father and the family's address is given. Children are usually baptised soon after birth, but not always. Sometimes you will find a bunch of siblings being baptised at the same time; perhaps the family has just moved into the parish and wanted to establish their 'parish of settlement'; this meant that they officially belonged to the parish and might be eligible for poor relief.

Burials

Entries in burial registers should not be neglected, as they often are, not least by modern indexers. You need to know if the individual you have found in a baptism register survived infancy to become your great, great, great, great ——. To do this you can go to the archives to look at the registers themselves (usually on film) or browse them at Ancestry. For deaths from 1813 you can try Ancestry's 'London Deaths and Burials 1813–1980'. The London Burial Index 1538–1812 (at SOG, via Origins) is a bit of lucky dip, but is worth a try. FFHS' 'National Burial Index' is an ongoing project which has, as yet, a slight East End coverage for the pre-1837 period.

People were usually buried within a few days of death. Until the mid-nineteenth century burials for all were, more often than not, in the parish churchyard. Nonconformists had their own burial grounds, although families did not always use them. Jews also had their own cemeteries (see p. 156).

Marriages

Sources for pre-1837 marriages:

- Entries in parish registers and bann books.
- Allegations and bonds associated with the issue of marriage licences (an alternative to banns).
- Fleet marriages (irregular or clandestine marriages), seventeenth century to 1754. A great many East Enders married 'in the Fleet'.
- Quaker registers (they were allowed their own marriages; see p. 124).
- Jewish marriages (see p. 155–6).

- Divorce. Before 1858 the only recourse for ordinary people (usually women) in an impossible marriage was to get a separation from 'bed and board' in the church courts. Separation proceedings for London, and much of the rest of the country, were dealt with by the London Consistory Court (records at LMA; depositions of witnesses 1700–13 accessible at Origins). It was more common than might be imagined.

Indexes (general) for pre-1837 marriages:

- IGI (few) and Ancestry databases (see above).
- Boyd's Marriage Index (available at SOG and the Origins website) covers the following: Shadwell St Paul 1671–1754; Stepney St Dunstan 1568–1754; Crispin Street Huguenot Chapel 1696–1711; Pearl Street Huguenot 1700 only; Whitechapel St Mary Matfelon 1616–25; St Benet Paul's Wharf Fleet marriages (some).
- The Pallot Index of London and Middlesex marriages (1780–1837) at Ancestry and Guildhall Library (LMA).
- Fleet (irregular and clandestine) marriages 1667–1754; indexes, transcripts and digitisation at The Genealogist (originals at TNA). Do not neglect this most important source – go to 'Research View' then 'Keyword Master Search' and select 'BMD' and under 'Census' or 'MBD' choose 'Nonconformist records'. The Fleet marriages appear under this title as the original registers and notebooks are grouped with Nonconformist registers at TNA.
- Licence indexes, see below.

Finding marriages can be a problem, and it is especially so in the East End. Couples tended to marry in the bride's parish, which may not be where they settled down. Thus, William Short married Elizabeth Bartlett at Christ Church Spitalfields in 1820 and their children were baptised in the adjoining parish of St Matthew Bethnal Green (see pedigree pp. 56–7). In addition, as throughout its history the East End has been continually expanding and new parishes being formed, you will not always know where to look. Before 1729–30, for instance, Limehouse, Spitalfields and Wapping-Stepney (St George-in-the-East) were all part of St Dunstan's enormous parish and details of the vital events of the populace should be sought among its immaculate records.

Before 1754 couples married all over the place (see below). For the period 1754–1837 couples married in the parish church, as they were obliged to do so by law, except Quakers and Jews. Either banns were called (an announcement of the intention to marry) on three consecutive Sundays in the church of bride and groom, or a licence might be procured. Couples in the East End tended to marry in the mother church, as their parents or grandparents had done, even after new parishes were formed. Thus, for example, after 1730 the inhabitants of Limehouse might marry at St Dunstan's Stepney even though they had their own church.

Fleet or Irregular Marriages
For this period, great numbers of East Enders married at one of the 'marrying churches' in the locality or at 'the Fleet', not in a church at all. The greatest event in East End genealogy since Thomas Colyer-Fergusson published his great St Dunstan marriage indexes (1898–1900) is the digitising and indexing of the Fleet registers. As a result, thousands of marriages have been made readily available for the first time.

Before the system was regularised by Hardwicke's Marriage Act, couples of all sorts and conditions resorted, for a variety of reasons, to marriage venues outside their parish. These 'clandestine' or 'irregular' (but legal) marriages were conducted either in churches that were empowered to issue their own licences or in non-ecclesiastical venues by dubious clergymen.

In the early seventeeth century the churches of St Faith-under-St Paul and St Gregory-by-St Paul were popular irregular marriage venues. From the mid- to late seventeenth century the east side of the City and Stepney was a marriage centre. From about 1644 Holy Trinity Minories was the favoured church; this was a parish created at the Dissolution and owned by the Crown, exempt from the Bishop's visitation rights. The other chief marrying churches were the two Aldgate churches of St James's Duke's Place and St Botolph's, which claimed exemption from ecclesiastical control. In the late seventeeth century about half of all London marriages were conducted in these three churches, but this had tailed off by about 1725. St Katharine's by the Tower, by charter of Edward VI free of diocesan authority, was a centre for clandestine marriages from about 1674. Other marrying churches were St Mary Bromley, St Leonard, St Mary Stratford Bow, St Mary Whitechapel and St Dunstan itself, where the parson was able to issue licences from at least 1669 and did so in large numbers. St Pancras, Mayfair and Southwark had popular venues but they were completely dwarfed by the East End centres. St Benet Paul's Wharf was always popular for weddings as it adjoined Doctors Commons, where Vicar General and Faculty Office marriage licences were issued. Couples would buy their licence and then go straight into the church to be married.

The original non-church centre was the Fleet Prison (off Farringdon Road), which claimed exemption from Church authority because the wardenship of the prison was in private hands and only the Crown had visitation rights. These marriages were cheap and no questions were asked. Unfrocked clergy and prison chaplains conducted a roaring trade in and around the prison in 'marriage shops'. Joshuah Lilley, for instance, advertised that at the Hand and Pen by the Fleet Ditch marriages were performed 'by a Gentleman regularly bred at one of our Universities and lawfully ordained'. It had been estimated that in the 1740s about 15 per cent of all marriages in England were celebrated in the Fleet, and most of them were from London and the surrounding neighbourhood, including great numbers from the East End. Stepney sailors and Spitalfields weavers feature prominently in the records.

A wedding in the Fleet, early eighteenth century. Author's Collection

The search for a marriage from this period is, therefore, far from straightforward. Fortunately, there are now modern searching aids and it is no longer a question of digging around in dusty registers all over the place. See Appendix 4 for a list of the popular marriage venues, registers and indexes. Mark D. Herber's *Clandestine Marriages in the Chapel and Rules of the Fleet Prison* (Francis Boutle Publishers, 1998–2001) has 3 volumes of transcripts of some of the notebooks, with a useful introduction.

Marriage Licences
Marriage by licence was popular for privacy or subterfuge and was regarded as the 'posh' way to marry. Between 1618 and 1641 a quarter of all marriages at St Dunstan's Stepney were by licence. 'Very few,' reported a French visitor in 1697, 'are willing to have their affairs declar'd to all the world in a publick place, when for a guinea they may do it snug'. In the eighteenth century probably one-third of marriages were conducted by licence. The records of licences are allegations and bonds; they may provide more information than a parish-register entry. A bond had to be entered into until 1823.

Licences were valid for three months. The associated oath (allegation) and bond provide a statement and undertaking of intention to marry and there are instances where the marriage did not actually take place. Sometimes the marriage took place at a different church from that mentioned in the allegation or bond. The records provide the names of the bride and groom, the name or names of the church for which the licence is issued and a note of consent by parent or guardian if either party is under age. See the allegation for Captain Cook's marriage on p. 80.

Licences were granted by various authorities. As has been shown, some incumbents granted their own licences. If the bride and groom lived in different dioceses they had to apply to the Archbishop of Canterbury's Vicar General. If they lived in different provinces (York and Canterbury) they had to obtain a Faculty Office licence. The rules were almost completely ignored, however.

Licences have long been a popular genealogical source. Before the bringing together and digitising of parish registers, they were an easier source to search; the Archbishop's licences are the largest collection for East Enders.

Archbishop's licences are held at Lambeth Palace Library, 1534–present. SOG and LDS centres have films for 1694–1850, and these are

Captain Cook's marriage allegation, 1762. Although both Cook and his bride were residents of Shadwell, they married in Barking church. Possibly Elizabeth was in service there or staying with Quaker friends. Lambeth Palace Library indexed at Origins; copies of the allegation or bonds have to be ordered. Published indexes are available: 'Allegations of the Faculty Office 1543–1869', *Harleian Society* 24 (1888) and '1632–1714', *British Record Society Index Library* 33 (1632–1714), access at Ancestry, 'Vicar General's marriage licences 1660–1679', *Harleian Society* 23.

Bishop of London's licences are at LMA 1521–1982, indexes for 1520–1828 in *Harleian Society* 25–6 and for 1597–1700 in *British Record Society Index Library* 72 and 76 (for 1597–1700, access at Ancestry).

The licences issued by the Royal Peculiar of St Katharine's by the Tower 1686–1802 are at the Guildhall Library, indexed at: www. history.ac.uk/gh/stkath.htm (names only, no addresses).

For further information about these records, see Melanie Barber, 'Records of Marriage and Divorce in Lambeth Palace Library', *Genealogists' Magazine*, Vol. 20, 4.

An example of a marriage allegation is that of Sherland Short (apprenticed to a Stepney Mariner, in 'Apprentices of Great Britian 1710–1774', accessed from SOG at Origins), who married Ann Piggot at St Benet Paul's Wharf in October 1727. The marriage was found in Boyd's Marriage Index, accessed at Origins. The marriage licence was issued by the Faculty Office on 9 October 1727; the index entry found at Origins and a copy of the allegation ordered. It reads:

> On which day appeared personally Sherland Short of the parish of St Michael Queenhithe London Aged above Twenty One years and a Batchelor and alledged that he intended to marry with Anne Piggott of the parish of St John Baptist London Aged above Twenty One years and a Spinster.
>
> Not knowing or believing any lawful Let or Impediment by reason of any Precontract, Consanguinity Affinity, or any other lawful means whatsoever to hinder the said intended Marriage, of the truth of the premises he made Oath, and prayed Licence to Solemnize the said Marriage, in the parish church of St Benedict Paul's Wharf London.
>
> Sherland Short [signed with a very educated flourish]
>
> Jurat' etc fiat Licentia [let a licence issue]
> W Bramston Sur[rogate] Signed

Chapter 4

OTHER MAJOR SOURCES

The following pages contain descriptions of a variety of significant genealogical sources from the sixteenth to twentieth centuries. Some may give you extra family members or fill in gaps, while some will flesh out what you know about your ancestors' lives.

Wills and Probate

Wills are invaluable. If you are lucky enough to find one for any family member it might tell you more about your ancestor than any other official record. But only a relatively small percentage of people left wills, mainly men. The poor did not usually bother.

Grants of administration, called admons in the records, might be made if the deceased had not made a will or none could be found. They are not as informative as wills, as they only supply the name of the dead person, address and grantee (usually wife or next of kin) and a valuation of the estate.

From 1858–Present

Wills proved and administrations granted from 11 January 1858 can be ordered from the Principal Probate Registry (PPR) in Holborn (see Appendix 8).

Death duty registers are an important source for supplementing will and admons to 1903. These are at TNA (see below).

The PPR has good, easy indexes, with names and addresses given and the value of the estate. There is no Internet access here, although many indexes are now on Ancestry. You can consult the indexes ('National

Probate Calendars, 1858–1943') at TNA, LMA, your local probate registry or the PPR. The procedure is very straightforward and the results usually most rewarding. A small fee (currently £5) is charged to read and obtain a copy of the will or grant of administration and there is a waiting time of about an hour. If you prefer, apply by post to Chief Clerk, York Probate Sub-Registry, Castle Chambers, Clifford Street, York YO1 9RG.

Few East Enders from this period left wills and, even if the did, they often did not go to probate and have been lost. Charles Dickens's character Sam Weller popped his mother-in-law's will into a teapot on the mantelpiece and left it there: 'As it's all right and satisfactory to us'.

As there are relatively few East End wills registered, if the name you are researching is not too common, it's a good idea to spend some time flicking through the index volumes and pick up on anyone who looks to be a likely member of your family, direct ancestor or not. One of your family may well feature as a legatee. Most families have something to say about a rich uncle. My mother's Uncle George came and distributed gold sovereigns to her and her sisters at Christmas!

Pre-1858: Wills at LMA and TNA
A few hints for researching these wills and probate records:

- They may not make any mention of a person's freehold or copyhold properties, i.e. their houses may not feature. Likewise, valuations of estates will not include the real estate.
- Don't worry about the Latin (pre-1733) piece at the bottom; it is the 'probate clause', which authorises the will. You just need the name and date from it.
- The children featured in the will may not comprise the whole family. Elder sons and daughters might already have been provided for in marriage or other settlements.

LMA/Guildhall Wills and Admons
The Bishop of London's Commissary Court proved most wills for Tower Hamlets before the nineteenth century, although the wills of seamen (and others) who died at sea or abroad (of which Stepney had many) were normally proved in the senior court, the Prerogative Court of Canterbury (see below the section on TNA/PCC wills).

The Commissary archive is a magnificent series of records; many of the wills are of ordinary working men who made good. You will find

Elizabethan mariners who made their fortune from gold from the New World, watermen grown wealthy by taking Londoners in their 'taxi boats', builders, limemen and all sorts. It is a particularly rich source for the sixteenth and seventeenth centuries, and thereafter wills from the area were increasingly taken for probate to the senior court, the PCC.

Commissary Court wills are now held at LMA and the registered copies, entered in Act Books (Guildhall MS 9171), may be read on microfilm. The original wills (MS 9172) can also be inspected; do this to see your ancestor's signature. Moreover, the court copies have been tidied up by the clerk and the original will, especially if it is a nuncupative or spoken will, dictated to a bystander, may use spellings of words that reveal how they spoke.

The Commissary Court wills are scheduled to be digitised and will be available at Ancestry in due course. For now you will have to go to LMA to read them. Published indexes are available for the periods 1374–1649 and 1661–1700 – British Record Society, *Indexes to Testamentary Records in the Commissary Court of London (London Division) now Preserved in Guildhall Library*. For the period 1750–1858 they are indexed (with other wills) in the *London Probate Index*, which belongs to Dr David Wright, who charges a search fee. Dr Wright can be contacted at: 71 Island Wall, Whitstable, Kent CT5 1EL; davideastkent@aol.com; www.canterhill.co.uk/davideastkent/. Alternatively, the indexes can be consulted at LMA.

The wills of people dying in the parishes of St Botolph's Aldgate (masses of sailors) and Holy Trinity Minories were proved by the Archdeacon of London, and those of residents of St Katharine's by the Tower were proved by the officials of the Peculiar Court of St Katharine. These wills are all held at LMA.

An index to Archdeaconry wills for the periods 1363–1649 and 1661–1700 has been published by the British Record Society, *Testamentary Records of the Archdeaconry of London*. The index for the period 1700–1807 can be found in Cliff Webb's *An Index of Wills Proved in the Archdeaconry Court of London* (SOG, 1996). Origins has Archdeaconry will indexes for the period 1750–1800 online.

Between 1650 and 1660 all wills in the country were proved in the PCC (records at TNA and available online, see below).

A few East Enders' wills may be found among the records of the London Consistory Court at LMA. This court had a jurisdiction that overlapped with the Commissary Court. It seems to have been the custom for clergy to have their wills proved in the Consistory Court.

Indexes for 1492–1547 are available in published form – *London Consistory Court Wills, 1492–1547*, ed. Ida Darlington (London Record Society 3, 1967), and for the period 1514–1858 a near complete index is available online via LMA's website.

Other Probate Records at LMA/ Guildhall

Letters of administration supply only the name of the widow or next of kin, but this can be very useful. They are indexed alongside wills in contemporary indexes.

Inventories (lists of goods and chattels excluding freehold property) survive for some estates (seventeenth and eighteenth centuries). The inventory for Thomas Short, weaver of Mile End New Town who died in 1724 (see pedigree on p. 56) is a good example:

> In the kitchen: a grate, shovel, tongs, poker, grid iron, spit pulley and jack, two brass candlesticks, one iron one, two tin pots, one oval table, one old chest of drawers, two pewter dishes etc.
>
> In the room adjoining, one sacking bottom bedstead and China furniture [hangings], one small feather bed, a chest of drawers, seven matted chairs,

Probate inventory for Thomas Short, weaver of Mile End New Town, 1724. London Commissary Court, LMA Guildhall MS 9147/43

one deal table, some wicker ware [where the family slept – Thomas, Mary and a child, perhaps].

In the workshop on the next floor three silk looms, one double wheel and jack, a chest of drawers and a bedstead [where young Thomas slept? He was 9 when his father died].

In the workshop on the top floor one silk loom and a double wheel and jack, a turner and bobbins.

The estate was owed £1 12s by one John Short for shop goods. The total value was £8 17s.

Dated 24 July 1725 and signed by Mary Short, widow and administratrix.

TNA Wills and Admons

These are wills proved in the Archbishop's court, the PCC. Individuals who died abroad or at sea (as many of our seafaring East Enders did) had their wills proved in the PCC. Sailors and adventurers apart, PCC wills tend to be those of rather richer people than those found at LMA, though from the late eighteenth century the London courts lost custom to the PCC and even quite humble individuals appear in the PCC records.

The will of William Short can be found in the PCC records at TNA and was accessed online:

> Will of William Short, of 9, Thomas Street, Bethnal Green milkman d. 1851 [see Short pedigree on p. 57], leaving his 'milk walks' to his dear wife Elizabeth and, after her death, to which ever of their children she shall name by will. He makes his mark [he cannot write]; the witnesses are: Joseph Cox of BG Road, and James P May and William Dance of 2, Princes Street, Spitalfields [probably lawyers].

These 'all to wife' wills are very common and rather disappointing. Much more interesting are the lengthy documents with specific legacies and lists of family members.

It is a good idea to be aware of the following:

- TNA/PCC wills can be read on film at TNA or, for a small fee, accessed through TNA's website – go to DocumentsOnline.
- PCC original wills are in class PROB 10; those that can be read online are the court copies (PROB 11). To see your ancestors's signature it is necessary to go to Kew and order the PROB 10 version.

- The online data base does NOT include admons. You will have to go to TNA to access these; they are indexed and in classes PROB 6 and 7. Entries only reveal the name of the deceased, address and name of next of kin, widow or creditor who got the grant. It is possible to find out more information about intestate estates from the death duty records (see below).
- Do NOT do a name search in TNA's main online catalogue for wills; they have not been indexed there.

Other Probate Records at TNA

There is a wonderful probate (PCC) archive, covering (mainly) 1666–1858, earlier records having been lost in the Great Fire. These are outlined in TNA's information leaflet, 'Wills and Probate Records', which can be downloaded, and described in Amanda Bevan's *Tracing Your Ancestors in the National Archives* (TNA, 2006) or Jane Cox's *Wills, Probate and Death Duties, Affection Defying the Power of Death* (FFHS, 1993).

Having spent ten years sorting these records, I am tempted to tell you a great deal. Suffice it to say, however, that there are many, many thousands of inventories (PROB 3, 4, 5, 31 and 32), the bulk of which date from the seventeenth century and a great many of these relate to East Enders, especially mariners. From these you might be able to find out what colour curtains your ancestor had or how many chamber pots etc. The inventory for Joseph Bolton, an eighteenth-century landlord of the White Horse at Mile End, itemises, room by room, the contents of this impressive coaching inn. This East End tavern had over twenty bedrooms, beds dressed with crimson, blue or green silk hangings, rooms hung with tapestries, mirrors and paintings and equipped with clocks, tea tables, candlesticks, glasses and cups for chocolate and coffee. In the bar the drinks on offer were mainly beer and 'mountain wine', costing about 7*d* a pint (TNA PROB 3/40/43, dated 1741).

To locate an inventory, simply search under your ancestor's name in TNA's online catalogue; a reference and description will appear. Thus, for Joseph Bolton (above):

> Bolton, Joseph, p. of St. Dunstans, Stepney, co. Midd., widower. (Innkeeper.) Philadelphia Barker, spinster, cousin german and only next of kin. (White Horse, Mile End.) 2 mm [2 membranes long], 12 May 1741.

It is necessary to travel to Kew to read the actual document.

Where an executor's account survives (it may be with the inventory) this could be a real find. People owing money to the estate are listed; often they are relatives and you may be able to find out what refreshments were taken at your ancestor's funeral.

If your ancestor's estate was subject to litigation, there may be pages and pages of detail. The depositions of witnesses in probate cases (in English) can be most revealing – tales told by servants and nurses, bitter relatives, apothecaries and the woman next door. The story of Betty Boulter of Restoration Whitechapel remains my favourite. She ran off with a soldier and her husband tried to claim her father's estate. She won the contest, but died soon after. The full details are given in Jane Cox's *Hatred Pursued Beyond the Grave* (HMSO, 1993).

It will be clear if your ancestor's will was the subject of a law suit, as it will say 'by decree' or 'by sent[ence]' on the will, and you can then set about researching the various different records. The majority of PCC suits had a parallel case going on in the Court of Chancery. Chancery records are described in Amanda Bevan's *Tracing your Ancestors in the National Archives* (TNA, 2006). See also P.W. Coldham's published list of 26,000 will/admon disputes, 1574–1714, which is accessible via Origins. Will disputes from 1858 were handled by the Probate, Admiralty and Divorce Division of the High Court; only a sample (large) of records have survived and these are held at TNA in J 121.

Reading and Understanding Probate Records

The TNA/ PCC wills can be difficult to read. If you simply can't, first order the original will; those online and on film at TNA are court copies (PROB 11). The original wills are classified as PROB 10 and are in a much easier hand. Also, you get the document itself. If you can't go to Kew, you could look at the handwriting samples for various periods provided by TNA online at: www.nationalarchives.gov.uk> DocumentsOnline>wills.

Formal court proceedings are in Latin until 1733, but the substance of the case will be found in the evidence given by witnesses, which is in English. For assistance with understanding the legal jargon, Stuart A. Raymond's *Words from Wills and Other Probate Records, 1500–1800: a Glossary* (FFHS, 2004) is helpful. For untangling the procedure, look at Jane Cox's *Wills, Probate and Death Duties, Affection Defying the Power of Death* (FFHS, 1993).

Death Duty Records

These records form a very useful and underused source. They document a series of taxes on estates passing at death. They may provide:

- Information to supplement the scant details in the Administration Act books. Names and addresses of children and other relatives entitled in the distribution of an estate may be given.
- A valuation and sometimes even a breakdown of the estate. You can see how rich your ancestor was!
- Information about the relationships of legatees and distributees to the deceased – even illegitimacy is noted. Thus, the letters Stra ND tells you that the individual was a 'stranger natural daughter', i.e. illegitimate. Nephews are indentified as son of a brother or sister and so forth. A full list of these abbreviations is provided in Jane Cox's *Will, Inventories and Death Duties* (Public Record Office, 1988).

Not all estates for which there were wills/admons are covered, but as the scope of the tax was widened over the years, more appear. Thus, you are much more likely to find the estate you are looking for in 1880 than you are in 1810.

The registers are at TNA at IR 26 and they are indexed at IR 27. For the period 1796–1810 they are online (www.nationalarchives.gov.uk> DocumentsOnline>wills and death duties), but it is the later volumes that are far more likely to be rewarding. To access these it is necessary to visit Kew. The records are described in Amanda Bevan's *Tracing your Ancestors in the National Archives* (TNA, 2006) and in Jane Cox's *Wills, Probate and Death Duties, Affection Defying the Power of Death* (FFHS, 1993).

Cemetery Records and Monumental Inscriptions

Monumental inscriptions (MIs) used to be a very popular genealogical source, but they have been rather over taken. They are not really the place to start looking, especially not for Londoners, but you might turn up trumps.

St Dunstan's Stepney was famous for its MIs, and they were regarded as an early example of cheery Cockney wit in the face of adversity. In the eighteenth century a trip around the churchyard was a popular outing for Londoners. The inscriptions are to be found in W.C. Pepys and E. Goodman's *The Church of St Dunstan, Stepney* (1905). My personal favourite is:

> Here lyes the Body of Daniel Saul
> Spitalfields Weaver, and that's all.

In addition, Lysons lists tombs of gentry in *Environs of London* (1792). See also MIs at Holy Trinity Mile End, EoLFHS, 1993 fiche; 'Inscriptions in St Katharine by the Tower', *Genealogists' Magazine*, 6; and *St Anne Limehouse* (SOG, 1978).

Cemetery Records

It is simpler to search for GRO death registration than to search cemetery records. No extra information is available from burial registers, but, if the cemetery is still open, as in the case of the City of London Cemetery, you might be able to locate the grave and read the tombstone inscription, if there is one.

Burials in London churchyards stopped in the mid-nineteenth century when there was no longer room for the bodies. Before that (Jews and Nonconformists apart) they were buried in the churchyard of their parish church; burials are entered in the parish registers (see above). From the 1840s, East Londoners were increasingly interred in the cemeteries described below.

- The City of London Cemetery in Manor Park, London E12 5DQ has burials from 1856 (from all over London) which can be searched on site. There is an ongoing digitisation programme (1856–7 available at the time of writing) which will allow you to inspect the original entries, which give addresses. Access is via the EoLFHS website, which will also tell you about the cemetery. An example of a typical entry would be:

  > 27th November 1856 William Muncton Smith, 9 months,
  > son of William Smith of 5, Popes Hill, Shadwell, parish of
  > St Paul Shadwell, [buried] in grave no. 105 at square 27.

- The City of London and Tower Hamlets Cemetery, alias Bow Cemetery, Southern Grove, London E3. This is now a park. The registers (burials 1841–1966) are at LMA, indexed on the National Burial Index for 1841–52 (available on CD-ROM from FFHS).

- Lists of civilian war dead are available at the Commonwealth War Graves Commission website at: www.cwgc.org and at THLHLA. Indexes to burials 1947–1965 are also at THLHLA.
- Victoria Park Cemetery, Hackney E3. The first burial took place in 1853; registers 1853–76 at TNA and online at The Genealogist (index and transcripts).
- From 1872 Poplar burials may have been made in the East London Cemetery in Plaistow. The records are not accessible to the public.

For details of cemeteries in Newham and the London parts of Essex, where East Enders may have been buried, either moving out, or staying with children who had, see the EoLFHS website. For Jewish and Nonconformist burials see the relevant sections in Chapter 5. For a description of burial places in Stepney access The London Burial Grounds website at: www.burial.magic-nation.co.uk/bgmileendold.htm.

School Records

These can be surprisingly useful for tracing the movements of your family from one address to another, as well as possibly informing you about your ancestors' behaviour and academic achievements. The records mainly date from the late nineteenth century.

My aunt told an amusing tale of when she was 5 at school in Bow (c. 1920). They had to use a rag and spit to clean their slates and she, being short of spit, borrowed some from her neighbour, one Ernie Slack. Imagine my delight when searching in the admission registers for Malmesbury Road School, I happened upon an entry for 'E. Slack'.

There are no central indexes of pupils; you will have to know where your individual went to school or be prepared for a good deal of digging around. LMA's school records are, however, scheduled for digitisation. Some records of the Jews' Free School are available online (see p. 159). School records are closed for sixty-five years, except admission and discharge registers, which are closed for thirty.

From the Middle Ages there were schools attached to monasteries and churches. The very first known rector of Stepney (in the twelfth century) was 'Master of the Schools' in the City. The earliest known school in Tower Hamlets is probably that established by Nicholas Gibson and his wife, Avice, in 1536 in what is now Ratcliff Highway. The school was entrusted to the care of the Coopers' Company and its direct descendant, Coopers and Coborn School, flourishes today in Upminster.

Private charities, parishes and livery companies funded and ran schools. East End families who had done well for themselves might send their boys away to be educated at a public school, or to one of the City schools and maybe then to university. Published registers of public schools are held at SOG, LMA, Guildhall and BL, and Ancestry has the Oxford and Cambridge Alumni and Charterhouse Registers. Protestant Nonconformists were enthusiastic about education and there were many 'Dissenters' Academies' in the East End from the seventeenth century; one such was attended by John Wesley's father. In Victorian times numerous small private schools appeared; you will find them in directories (see p. 100) but virtually no records have survived.

In 1844, Lord Shaftesbury established the Ragged School Union and free schools were set up under its auspices for the education of poor children. One such school was Dr Barnardo's ragged school, which is now the Ragged School Museum, 46–50 Copperfield Road, London E3 4RR; tel: 0208 9806405; www.raggedschoolmuseum.org.uk.

From the beginning of the nineteenth century serious attention began to be paid to education and many National (Church of England) and British (Nonconformist) schools were set up; in some cases the societies took over existing schools. In 1870, the London School Board established many more (elementary schools), absorbing the old National and British schools. In 1904, these were taken over by the LCC and in 1965 by the Inner London Education Authority. Children from ordinary families rarely had any secondary education until the 1920s.

Industrial schools (reformatories) existed from 1857 when an Act of Parliament authorised magistrates to send young offenders to these institutions, of which there were sixty in England by 1865. There were a number in the East End, including the East London Industrial School and Shoeblack Society in Mansell Street and then Leman Street, and the Boys' Refuge Industrial School in Commercial Street.

From the late nineteenth century most East End children were enrolled at local elementary schools (although the truancy rate was high) and you have a good chance of finding your family members in the admission/discharge registers or the log books, where these survive.

Records of East End schools comprise a vast archive, and are mainly held at LMA, although some are at THLHLA (see Appendix 5). Admission registers among school records at LMA (to 1911) are currently being digitised by Ancestry.

Class 7, Malmesbury Road School, c. 1920. Author's Collection

A number of independent schools have retained their own records. For Nonconformist school records not at LMA or THLHLA contact Dr Williams's Library, Friends House (for Quaker Schools), the Catholic Education Council or the British and Foreign Schools Archive Centre. For Jewish schools see Chapter 5.

Cliff Webb's *An Index of London Schools and their Records*, 3rd edn (SOG, 2007) is an invaluable guide for the location of school records. It lists, alphabetically, all the schools that he could locate in the old London County Council area, with details of their records, if known. There is an also an alphabetical list of all the schools by postal district. The book does not include ephemeral private schools where no records are known to exist. Webb's entry for Approach School in Bethnal Green, for example, reads:

> Approach Road School Bethnal Green E 2 (Wesleyan). Op[ened]; cl[osed] 1927 (LMA: EO/DIV 5 APP) A[dmissions] & D[ischarges] 1890–1927 (inf[ants]); 1906–27 (m[i]x[e]d); L[og] B[ooks] 1869–1927 (mxd); 1869–1927 (inf).

You can also search LMA's website under the name of the school to see whether the records they have will be of use to you. An example of the type of information that can be discovered is in the admission register for Malmesbury Road School, Bow, 1920. This lists the pupils with name and date of birth, name of parent and address and school to which the child was moved.

> A Jewish boy from Jubliee Street, named Nadelsticher, was removed from Malmesbury Road to the Serab Street [Jewish] School in May 1915, 'an intelligent lad' remarks Mr Woodward, the head teacher. (LMA X0 95/2770.)

See the photograph of pupils at this school taken in about 1920 on p. 93.

To make contact with old boys/girls try www.friendsreunited.co.uk, or contact the school's old pupils' association, if there is one.

In the nineteenth century Sunday schools were very important for East End children. Many children attended in order to learn to read and write, so that they could earn money to support their families during the week. Graces Foakes and her sister, Kathleen, were sent to Sunday school morning and afternoon and to a service in the evening, even though their parents were not church-goers (Foakes, *My Part of the River* (Shepheard-Walwyn Publishers, 1972)). What records survive can be found with other parish records.

Poor Law schools (boarding) were set up by the 1834 Poor Law Commission. Children from Poplar (1868–97) and Whitechapel (1868–97) were sent to the Forest Gate School, Essex (1854–1907) and the training ship *Goliath* (1870–5). Children from the Stepney Poor Law Union (along with children from Bermondsey, Woolwich etc.) were sent to the Brighton Road School/Belmont House, Sutton (1855–1902), the Banstead Road School, Sutton (1844–1902), Herne Bay School, Kent (1876–97) and Witham School, Essex (1882–1900). The records of these institutions are at LMA. Will Crooks, chairman of the Poplar Board of Guardians, spent a short time at Belmont House and he recalled that 'every day spent in that school is burnt into my soul' (www.workhouses. org.uk).

Some of the best-known East End schools are:

- Bancroft's School. Founded in 1737 by the Drapers' Company in Mile End (where Queen Mary and Westfield College now is). It moved to Woodford, Essex in 1889; now an independent co-educational school: Bancroft's School, Woodford, Essex IG8 ORF. See K.R. Wing's *A History of Bancroft's School* (1987).
- Sir John Cass Foundation. This school started life in the City in Duke's Place, Aldgate, where it was 1710–62; in Church Row

1762–1869; in Jewry Street 1869–1908; in 1944 its secondary half was amalgamated with the Stepney Red Coat School (see below) on a site in Stepney Way E1. The primary school is still based near the original site.

Records at LMA/Guildhall: admission and discharge 1896–1935 (mixed), 1896–1905 (girls); 1913–45 (upper school); log books 1905–13. LMA: log books (infants) 1909–13; minute books and apprenticeship indentures 1863–1910, 1975. See 'Sir John Cass and his School', *Transactions of the London & Middlesex Archaeological Society*, n.s. 2, 1911–13.

- Coborn School for Girls. Founded by Prisca Coborn, a brewer's widow, as a mixed school in Bow in 1701. Moved to Old Ford Road then Fairfield Road and to Bow Road in 1891, when it became a girls' school. Coborn was a most genteel establishment which changed the lives of many local girls. It merged with Coopers in 1971 (see above) and is now at Upminster. See photograph on p. 96.

  Estate and administrative records only at LMA. See Churchett's history (see below) and *Cockney Ancestor*, 89 (Winter 2000). For tracing old pupils try the school association at: www.occa.co.uk.

- Coopers School/Ratcliff Charity School. Founded by Nicholas and Avice Gibson in 1536 on Ratcliff Highway; handed over to the Coopers' Company in 1540. Moved to Tredegar Square, Bow, 1891 (boys). Merged with Coborn girls (see above) and moved to Upminster 1971.

  Estate and administrative records only at LMA/Guildhall from 1520. See W. Foster's *Nicholas Gibson and his Free School at Ratcliff* (1936), Colin Churchett's *Coopers' Company and Coborn School Anniversary History* (1986) and the *Victoria County History of Middlesex*, Vol. 1 (online at: www.british.history.ac.uk/catalogue. aspx?gid=66). Present address: St Mary's Lane, Upminster RM14 3HS. For tracing old pupils try the Old Coopers' Coborn Association at: www.occa.co.uk.

- Davenant Foundation Grammar School, St Mary Street, White-chapel Road E1. Founded 1686, elementary school closed 1950; secondary school moved to Debden, 1965.

  Records at LMA: admission and discharge 1906–39 (infants); 1915–64 (gaps, boys); log books (infants) 1911–13; punishment books 1946–64; minute books 1888–94, 1909–64. See R. Reynolds' *History of Davenant Foundation Grammar School* (1966). Davenant's

Upper sixth form, Coborn School, 1932. Violet Short (see Short pedigree on p. 57) is second from left in the front row. Author's Collection

history is complicated; see the account in the *Victoria County History of Middlesex*, Vol. 1 (online at: www.british.history.ac.uk/catalogue.aspx?gid=66).

- George Green's School, Poplar, East India Dock Road and Manchester Road E14. Opened 1828. Will Crooks was its most famous old boy.

  Records at LMA: admission and discharge registers 1884–1909 (boys), 1884–1910 (girls). THLHLA: 1898–1919 (girls), 1902–24 (9 boys), 1932–46 (mixed); 1946–76 and misc., staff testimonials. See H.C. Wilks's *A History of George Green's School 1828–1978* (1979) and A.J.C. Read's *George Green's School; Reminiscences of School Life, 1907–1936* (1986).

- Jews's Free School. See Chapter 5 and for other Jewish schools contact Jewish School Records, Jewish Historical Society, 33 Seymour Place, London W1H 5AP.

- Raine's Foundation School. Now in Approach Road, Bethnal Green E2. Endowed in 1719 by Henry Raine, brewer, and opened *c.* 1719; schools for fifty boys and fifty girls, in Fawdon Fields, Wapping-Stepney. Moved to Cannon Street Road in 1875 (boys) and 1880 (girls). In 1897 recognised as a secondary school (boys) and in 1904 (girls). In 1913 the schools moved to Arbour Square and in 1977 were merged with St Jude's as a comprehensive school in Approach Road. See *Victoria County History of Middlesex*, Vol. 1 (online at: www.british.history.ac.uk/catalogue.aspx?gid=66).

Records at LMA: admission and discharge 1736–1955; log books 1818–1949; minute books (some) 1736–1941. THLHLA: records of the Old Raineians Association 1910–94.

- Red Coat Secondary School, Stepney Green E1. This school opened in 1714 as the Hamlet of Mile End School; secondary part merged with Cass (see above) in 1944.

  Records at LMA/Guildhall: admission and discharge 1776–1837, 1874–1918; log books 1863–89, 1913–39 (girls), 1883–1936 (infants), 1930–39 (boys); minute books 1811–22, 1851–89. LMA: 1962–6 (mixed); roll of service 1914–18. THLHLA: 1912–27 (mixed); minute books 1795–1809.

- Stepney Green Coat School. Opened in 1710 in Whitehorse Lane as Hamlet of Ratcliff School; girls from 1723. Moved to Limehouse (Norbiton Road), 1970.

  Records at THLHLA: log books 1877–99 (boys and girls), 1881–1924 (infants), 1899–1939 (mixed); punishment books 1900–14; list of subscribers 1710–1859; minute books 1710–1850, 1867–1942. See J.V. Pixell's *A Short History of the Hamlet of Ratcliff School* (1910) and photograph on p. 98.

For information on denominational schools contact the following:

- Wesleyan Committee of Education Records, Methodist Church Division of Education and Youth, 2 Chester House, Pages Lane, Muswell Hill N10 1PZ.
- Dr Williams's Library, 14 Gordon Square, London WC1H OAG.
- Quaker Schools Information, Friends House, Euston Road, London NW1 2BJ.
- Catholic schools' records at Catholic Education Council, 41 Cromwell Road, London SW6 2DJ.
- British schools' records at British and Foreign Schools Archives Centre, West London Institute of Higher Education, Borough Road, Isleworth, Middlesex TW7 5DU.
- National Society, Church of England Record Centre, 15 Galleywall Road, London SE16 3PB.

Children from Stepney Green Coat School, c. 1910. J.V. Pixell, *A Short History of the Hamlet of Ratcliff School* (1910)

For records of ragged schools contact the Shaftesbury Society, 18–20 Kingston Road, London SW19 1JZ. A list of industrial schools (with some links to their census entries) can be found at: www. missing-ancestors.com. See also Colin Chapman's *Basic Facts about Using Education Records* (FFHS, 1999).

Teachers

Before the national registration system was introduced teachers were supposed to be licensed by the Church and the names of teachers, including dissenters, may appear in episcopal and archiepiscopal visitation records at LMA (Guildhall) and Lambeth Palace Library. The following is a typical example:

> The visitation of Stepney church in August 1673 tells us that Mistress Payne, wife of Ralph, runs a school in Trinity House and makes her pupils attend school on holy days, forbidding them to observe the holidays proscribed by the church. William Ludinager [this name means teacher, so, presumably they did not know his proper name] has a school at Bishop's Hall in Bethnal Green and takes his scholars to conventicles. Mr Ellwood, the schoolmaster at Green Bank in Wapping was formerly excommunicated for teaching without a licence. (LMA/Guildhall MS 9537/20.)

For teachers working between 1870 and 1948 there is a fairly useful source at SOG (access index and digitisation at Origins). This is a register of teachers, giving their details, including place of training and curriculum vitae. Registration, which started in 1914, was voluntary, however, and many teachers are not included. Names of teachers and other details may appear in the records of the individual schools.

Directories and Voters' Lists

These date from the seventeenth century, and are particularly useful for the post-census (1911) period.

Trade and Street Directories

Directories are widely available on most general genealogical websites and on the website www.historicaldirectories.org. there are eighty for London dating from 1808. It is also useful to consult LMA's 'Directories of London and the Home Counties'. The earliest directory is that of 1677. Pigots' directories for 1825 and 1839 and the London and County Directory for 1811 are available at Ancestry. There are sets of varying completeness at BL, Guildhall Library, LMA, TNA, SOG and THLHLA. See also SOG's *Directories and poll books, including almanacs and electoral rolls in the Library of the Society of Genealogists*, 6th edn (1995) or search the SOG website via the online catalogue>London/Middlesex-Directories; London.

Tower Hamlets is normally included in London directories, but many of our poor East End ancestors, as short-term sub-tenants or lodgers, may not feature at all.

Businesses, including shops, will be in the commercial section and there are alphabetical lists of residents in some. If you know what trade or occupation your ancestor was in, you could look in the trade or commercial section under that trade heading. For example, a search in the list of 'oil and colour men' in the trade section of the 1882 *Post Office Directory* reveals:

> Williams, Samuel 366, Bethnal Green Road, 69 Chrisp Street Poplar & 306 Roman Road. [This was Thomas Short's employer; see the pedigree on pp. 56–7.]

In the streets section, a search under Bethnal Green Road, eleven houses down from the turning with Hague Street, turns up:

> Bethnal Green Road, 364: Young, Mrs Eliza, coffee rooms. [This is the daughter of William and Elizabeth Short's daughter; see the pedigree on pp. 56–7.]

Telephone Directories, 1880–Present
These can be immensely useful for tracking people down, especially in the post-census period, although not many East Enders had telephones until the 1950s. You can consult the directories at the British Telecom Archives in Holborn, the Guildhall Library or access them online at Ancestry, for the period 1880–1984.

Electoral Registers and Poll Books
Electoral registers are lists of people eligible to vote. Only a small proportion of men before 1867 and no women until 1918 were eligible, and then they had to be over 30. From 1928 all adults were eligible.

Poll books (to 1872) are lists of people who actually voted; they are more informative than electoral registers, providing occupations and even noting who the individual voted for.

LMA has a number of poll books from 1749/50 and electoral registers from 1832/3 (download information leaflet 10 'Electoral Registers at the London Metropolitan Archives'); none were published during the First and Second World Wars. The BL holds the most complete set of electoral registers and THLHLA has registers for the East End from 1901. There is a collection of poll books at SOG; see SOG's *Directories and poll books, including almanacs and electoral rolls in the Library of the Society of Genealogists*, 6th edn (1995), or search the SOG website via the online catalogue>London/Middlesex-Poll Books. These registers are of limited use as there are no name indexes and you need an address. They are fully listed in Jeremy Gibson and Colin Rogers' *Poll Books, 1692–1872* (FHP, 2008) and Jeremy Gibson's *Electoral Register, 1832–1948* (FHP, 2008).

Hospital Records

These records are probably only useful to confirm something you know, or suspect.

To locate extant archives of hospitals (including workhouse infirmaries, lunatic asylums and lying-in hospitals) use the Hospital Records Database at TNA's website or search under 'Tower Hamlets' at LMA's online catalogue. See also LMA information leaflets 34 and 35, 'Hospital Records' and 'Records of Patients in London Hospitals'. These records are subject to an extended closure period and you may not be able to consult all of them.

There were specialist hospitals, for tuberculosis, cholera etc., and your ancestors may well have been sent out of the borough to one of these. London hospitals are listed at Gendocs: http://homepage.ntlworld.com/hitch/gendocs/index.html. From 1867 there were infirmaries attached to workhouses (see pp. 129–33); where extant, the records are at LMA.

The most important source for sick East Enders is the magnificent archive of 'the London', now the Royal London Hospital in Whitechapel. This started life in Featherstone Street in 1740, quickly moved to Prescot Street in Whitechapel and to the Mile End Road in 1757. The records may be consulted (by appointment) at the Royal London Archives

Centre at 9 Prescot Street, London E1 8PR; email: jonathan.evans@ bartsandthelondon.nhs.uk. The records are outlined at the TNA hospital database but the main means of reference is via the archives. There are patient records from 1761; staff records from 1880.

Private madhouses in the period 1798–1812 are listed, with names of patients, in the 'County Register' at TNA (MH 51/735). One such establishment was the celebrated Bethnal Green madhouse, which was set up between 1726 and 1770, closed in 1920; in 1851 there were 558 inmates. Lunatics from the East End might have been sent to 'Bedlam', and records of the Bethlehem Hospital from 1720 are held at the Royal London Hospital Archives. Lists of pauper lunatics who were chargeable to the parishes and some committal orders are to be found in the Middlesex Sessions records at LMA. The following extract detailing the committal of a lunatic is a sample from the Sessions records:

> Elizabeth Taylor represents to the Court that her daughter, Elizabeth Hurst, wife of John Hurst, anchorsmith, late of Limehouse, has been distracted in mind and very outrageous; that the churchwardens etc. of Limehouse have permitted her to go about the streets day and night, so that the petitioner had taken her into her own home, but she is very unruly and bites and wounds, and threatens to fire the house. The petitioner prays that the churchwardens may be ordered to place her in Bethlehem hospital. Order made accordingly. (*Calendar of the Sessions Books* (1689–1709), 201.)

From 1808 there were county lunatic asylums, for Middlesex these were the Hanwell Asylum (1831) and Colney Hatch (1851). Among the Middlesex Sessions records at LMA you will find notices of death and discharge from Hanwell 1846–53 and Colney Hatch 1852–3 and other references to lunatic paupers who were chargeable to the county 1853–90. There are lists of lunatics and admission and discharge registers for them among the records of the Poor Law unions (see pp. 129–33).

Babies were born at home, or in the workhouse, by and large, until the twentieth century. There were some lying-in hospitals, notably that at Endell Street in Holborn, and the children of some East Enders (mainly soldiers) might be located there during the period 1749–1869; access these via the International Genealogical Index, on the LDS website FamilySearch; originals held at TNA in RG 8.

It is well worth visiting the London Hospital Museum at St Philip's Church, Newark Street, London E1 2AA.

Parish Magazines

Magazines were produced by most parishes from the 1890s, and, although they are not always easy to locate, they really bring to life the activities of our more recent ancestors. Some also list baptisms and marriages. They may be found among the deposited records at LMA or THLHLA, but, if the church in question is still in existence, it is probably best to try there first. For addresses and phone numbers consult the *London Diocesan Year Book*. St Dunstan's Stepney has a good run of magazines from 1902 (at THLHLA and BL). There are some magazines among the parish records for the following Bethnal Green churches at LMA: St Matthew's, St Bartholomew's, St Jude's and St Peter's (newsletters).

The period from the 1890s to the First World War was the era of the great welfare parishes in the East End and the many organisations attached to churchs (and chapels) involved a great number of people, who may feature in the magazines. In 1900 St Dunstan's, for instance, boasted the following: 2 communicants' guilds, 2 temperance societies, a children's guild with 10 branches, Sunday schools with 1,200 on the books and between 50 and 60 teachers, Bible classes (15 on Sunday and 8 in the week, with 589 on the books), 4 Mothers' Meetings, a Mothers' Union with 2 branches, an Old Boys' Association and 2 boys' clubs, a girls' friendly society and 4 'rough' girls' classes, 3 work parties, sewing classes, 2 day schools, a benefit society, a penny bank, a football club and a drum and fife band led by Mr G. Merriman of 116 Shandy Street. In addition there were 2 Scripture readers, 60 district visitors, 15 temperance workers, 10 club workers and a parish nurse.

In August 1908, the members of St Dunstan's Old Boys Association took part in a special event, which was written up in the magazine. The choirmaster and organist Percy Downes, a young draper's son from Commercial Road, took them camping to Skegness, boys in one field, men in another. They walked and swam and played cricket, and after tea it was 'ties, collars and dickeys' and down to the front to 'try and captivate the youth and beauty of Skegness'.

In the 1950s the go-ahead Canon Young relaunched St Dunstan's magazine as *Stepahoy*. This was no dull church newsletter, but a tabloid newspaper containing lots of pictures, a good many of which featured a beaming rector, arms linked with Alan Ladd, Pearl Carr and Teddy Johnson, the Beatles, Matt Monro, Petula Clark, Harry Secombe and a whole host of other celebrities. A useful aspect for Stepney ancestor hunters are the series of interviews with local publicans and shop-keepers, such as Mr Bert Moore who kept the sweet shop in Ben Jonson Road.

Local Newspapers

It is so fascinating reading through old newspapers, especially looking at the advertisements and the property pages, that you may well forget what you have come for and spend the rest of the day idling away in the pages of the *East London Observer* for the 1880s!

Do not expect to find obituaries or birth, marriage or death announce-ments unless your ancestors were among the few who 'made it'; and there are precious few advertisements put in by solicitors seeking the next of kin of wealthy intestates. Newspapers are mainly useful for getting a feel for the period and the locality; you may want to read an account of the General Strike or the Battle of Cable Street. You never know, you may find an advertisement put in by someone in the family, an account of someone who has broken the law or your ancestor listed as a member of a local football team.

THLHLA is the best place to browse through local papers (on film); a list of their holding is found in Appendix 5. In the library you can consult a list that tells you which political complexion the various papers have. The BL's comprehensive holdings of newspapers may be read at its Newspaper Library at Colindale; you will need to get a reader's ticket there. The library is closing in 2012 and as a result, a massive project is underway to digitise newspapers. Some are already at: http://newspapers.bl.uk.

Although there are no specifically East End newspapers until the mid-nineteenth century, you may find it rewarding to browse through the earlier London papers. There is a great deal about the operations of the East India Company, for instance, and many a tale from rackety sailor town, Wapping, Shadwell and Limehouse. The Burney Collection of seventeenth- and eighteenth-century newspapers is available at the BL at St Pancras (photostats are on the open shelves). TNA has a set online.

Rate Books

These contain lists of names of inhabitants, the better off who were liable for local taxes of one sort and another. They are not a comprehensive index of names, and are useful mainly for the pre- and post-census period, i.e., pre-1841 and post-1911.

The following list details rate books and valuation records for pre-1841 and post-1911 held at THLHLA (not including those that fall within the census decades); a few are also included from LMA (formerly Guildhall).

- Aldgate: list for Upper East Smithfield 1820–2 at LMA (Guildhall 6196).
- Bethnal Green: Army Reserve Rate 1803; Church Rate 1743–51; 'Election Book' 1772; Highways Rate (2nd Division) 1791; Church Division 1838; Poor Rate 1744, 1794 (1st Division); Scavenger Rate 1728; Tithe Rate 1775, 1791 (2nd Divison); Window Tax 1793.
- Bow: Poor Rate 1773–1867; Church and Churchyard Rate 1810–73; Church Rate for 1765 at LMA (Guildhall).
- Bromley: Poor Rate 1783–1836 (gaps); Church Rate 1812–62 (gaps); Highway Rate 1816–42 (gaps).
- Limehouse: Poor Rate 1762–72 (transcript), 1782–3.
- Poplar and Blackwall: Poor Rate 1798–1840 (gaps); Church Rate 1799–1868; Army Reserve Rate 1803; Highway Rate 1809–11; Conjunct Rate 1813–37; Valuation Lists 1818–19.
- Ratcliff: Church Rate 1710.
- St George-in-the-East: Poor Rate for Wapping-Stepney Lower Town 1719; LMA has a Poor Rate list for 1727 for Wapping-Stepney, the name of the hamlet before the parish was formed.
- Shadwell: Poor Rate 1725 (photocopy).
- Spitalfields: hamlet, Standard Rate for Old Town, 1700.
- Wapping: St John's parish, Watch Rate 1800.
- Wellclose Liberty: Rate for raising funds for disbanding HM forces and paying seamen, 1698 at LMA (Guildhall 3041/10);
- Whitechapel: Watch Rate (2nd Division) 1800, 4th Division 1805–6. Whitechapel tithe collector's book (like rate books) 1753–1854 at LMA with parish records at P93/MRY1/117-168 and 177-206.

Valuations from *c.* 1905 are at THLHLA for Bethnal Green and Poplar Boroughs. A very few from 1935 survive for Stepney Borough.

The following list details records of tax payers from the Sewer Rate Books (omitting those for census decades) held at LMA:

- Aldgate 1732–1846 (gaps).
- Bethnal Green 1723–1846 (gaps).
- Bow 1726–1812 (gaps).
- Bromley 1703–1844 (gaps).
- Goodmans' Fields 1721–2.
- Limehouse 1717–1845 (gaps).
- MENT 1703–4, 1743–1846 (gaps).
- MEOT 1717–46 (gaps).
- Holy Trinity Minories 1721–1838 (gaps).
- Norton Folgate 1812–48.
- Old Artillery Ground 1766, 1773, 1783.
- Old Ford 1763.
- Poplar 1717–1855 (gaps).
- Ratcliff 1743–1846 (gaps).
- St George-in-the-East 1739–1846 (gaps).
- Spitalfields 1713–1846 (gaps).
- Tower Liberty 1719–1838 (gaps).
- Whitechapel 1713–1846 (gaps).

Land Tax Records

These records are most useful for eighteenth- and early nineteenth-century ancestors. There are no comprehensive name indexes, so you need to know roughly where an individual lived to find them. They comprise a limited 'census' of 'heads of household'.

Owners and/or occupiers of all properties are listed in these records, which are held at LMA and THLHLA (see below). The tax was levied from 1692 to 1963, but the records that are of most use to genealogists are those for the eighteenth century.

All Land Tax assessments provide, year by year, the name of the owner/occupier (occupiers are not always there) and the amount for which each property was assessed (the latter is unreliable as after 1698 no revaluation was made). There may be additional information about the personal estate (cash, salary, leases) of the owner/occupier in the earlier records.

The records are mainly at LMA (at MR/PLT; Ancestry plan to digitise these), with some at THLHLA, as noted:

- Whole district 1693–4 (formerly CLRO).
- Aldgate parish of St Botolph Without/Manor of East Smithfield 1767–1832; former Guildhall MSS: East Smithfield Manor 1731–1926; photocopy of East Smithfield list for 1793 at THLHLA.
- Bethnal Green, hamlet and parish 1767–1832; former Guildhall MSS: 1829–1930 (gaps); THLHLA: 1744–1824.
- Bow parish 1767–1832; former Guildhall MSS: 1747, 1755 and 1763; THLHLA: 1741–1825.
- Bromley parish 1780–1832; former Guildhall MSS: 1783–1826–1926 (many gaps); THLHLA: 1744–1825 (gaps). Bromley Land Tax list for 1750 is included in EoLFHS's CD-ROM 'Tower Hamlets Collection of Rate Books'.
- Limehouse parish 1767–1832; former Guildhall MSS: 1717–1825 (gaps); THLHLA: 1724.
- Mile End New Town hamlet 1767–1832; former Guildhall MSS: 1743–1823, 1837–1930.
- Mile End Old Town hamlet 1767–1832; former Guildhall MSS: 1738–1824, 1837–1930. See EoLFHS's CD-ROM 'Mile End Old Town Residents 1741–1790', compiled by Derek Morris from the Land Tax records.
- Holy Trinity Minories; former Guildhall MSS: 1744–1825.
- Norton Folgate liberty 1767–1832; former Guildhall MSS: 1743–1825, 1844–1923.
- Old Artillery Ground 1767–1806 (gaps); former Guildhall MSS: 1743–1923 (gaps); THLHLA: 1847.
- Poplar and Blackwall, hamlet and Poplar parish 1767–1832; former Guildhall MSS: 1743, 1815, 1831–1931; THLHLA: 1705–1826.
- Ratcliff hamlet 1767–1832; former Guildhall MSS: 1730–1843, 1835–1931; THLHLA: 1799–1810 (details of tax redeemed only).
- St George-in-the-East parish 1767–1832, also assessments for 1752–3 in parish records at P 93/GEP/152-3; former Guildhall MSS: 1730–1923; THLHLA: 1801 (1801 records on EoLFHS's CD-ROM 'Tower Hamlets Collection of Rate Books').
- St Katharine's precinct 1767–1832; former Guildhall MSS: 1732–1822.
- Shadwell parish 1780–1832; former Guildhall MSS: 1731–1823, 1831–1917.
- Spitalfields parish 1767–1832; former Guildhall MSS: 1743–1923 (gaps).

- Tower Within liberty 1767–1806 (gaps); Without *ibid.*; former Guildhall MSS: Tower Liberty: 1744–1823 (gaps; LDS film).
- Wapping parish 1767–1832 (gaps); former Guildhall MSS: 1730–1826.
- Wellclose liberty 1780–1819 (gaps); former Guildhall MSS: 1729–1923 (gaps).
- Whitechapel parish 1767–1832 (gaps); former Guildhall MSS: 1733–1922 (gaps).

THLHLA has a handlist of personal name indexes, some of which relate to Land Tax records.

From 1798 tax payers might pay a lump sum and, if they did, they do not appear in the lists, which cease to be of much use as a 'census' of inhabitants. This deficiency might be supplied by a visit to TNA where you can consult the Land Tax Redemption Quotas and Assessments (IR 23, 1798–1914).

It was a search of the Land Tax records that revealed exactly where Captain Cook lived before he moved to Mile End. Julia Hunt of the Stepney Historical Trust made the discovery in 1990, and the Trust put up a blue plaque to mark the spot, on the Highway in Shadwell. In 1762, Cook married Elizabeth, daughter of Samuel Batts, landlord of the Bell alehouse. The Land Tax records showed that the young couple set up home at 126 Upper Shadwell, North Side, where Elizabeth's mother and stepfather, John Blackburn, had lived. (See J. Hunt's *From Whitby to Wapping* (Stepney Historical Trust, 1991)).

Apprenticeship Records

These relate mainly to seventeenth- and eighteenth-century ancestors. Before the advent of industrialisation it was the norm for boys to serve a seven-year (usually) apprenticeship, normally paid for by their parents (or the parish) before practising a trade or craft. It was a legal requirement until 1814. Poor boys and some girls were often put to apprenticeship by the parish; an Act of 1801–2 obliged masters to accept parish apprentices.

Apprentices would normally live with their master, as part of his household; they were not allowed to marry. Once their term was up and they were qualified practitioners of the chosen trade they would become 'journeymen' and then they might go on to be masters. As the

East End is the 'working end of town', one might expect to find a good number of our ancestors among apprenticeship records. However, do not raise your hopes too high – you are unlikely to find poor weavers, there, for instance, or unskilled workers of any sort. Also, sons might follow fathers into their family 'business' and no legal contract was entered into; it was quite expensive.

The good news is that the East End was within the 'catchment area' for most City livery companies (usually a 10-mile radius of London) and their apprentice records may include lads from Whitechapel, Stepney, Wapping and the rest. In addition, people came from all over the country to be apprenticed to London craftsmen and often stayed, and the records can link a family to their country origins.

When researching livery company records, it should be remembered that although tradesmen and craftsman operating in and around London were obliged to join a company, it could be any company, not necessarily the one linked to their occupation. From about 1650, it was common, for instance, for Bethnal Green weavers to attach themselves to the Wax Chandlers' Company. Oliver Cromwell was a Fishmonger.

Sources for apprentices are:

- Apprentices of Great Britain 1710–74 (countrywide), based on a tax on apprentices. Original records at TNA (IR1); available on fiche (indexed) at SOG (also at Origins) and at LMA.
- Freedoms. The admission papers of livery company members and apprentices who became freemen (1681–2004). These are held at the Guildhall Library and entries indicate to which company an individual was attached.
- London Apprentice Abstracts 1442–1850, taken from livery companies' records, SOG and Origins. See also Cliff Webb's *London Apprentices* (SOG, 1996–2000), which contains lists of apprentices and masters taken from forty livery company records. These include the following companies (more indexes are planned): Brewers (1685–1800), Broderers (1679–1800), Coach Makers and Coach Harness Makers (1677–1800), Combmakers (1744–50), Cooks (1654–1800), Distillers (1659–1811), Farriers (1619–1800), Fanmakers (1755–1805), Framework Knitters (1727–30), Fruiterers (1750–1815) Gardeners (1764–1850), Glass Sellers (1664–1812), Gold and Silver Wyre Drawers (1693–1837), Gun Makers (1656–1800), Horners (1781–1800), Innholders (1682–1800, gaps), Ironmongers (1655–1800), Masons (1663–1805), Musicians (1765–1800), Needlemakers

(1664–1801), Pattenmakers (1673–1805), Paviors (1568–1800), Pin-makers (1691–1721), Plumbers (1571–1800), Poulterers (1691–1729, 1754–1800), Makers of Playing Cards (1675–1760), Saddlers (1657–66, 1800), Tobacco Pipe Makers (1800), Woolmen (1665–1828). These records give name, address and parentage of apprentice and name and (address) and occupation of master. An example from Webb's *London Apprentices*/Origins:

> John Short son of John of Whitechapel corn chandler was bound to William Peet Blacksmith 5 July 1733.

- Records of merchant seamen apprentices 1780, 1818–45 at LMA (Trinity House records, access at Origins); 1824–53 (TNA BT 150).
- C.H. Ridge (ed.)'s *Records of the Worshipful Company of Shipwrights* (2 vols, Phillimore 1939–46) – a list of freemen and apprentices 1428–1858. These records include a lot of related trades, such as watermen.
- Parish apprentices, St Mary Stratford Bow 1803–27; THAOL: digitised and indexed; originals at THLHLA. A sample record of a parish apprenticeship from the Bow Apprenticeships at THAOL:

> On 24th October 1821 James Riley, 12 years old, son of Elizabeth Riley, of Bow Middle, was bound to George Porter, weaver of 6, Underwood Street Mile End New Town, for 9 years or until he shall reach the age of 21. The fee is £4 2s. The contract is authorised by churchwarden, overseer and magistrates [named].

- There are many references to apprenticeships among the Sessions records at LMA, discharges, disputes between master and apprentice etc. (see section on Criminals in Chapter 5). An example from the *Calendar of Middlesex Sessions 1689–1709*, 218:

> Order of October 1700 discharging Mary Farr, daughter of Thomas Farr, mariner of Limehouse, from her apprenticeship with Jane Dowse of the same parish, child's coat maker, on grounds of ill usage etc.

For watermen's apprenticeships 1759–1897 see the relevant section in Chapter 6, and for Huguenot and Poor Law union apprenticeships see Chapter 5.

Livery Company Records and Links with the City

These records are of most use for seventeeth- and eighteenth-century ancestors. Boyd's Inhabitants of London at SOG (access via Origins) is a compilation from a variety of sources, and is especially useful for the sixteenth–eighteenth centuries. See also Apprenticeship Records (above) and Watermen and Lightermen in Chapter 6.

From medieval times wealthy City merchants tended to 'look east' for their leisure and bought fine country houses in Mile End and Stepney. Links with the City of London were very strong, more so than in the western suburbs, which had grown up around the royal palace and Law Courts at Westminster. The City livery companies operated a 'closed shop', controlling the operation of crafts and trades in and around London and all of Tower Hamlets was in their patch. Thus, although from an administrative point of view, the East End belonged to the county of Middlesex, as far as trade and industry were concerned, it was very much part of London.

If you find an ancestor described as 'Citizen and Mercer', 'Citizen and Brewer' etc. it indicates he belonged to a City livery company and you may be able to find out more about him among the records of that company, most of which are deposited at the Guildhall Library. A few companies still hold their own records, as indicated in the list on p. 112.

There are no general indexes (apart from the apprenticeship indexes listed on p. 109) to the companies' records, and you may be in for a long search. For an introduction to the types of livery company records, see C.R.H. Cooper's 'The Archives of the City of London Livery Companies and related Organisations', *Archives*, XVI, No. 72, 1984.

Although the companies controlled crafts and trades in the early days, by the mid-eighteenth century, links with them were declining and by the mid-nineteenth you will find very few apprenticeships. Most individuals who joined companies did so by 'Redemption' (paying) or 'Patrimony', and the companies were becoming clubs for merchants and professional men.

When researching these records remember that craftsmen and tradesmen from about 1650 might join any company, not necessarily one related to their occupation. Thus, Susanna King, buried at Shadwell church in May 1720, is described as the widow of John King, 'Cheesemonger, but free of the Pewterers' Company'. However, some companies had special East End links, as described below, reflecting the occupations of the locals.

111

The Mercers' Company owned a great deal of land in Stepney from the early sixteenth century, when Colet land was given over to them as an endowment for St Paul's School. Until the mid-twentieth century the Company was landlord to many East Enders. The Mercers' almshouses were near Stepney church; the Coopers' Company School and alms-houses were in Ratcliff, and the Drapers, Vintners and Skinners had almshouses in Mile End. Other companies with special links were the Brewers and the Weavers, the Watermen and the Lightermen (see p. 183), there being great numbers of men employed in these trades.

Searchable List of London Livery Company Men in 1696

Following a plot to assassinate William III, all people of standing and office holders were asked to take an oath of loyalty. These Association Oath Rolls survive at TNA (C 213) and the London lists may be accessed at Origins; search by name or company. Included are 2,738 weavers and 1,445 watermen, 4,000 of the latter already being in the King's service did not take the oath.

The Companies are listed below, in order of precedence:

Mercers*, Grocers, Drapers*, Fishmongers, Goldsmiths*, Merchant Taylors, Skinners, Haberdashers, Salters, Ironmongers, Vintners, Cloth-workers*, Dyers, Brewers, Leathersellers*, Pewterers, Barbers, Cutlers, Bakers, Wax Chandlers, Tallow Chandlers, Armourers and Brasiers, Girdlers, Butchers, Saddlers*, Carpenters, Cordwainers (shoe makers), Painter Stainers, Curriers (leather dressers), Masons, Plumbers, Innholders, Founders, Poulterers, Cooks, Coopers, Tylers and Brick-layers, Bowyers, Fletchers, Blacksmiths, Joiners and Ceilers, Weavers, Woolmen, Scriveners, Fruiterers, Plaisterers, Stationers*, Broderers, Upholders (upholsterers), Musicians, Turners, Basketmakers, Glaziers and Painters of Glass, Horners, Farriers, Paviors, Lorimers (makers of bits, bridles etc.), Apothecaries, Shipwrights, Spectacle Makers, Clockmakers, Glovers, Feltmakers, Framework Knitters, Needlemakers, Gardeners, Tin Plate Workers alias Wire Workers, Wheelwrights, Distillers, Pattenmakers, Glass Sellers, Coachmakers and Coach Harness Makers, Gunmakers, Gold and Silver Wyre Drawers, Makers of Playing Cards, Fan Makers, Carmen (carters), Master Mariners, Solicitors, Farmers, Air Pilots and Air Navigators, Tobacco Pipe Makers and Tobacco Blenders, Furniture Makers, Scientific Instrument Makers, Chartered Surveyors, Chartered Accountants, Chartered Secretaries and Administrators, Builders Merchants, Launderers, Marketors, Actuaries,

Insurers, Arbitrators, Chartered Engineers, Fuellers, Lightmongers, Environmental Cleaners, Chartered Architects, Constructors, Information Technologists, World Traders, Water Conservators, Firefighters, Hackney Carriage Drivers, Management Consultants, International Bankers, Tax Advisers, Security Professionals. The Parish Clerks' and Watermen's Companies are without livery.

*Companies still holding their own records.

The records of all these companies, except those marked with an asterisk, are at the Guildhall Library. For a link to their websites go to: www.fishhall.co.uk.>The Livery Companies Database. Otherwise, get addresses, phone numbers and information about access to their archives from the Library. A useful catalogue of deposited LMA/Guildhall records is in *City Livery Companies*, Guildhall Library Research Guide 3 (1989).

Some Seventeenth-century Census-type Records

These records comprise Protestation Returns, hearth, poll and other tax records and Association Oath Rolls.

Protestation Returns, 1641–2

These are lists of everyone (men over 18) taking oaths of loyalty to the government, although the lists for Old Ford include some women (see document on p. 114). Not everyone took the oath. The records at the Parliamentary Archives include:

- Limehouse: 843 names (population *c.* 5,000). The areas listed are Green Dragon Lane, Nightingale Lane, 'Land Side', Ropefield and Three Colt Street. Many are 'at sea'. The churchwarden is Edward Kedden and the sideman John Archer.
- Spitalfields (including Artillery Lane and Wentworth Street): 314 names, of which about one-third are French or Dutch names, the churchwarden is James Denteer/Dentier. Names include Clement Defoe and John Stripe. Some are clearly invented French names, showing the usual resentment towards immigrants: Charles Lepoxon, Jacques Monsieur.
- Bethnal Green: 126 names.
- Mile End: 125 names.
- Poplar and Blackwall: 405 names.

Protestation Returns for Old Ford, 1641–2. Unusually, women are listed. Parliamentary Archives

- Ratcliff (many 'at sea'): 978 names (population *c*. 5,000), including Peter Pett, the shipwright.
- Bow: 330 names.
- Old Ford: 46 names. (See p. 114.)

Hearth and Poll Tax Returns, 1662–95

These records provide the nearest thing there is to a census for the Restoration East End (and most of the rest of the country).

The hearth tax (records from 1662–6 and 1669–74) was levied on fireplaces; one shilling for each had to be paid by the occupants of houses, not the landlords, every Lady Day (25 March) and every Michaelmas Day (29 September). There was widespread evasion of the hated 'chimney money', but records have an excellent survival rate and are very good for the East End. The TNA record E 179/252/32, for instance, comprises thirty-nine books for London and Middlesex for 1666. A note by William Millman in Stepney's book (pt 36, covering Limehouse, Poplar and Blackwall, Spitalfields, Ratcliff and Shadwell) says:

> All the collectors imployed by the Farmers had Instructions to return Every Individual house within their precincts whether chargeable or not; which is the reason that the Arreares in many poor parishes and places are farr greater than otherwise they would have bin.

Only the name of the head of household is given, and the number of hearths he has is a clue to wealth and status. Thus the riverside cottages of Wapping and Shadwell have only one hearth, while the Bethnal Green mansion of Samuel Pepys's friend, Sir William Ryder (popularly thought to be the 'very house ... built by the Blind Beggar of Bednall-green' (*Diary*, 26 June 1663)), had no less than seventeen (TNA E 179/143/407 pt 10). Even the very poor may make an appearance, in lists of exemptions. But bear in mind that if your ancestor has ten hearths, it may mean that he was an innkeeper rather than a man of great means.

There are records at TNA (E 179) and LMA, but the TNA collection is far greater. Download or obtain from TNA the research guide, Domestic Records Information 32: 'The Hearth Tax 1662–1689' and Domestic Records Information 10: 'Taxation Records before 1689'. The E 179 database website at: www.nationalarchives.gov.uk/e179 provides a place index for hearth and other taxes, but no names, and is not easy to use. Go to 'search by place' and under the heading 'document type' click on 'documents containing the name of individuals'. The places to choose are: Bishopsgate, Aldgate, Whitechapel, Stepney, Wapping, Bethnal Green, Poplar and Blackwall, Ratcliff and Mile End. This will give you the reference for the tax list, for example, E 179/143/342 a schedule of poll tax defaulters for Poplar and Blackwall, April 1667.

A list of the records of hearth and other taxes for this period can be found in Jeremy Gibson's *The Hearth Tax and Other Later Stuart Tax Lists and the Association Oath Rolls*, 2nd edn (FFHS, 1996); look under 'London' and under 'Middlesex'. The 1666 records for London and Middlesex are being indexed by Roehampton University in conjunction with the British Records Society; this most welcome publication should appear in 2011.

The poll tax records sometimes list the whole family, women, children and even servants. They are at LMA, formerly in the Corporation of London Record Office and span 1660–95, ref. COL/CHD/LA.

For 1693–4 there is a set of tax records which can be consulted online at: www.british-history.ac.uk/source.aspx?pubid=26. It is based on the assessments for the 'Four Shillings in the Pound Aid', held at LMA (formerly CLRO), abstracted by the Centre for Metropolitan History. The tax was on personal estate (investments), salaries and property worth over £1 a year, so it is mainly a list of landlords. Thus:

> Mrs Webster paid for her sixteen houses on the north side of Ratcliff Highway and a warehouse in Pennington Street; William Russel has a £22 house in Brick Lane (annual rent) and pays for himself and his tenants.

Association Oath Rolls, 1696

The Association Oath Rolls contain the names of men who took an oath of loyalty to the Crown following a Jacobite plot. All office holders were obliged to do this and it was open for all to sign if they so desired; men of some standing were encouraged to do so and the records provide a list of substantial inhabitants. The rolls are at TNA in class C213. Those for London may be accessed at Origins. The roll for Tower Hamlets' parishes is C213/152; for the Middlesex Militia officers C213/153; for the county's tax commissioners C213/154; for the officers at the Tower C213/395.

For all the above records, see Gibson's *The Hearth Tax and Other Later Stuart Tax Lists and the Association Oath Rolls*. LMA records are listed in the most useful publication (now out of print) *London Rate Assessments and Inhabitants' Lists in Guildhall Library and the Corporation of London Records Office*, 2nd edn (Corporation of London, 1968). Boyd's Inhabitants of London at SOG (access via Origins) is a compilation from a variety of sources, and is especially useful for the sixteen to eighteenth centuries.

Manor Court Records

These are mainly used in searching for ancestors before the existence of parish registers, i.e. from the mid-sixteenth century backwards.

Manors were estates of varying sizes; some might just be one farm and others covered huge areas. Some had courts that regulated the tenants. The various Stepney manors are described in *Victoria County History of Middlesex*, Vol. 11 *Early Stepney: Manors and Estates* (online at: www.british.history.ac.uk/report.aspx?compid=22732). Extant records of manor courts for Tower Hamlets are listed below. By far the most important and useful are the records of the great Manor of Stepney, which was responsible for the majority of medieval East Enders and continued to be landlord to some until the 1920s. You may find lists of the leading inhabitants, prosecutions of minor offences, lists of tenants, the records of property transactions and deaths of people who held their lands and houses from the local lord by 'copyhold', the most common form of tenure for ordinary folk in the medieval period (often converted to leasehold from the sixteenth century).

- Stepney Manor: records (1318–1925) at LMA; some at TNA. The largest and most important manor, comprising all Stepney's hamlets and Hackney. Owned by Bishops of London to 1550, then by the Wentworth family. The records are full and informative. Particularly useful are two items which, taken together, provide a list of tenants hamlet by hamlet (in some cases giving street addresses) from *c.* 1400 (TNA SC 12/1/31; LMA Guildhall MS: 25, 422). See Patricia Croot's 'Settlement, Tenure and Land Use in Medieval Stepney', *London Journal*, Vol. 22, no. 1, 1997. Copyhold was not abolished until 1922–4 and many Stepney folk continued to be tenants of the Lord of the Manor until then, featuring in the court rolls, which survive at LMA in unbroken series from the seventeenth century until the 1920s.

- East Smithfield: a rough patch, owned by the Abbey of St Mary Graces by Tower Hill. Records include numerous prosecutions for gaming and brothel keeping in the fifteenth century. Records at TNA: 1409–1623 (some); LMA/Guildhall: 1728–1862 (some).
- Poplar: belonged, also, to the Abbey of St Mary Graces before the Reformation. Records at TNA: 1423–1620 (some); Duchy of Cornwall Office: 1603–4; THLHLA: 1810–1921.
- Norton Folgate: another rough manor in the fifteenth century. Records at Hereford Cathedral Library and Archives: 1340 court roll; LMA/Guildhall: court roll 1439–1518, Parliamentary survey of 1649, court roll 1720–63; THLHLA: court rolls 1704–20.
- Bromley Manor: few surviving records: Duchy of Cornwall Office: court roll 1602–6; TNA: estreats 1618–19; THLHLA: court books 1806–93; LMA: map 1823 and terrier 1840.
- St Katharine's: records at LMA: 1779–1824 (some).
- Stratford at Bow: only a few records: Cambridge University Library: extent *c*. 1300–1400; BL: court roll extracts 1540, extent 1540–1.
- Shadwell: few records. At LMA/Guildhall: a 1300 survey and a visitation of 1334, survey 1650, court roll for 1664, accounts 1705.

The records are described in detail on TNA's Manorial Documents Register, or you can go to TNA and consult the Register. Remember that many Guildhall records are now at LMA.

The early records are not easy to read and understand, and there are no indexes. You will have to persevere if you are lucky enough to trace your family back that far. Some books that may be of help are:

M. Ellis, *Using Manorial Records* (PRO, 1994)

D. Stuart, *Manorial Records, an Introduction to their Transcription and Translation* (Phillimore, 1992)

P.D.A. Harvey, *Manorial Records* (British Records Association, Archives and the User No. 5, 1984)

B.P. Park, *My Ancestors were Manorial Tenants* (SOG, 1990).

For some more about sources for medieval ancestors, see Appendix 6.

Chapter 5

RECORDS OF GROUPS

This chapter deals with special sources for particular groups of East End people.

Nonconformists

This section provides information on locating ancestors who were Methodists, Independents (Congregationalist), Prebyterians, Baptists or Unitarian or of the Countess of Huntingdon's Connexion (Methodists under the personal direction of Selina, Countess of Huntingdon, d. 1791). Quakers, Irish/Roman Catholics and Huguenots are considered separately in this chapter.

Many East Enders were Nonconformists and their baptisms will not therefore appear in the Church of England records described above, although their marriages will. Lists of Nonconformist chapels can be found in Appendix 3. For details of Nonconformist chapels and their records, arranged by parish, see EoLFHS parish information at: www. eolfhs.org.uk.

The Tower Hamlets were well to the left in terms of religion and politics from the late sixteenth and early seventeenth centuries when Protestant sects were challenging the authority of the established church. Stepney Meeting (the Bull Lane Chapel) was the first Independent/ Congregational chapel in the world; its registers start in 1644. Protestant Nonconformity continued to flourish, even during the Restoration period of prosecution.

John Wesley's 'Methodism', which addressed the social problems of drinking, gambling and sexual licence, a new Puritanism, attracted vast numbers of our eighteenth-century East End ancestors. In the year of his famed 'Aldersgate experience', and his conversion to a new brand of evangelical Christianity, 1738, Wesley preached several times in Wapping church. That October he was at St George-in-the-East and the following February delivered his first sermon at Spitalfields, which was to become one of his strongholds. The Methodists took over the French Huguenot chapel in Brick Lane, l'Eglise Neuve (later the Spitalfields Great Synagogue and then a mosque). In March 1764, Wesley opened a new chapel in Wapping. It is not surprising that Wesley's greatest success was in Spitalfields with its Huguenot traditions.

Brick Lane mosque. A Huguenot church, turned Wesleyan chapel, turned synagogue, turned mosque. Yvonne Hughes

120

After the early eighteenth-century slumber, when religious activity waned, Nonconformity in all its manifestations revived and, again, took over many, many East End souls. Methodism continued to be the chosen creed of many of them into the twentieth century. By the mid- to late nineteenth century there were a myriad chapels in the East End and a good half of families were probably attached to them rather than their parish church, although they were required to marry in their parish (Church of England) church until 1837, with the exception of Quakers.

Searching for Nonconformist ancestors in chapel records is going to be, in the main, something that is done for the pre-registration, pre-census period; after that everyone is more easily found in the central GRO and census indexes described above. Most of the pre-1837 registers of baptisms/births are easily accessible at TNA (RG 4) or online for a fee. Go to bmdregisters.co.uk or thegenealogist.co.uk. Together with them are lists of burials from the Nonconformist burial grounds at Bunhill Fields (1713–1854) and Gibraltar Row in Bethnal Green (from 1793) and also the registers and certificates of the central registry (voluntary) of Baptists, Independents and Presbyterians (1716–1827), and of the Wesleyan Metropolitan Registry of births/baptisms 1818–37 (with some backdated entries: RG 4; certificates: RG 5). The Genealogist provides a single index for this great block of Nonconformist records, and this group of records is also on film at THLHLA and at LDS libraries.

At Guildhall (LMA) are transcripts of the Bunhill Fields burial ground registers (1789–1854) and an index for 1788–1853: J. Hanson and M. Stevens, *Bunhill Fields Burial Ground*; microform index 1799–1853 (Guildhall (LMA), 1999). For inscriptions on the tombs in Bunhill Fields, see J.A. Jones (ed.), *Bunhill Memorials* (J. Paul, 1849); E. Curll, *The Inscriptions upon the tombs, grave stones etc. in the Dissenters' burial place near Bunhill Fields* (1717); A.W. Light, *Bunhill Fields* (2 vols, C.J. Farncombe and Sons, 1913 and 1933); *History of Bunhill Fields Burial Ground, with some of the Principal Inscriptions, London and Middlesex Tracts*, Vol. 1 (City Lands Committee of the Corporation of London, 1902).

Remember marriages (except Quakers) usually took place in the parish church (though not always) in the period 1754–1837 and burials might also be in the parish churchyard. For the post-registration/census period the search is more difficult as the registers (see list in Appendix 3) are not, by and large, indexed.

The following is a sample entry in a Nonconformist register (TNA RG 4/4511 f. 3):

> Thomas Short of Petticoat Lane, son of Nathaniel and Mary was baptised 17 April 1757 at the Prebyterian Chapel in Great Alie Street, Goodman's Fields.

Adults might be baptised or initiated into the congregation, as this extract from the records of Sion Chapel shows:

> Edward Charles Short, son of Edward and Ann of Christ Church, Spitalfields, born March 1814, was baptised at the Sion Chapel in Mile End in October 1836.

The original 'birth certificates' from the Dr Williams's Registry look like this one:

> These are to certify that Benjamin son of Nathaniel Short and Mary his wife who was the Daughter of Thomas Matthews was born in Pettycoat Lane in the parish of St Botolphs, Aldgate in the City of London this 4th Day of July in the year 1760 at whose Birth were present Ann Hatton Elizabeth Kirk [signed; these witnesses were probably midwives]

The birth was registered at Dr Williams's Library, near Cripplegate, London, 1 August 1781.

Useful reference works include:

Nonconformist, Roman Catholic and Burial Ground Registers, Guildhall Library Research Guide, 3rd edn (2002); this lists published and MS material held by the library; MSS are now at LMA

G.R. Breed, *My Ancestors were Baptists*, 2nd edn (SOG, 1988)

D.J.H. Clifford, *My Ancestors were Congregationalists* (SOG, 1992)

A. Ruston, *My Ancestors were English Presbyterians/Unitarians* (SOG, 1993)

W. Leary, *My Ancestors were Methodists*, rev. edn (SOG, 1999).

Dissenting academies and chapels in St George-in-the-East are described at: www.stgite.org.uk/media/dissenters2.

Quakers

In the late seventeenth and eighteenth centuries Quakerism was very strong in Tower Hamlets, especially in Wapping and Ratcliff, where the stern, hard-working, God-fearing folk were much involved in the drink and cooperage trades. Their presence ceased to be felt much thereafter, although there were notable middle-class families to the east in Barking and West Ham.

The first Friends Meeting House was probably established in 1654 and met at the house of Captain James Brook on Mile End Green. From about 1656 there was a meeting house near the corner of Wheeler Street in Spitalfields; the street is now known as Quaker Street. In 1666–7 the Mile End Quakers' Meeting moved to a site in Ratcliff, at the corner of School Lane and Ratcliff Highway. From 1770–9 there was a Meeting in Wapping. See W. Beck and T.F. Ball's *The London Friends Meeting* (F.B. Kitto, 1869). The Ratcliff Meeting was a constituent meeting of the London and Middlesex Quarterly Meeting. Many East Enders were attached to the Monthly Meeting at Devonshire House in Houndsditch.

The Quakers operated as a 'state within a state', looking after their own poor and had a system of 'house visits'. E. Milligan and M. Thomas's booklet, *My Ancestors were Quakers*, 2nd edn (London, 1990), explains how their meetings were organised. They were regularly prosecuted for not paying tithes, refusing to serve in the militia etc. (1659–1836), and many appear in the records of the Sessions (see pp. 171–2). You may identify Quakers in wills and related records by the fact that they refused to take any oath and would 'affirm' instead.

Quakers were a thorn in the flesh of Stepney's eighteenth-century rectors because of their refusal to pay tithes. One such defaulter was Benjamin Batts of Ratcliff Square who refused to pay the tax due to the rector for his 11 acres. He was almost certainly a relative of Elizabeth Batts who married Captain Cook. (LMA P 93/DUN/ 200, 202, 207: lists of tithe defaulters.)

Records

From the seventeeth century Quakers kept their own meticulous and full records of births, marriages and deaths. Unlike other Nonconformist groups, Quakers used their parish church hardly at all and their records are usually quite separate. They were permitted to marry in their own meeting houses, being exempt from the 1754 Marriage Act.

If you have found Quakers in your family, you will be well advised to further your research at the archives held by the Library of the Religious Society of Friends at Friends House, although the main series of registers is available online (originals at TNA).

The following lists details the key sources:

- Pre-1837 Quaker registers (births, marriages and deaths) are at TNA (RG 6; available there or online at The Genealogist; indexed and at LDS libraries). These include: Ratcliff and Barking Monthly Meeting 1656–1838; Devonshire House, Houndsditch, Quarterly Meeting 1655–1837; London and Middlesex Quarterly Meeting 1646–1836.
- Alphabetical digests of the registers are kept at the Friends House Library. For further details, see D.J. Steel's *National Index of Parish Registers*, Vol. 2 (Phillimore, 1973) and *Society of Friends Registers, Notes and Certificates of Births, Marriages and Deaths*, Vol. 267 (List and Index Society, 1996).
- Burial notes are included in the main series of registers at RG 6. There are some burials in parish graveyards, but in London they were often buried in the Bunhill Fields burial ground (described above, access at The Genealogist) or in the Whitechapel Quaker Burial Ground: interment order book at LMA/Guildhall: MS 22,364, with alphabetical abstract (1777–81).
- At Friends House you will find: records of Ratcliff Meeting 1667–1821 (in 1821 this was amalgamated with the Barking Monthly Meeting); records of the Ratcliff and Barking Meeting 1821–2007. Also included are the records of the Wapping Constituent Meeting 1700–79 (when it was discontinued) and of the Plaistow Meeting from 1729. Records include: Men's minutes 1681–1970, Women's minutes from 1755, Suffering Books (records of prosecutions) from 1763–1856, registers of Members from 1784–1955, removal certificate books 1688–1832, marriage registers 1839–1914, burial notebooks for Ratcliff 1797–1857.

The records are much more informative than those of the established church. Thus, the marriage entry for Mary, daughter of John Selwood, a wealthy Ratcliff brewer, gives:

Thomas Bond of Radcliff mariner, son of John Bond of Devon Yeoman marries Mary Selwood daughter of John Selwood of Radcliff brewer on 3 January 1689. 38 named witnesses (members of Ratcliff Meeting). (TNA RG 6/674 f. 27.)

Birth (not baptism) entries are likewise informative and give the name of the midwife.

John Sansome son of John Sansome, cooper, and Elizabeth his wife, was born in Meeting House Alley in Wapping 10th of 'the 11th month called 'January' [Quakers had a different calendar] in the presence of 8 named witnesses including the midwife who delivered him, Abigail Joyce.

The same is true of death entries. The records for the Devonshire House Monthly Meeting (Bishopsgate) record:

Mary Short of Whitechapel, wife of William, aged 38 years [one index entry for this gives her age as 13] died 23 September 1735 and was buried 27th in the Quaker Burial Ground at Whitechapel; the 'searchers report consumption'.

The Quaker Family History Society has a useful website at: www. qfhs.co.uk.

Paupers and Orphans

The words 'pauper' or 'poor' may appear against your ancestor's name in parish registers or other records; you may find one (or a whole family) listed in one of the workhouses in census returns. If so, you may want to try and find out more from these records, which can be full and informative. For the post-1911 census period they can be useful for tracing family members.

Pre-1834: Poor Kept by the Parish

The poor are always with us and, although the East End did not become a byword for poverty until the second half of the nineteenth century, there was a poverty problem in parts of Tower Hamlets from Elizabethan times. Burials and baptisms in the parish registers for St Dunstan's Stepney for the late 1580s and 1590s 'out of the parsonage barn' show us that there was a parish shelter for the poor in the rector's tithe barn.

Contrary to what you might be led to believe, the poor were not left to starve in the past. From the late sixteenth century householders had to pay a poor rate and each parish looked after its own, sending off those who had not established their 'settlement' locally to be kept by another parish. Settlement was established by having been baptised, employed or apprenticed in the parish, or by renting a substantial property, holding parish office or, in the case of women, marrying a man who was 'settled' there. There are a whole range of useful records emanating from this requirement, best described in W.E. Tate's *The Parish Chest*, 3rd edn (Phillimore, 1983). Settlement examinations may be especially revealing, describing whole families and their movements.

As a result of the great numbers of sailors living there in the seventeenth and eighteenth centuries, Stepney parish became a favourite place for parishes to offload paupers who were, or claimed to have been, born at sea. If a constable found a vagrant 'old salt' wandering the streets of Liverpool or Bristol, he might get sent off to Stepney. The *National Gazeteer of Britain and Ireland*, published in 1868, stated: 'Paupers born at sea have been sent here from all parts of the country, but the recent decision of the superior courts refuse to establish this traditional law.' This is explained by Tom Ridge in 'All at Sea', *Archives*, Vol. 6 (1964).

Mostly paupers, the aged and indigent were allocated 'out relief', a small sum of money to keep the wolf from the door. There were workhouses in Tower Hamlets, as elsewhere, from the mid-eighteenth century. The Whitechapel Workhouse was in Ayliffe Street (1724); by 1776–7 it had 600 inmates. The Limehouse Workhouse was established in 1725, as was the one in Ratcliff; Shadwell followed a year later. The Spitalfields house was in Bell Lane (1728); there children were set to silk winding. The Aldgate Workhouse was in Rose Lane (1730), the Poplar workhouse on the north side of the High Street (1735), the Stepney Workhouse (1725) in White Horse Lane. The Wapping house was in Virginia Street (1723, High Street 1817). In 1803 a house in Mile End (Alderney Place) off Globe Road was rented from Thirwall, curate of Stepney church.

Orphans and foundlings were kept by the parish, often fostered out initially. Poor girls who conceived a child out of wedlock often went into the workhouse to have their babies. Fathers were chased up by the parish with a view to their providing maintenance.

Records

The records of poor relief pre-1834 were kept with other parish records and are now to be found, in the main, at THLHLA.

Much of the East End belonged to the huge parish of Stepney at this time; poor relief was administered by the respective hamlets (see p. 205

for lists of hamlets) and survival is patchy. Unfortunately, there are no records for Mile End New Town, the poorest area, virtually nothing for Shadwell, Wapping or Whitechapel and a few removal orders for Ratcliff. The following list details what is available:

- THLHLA has extensive records of poor relief and lists of paupers (in and out) for Poplar, Bow and Bromley and a very few items for Ratcliff, Limehouse, Bethnal Green, St George-in-the-East (some records at LMA) and virtually nothing for Mile End or Shadwell.
- Poplar hamlet and parish: registers of parish poor children 1705–40, overseers' accounts, list of persons in receipt of in and out relief, workhouse lists and accounts spanning 1712–1836. Not complete but a very good coverage. Until 1817 Poplar was a hamlet of Stepney. These records include those of Stepney's hamlet of Poplar, of the East India Company's chapel and, from 1817, those of the parish of Poplar All Saints.
- Bow parish: overseers' accounts 1719–68, pauper examination books 1739–1861, payments to paupers 1805–29, removal orders 1807–66, registers of paupers in the workhouse 1806–25, apprenticeship registers 1802–27 (access at THAOL), out relief 1859–65.
- Bromley parish: churchwardens' accounts 1650–1819, which have details of relieved paupers, overseers' accounts 1667–1839 with names, paupers' examination books 1778–1843 indexed, vestry books 1722–1825, which include recipients of poor relief, removal orders 1839–65. See EoLFHS's CD-ROM 'Settlement Examinations: Bromley 1778–1791'.
- Limehouse: disbursement books of overseers 1766–73.
- Bethnal Green: account of payments made by overseers to persons drawn for militia service 1798, records of out relief 1812–22, posting book overseers of poor for BG hamlet 1729–30, includes lists of payment of weekly pensions, and account book of overseers 1737–8.
- St George-in-the-East (Wapping-Stepney): a few bastardy bonds and oaths (eighteenth century). LMA has workhouse admission and discharge registers 1811–43, 1854–6 and settlement exams 1828–36.
- Ratcliff: a few removal orders.
- St Botolph's Bishopsgate: parish records are at LMA (P 69/BOT 4).
- Old Artillery Ground: settlement examinations for 1792–1826; EoLFHS CD-ROM.
- St Botolph's Aldgate: Poor Law records 1742–1868 available at Origins (originals at LMA/Guildhall).

The following extract is an example of a settlement examination, from St Botolph's Aldgate, LMA/GL MS: 2676/22:

> Eleanor Bleak (X) widow of William Bleak married 22 years ago at St Botolph Aldgate and he bound apprentice to (Mr) Smith of the Green Yard near Black Jack Alley now called Coopers Court, St Botolph Aldgate and served 3½ years when master died and he turned over to (Messrs) Watherley and Crowdie, glass blowers and served rest with them whose factory was near Green Yard, but in last year he usually slept in his father's house on the east side of Green Yard. 12 Dec 1797.

There are many references to removal and settlement in the records of the Middlesex Sessions and it is worth a look at the indexes to the published volumes of Session Books in *Middlesex County Records* (Sessions records at LMA). This extract is from the *Calendar of Middlesex Sessions 1689–1709*, 29:

> Dispute between the overseers etc. of the hamlet of Mile End new Town, in the parish of Stepney , and the churchwardens etc of Stratford ... respecting the last legal settlement of Thomas Woodall, who has three children, Mary, John and Hannah, chargeable to Mile End ... January 1691.

The Poor Law Unions and the Harsh New System, 1834–1929

See map on p. 129 for areas covered by the unions. The best place to do an initial search for workhouse ancestors is in the census returns, 1841–1911 (every ten years). The inmates of Tower Hamlets' workhouses in 1881 are all listed at: www.workhouses.org.uk.

The records kept by the Poor Law unions, listed below, may include admission and discharge registers and creed registers (the latter give dates of admission and discharge or death), lists of lunatics, of children put to apprenticeship or sent to Canada, birth and death registers, names of family and friends (visitors), lists of people receiving out relief and settlement examinations. Most records are at LMA; some are available online at Ancestry. A most useful tool for understanding the records is at: www.workhouses.org.uk.

The inmates comprised orphans and destitute children, single mums and pregnant paupers, the sick, lunatics, the old and the unemployed. Some people stayed just a night or two, while others kept coming back;

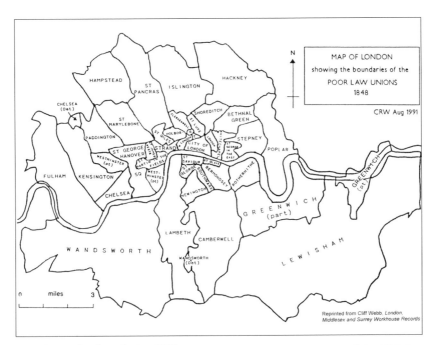

Poor Law union boundaries, 1848. Reproduced from J. Gibson, C. Rogers and C. Webb's *Poor Law Union Records: South East England and East Anglia,* 2nd edn (FFHS, 2005)

they were called 'ins and outs' – the vagrants, tramps and the homeless, usually to be found in the casual wards, where they had to break stones or pick oakum. They did not have to belong to the parish to gain entry. The casual ward at Whitechapel was described by Jack London, in *The People of the Abyss* (Macmillan, 1903).

The terrible poverty problem in the late nineteenth-century East End is described above at p. 37. The very worst areas on Booth's poverty map for the East End are parts of Bethnal Green and the parish of St John the Evangelist. The government's solution was the 1834 Poor Law Amendment Act which was intended to abolish all out relief for the able-bodied. This never happened; out relief was still paid, although many more people went into the workhouse than had been the case before. In the 1870s, the Charity Organisation Society took over the co-ordination of London's charitable endeavour, introducing a rigorous system of investigation of claims. From this time little out relief was paid by the Poor Law unions in St George-in-the-East, Stepney or

The Bow Road workhouse, later St Clement's Hospital. Built as the workhouse for the City of London Union, it opened in 1849. In 1869 it became the infirmary for the combined West and East London Unions. Yvonne Hughes

Whitechapel and applicants were directed to seek charitable relief (see below, p. 139).

Great workhouses were built where conditions were deliberately harsh to discourage malingerers. If an able-bodied man went into the workhouse, his family had to enter with him. From 1867, separate infirmaries were built and later there were experiments with farm colonies for families and 'cottage settlements' and 'scattered homes' for children in the countryside. Children might also be boarded out. Poor Law schools were established (see p. 94).

The saintly George Lansbury, a Christian Socialist who fought for the poor of the East End all his life, becoming leader of the Labour Party in 1931, was elected to the Poplar Board of Guardians in 1892. In *Looking Backwards and Forwards* (Blackie, 1935), he described the appalling brutality of the people who ran these institutions, where 'every vestige of kindliness' was destroyed.

The whole country was divided into 'unions', collections of parishes, and treated as one unit for Poor Law purposes. The unions for the East End were: Stepney/Limehouse, Poplar, St George-in-the-East, Whitechapel, Bethnal Green and London East. Mile End New Town, originally part of Stepney Union, broke off in 1857. In 1925, the Hamlet of Mile End Old Town, the Parish of St George-in-the-East and the Whitechapel Union were added to the Stepney Union; it was renamed the Parish of Stepney Union in 1927.

Stepney Union, 1837–1925 (called Limehouse Union, 1921–5)
It covered Limehouse, Ratcliff, Shadwell and Wapping and Mile End Old Town (until 1857).

Mile End Workhouse, for its time with Stepney Union, was the old hamlet workhouse in Alderney Place. Wapping Workhouse (described by Dickens in *The Uncommercial Traveller*; and closed 1863) was in Green Bank. Limehouse Workhouse was the old parish establishment in Ropemakers' Fields. The Hamlet of Ratcliff Workhouse in York Street West (now Barnes Street) became union offices and housed the casual ward. A new workhouse was built in Bromley, St Leonard Street 1861–3. The sick asylum was in Devon's Road, Bow. In 1901 children's cottage homes opened in Stifford, Essex.

LMA records: removal orders 1850–1927, registers of lunatics 1871–1927, lunatic reception orders 1872–1911, registers of servants and apprentices 1862–3, 1886–96, 1902–23, lists of children 1873–1927, registers of deserted children 1889–1924, emigrant children 1911–15; Limehouse Children's Establishment admission and discharge registers 1838–73, creed registers 1869–73, deaths 1866–73, visitors 1850–71; Mile End Old Town Workhouse admission and discharge registers 1840–57, deaths 1854–7; Ratcliff Workhouse admission and discharge registers 1839–72, 1893–1908; Children's Receiving Homes admission and discharge registers 1909–19, creed registers 1893–1916, births 1895–1913, deaths 1894–1911; Wapping Workhouse admission and discharge registers 1848–63 (closed 1863); Bromley House (1863–1913) admission and discharge registers 1866–1913, creed registers 1874–1923, births 1866–1923, deaths 1866–1923; Stepney Union Infirmary admission and discharge register 1913–16. Bow and Thavies Inn Institution admission and discharge registers 1923–4; Stifford Children's Homes admission and discharge registers 1902–23, creed registers 1902–21, birth-certificate copies 1890–4.

For inmates of Stepney and Bromley workhouses 1899–90, see below.

St George-in-the-East Union (formerly Wapping-Stepney), 1836–1925
A parish workhouse had been established here by 1824, on a site between Prusom Street and Princes Street (now Raine Street). It was taken over by the Union in 1837 (Raine Street/Charles Street/Old Gravel Lane Workhouse) and subsequently became St George-in-the-East Hospital. An industrial school was set up in Green Lane, Plashet in 1851. The casual ward was in Raymond Street, Wapping. For some years pauper children from the Union were farmed out to Mr Drouet's private establishment in Tooting, which became notorious folllowing a cholera epidemic. Dickens wrote of it:

> His establishment is crammed. It is in no respect a fit place for the reception of the throng shut up in it. The dietary of the children is so unwholesome and insufficient, that they climb secretly over pailings, and pick out scraps of sustenance from the tubs of hog-wash. Their clothing by day, and their covering by night, are shamefully defective. Their rooms are cold, damp, dirty; and rotten.

LMA records: settlement exams 1837–1921, removal orders 1876–1925, lunatic reception orders 1901–21, registers of lunatics 1859–1926, apprenticeship indentures 1900–14, pauper children 1866–8, 1887–1927, adoption registers 1900–24; St George-in the-East Workhouse admission and discharge registers 1811–43, 1854–6, settlement exams 1828–36; Raine Street Infirmary admission and discharge registers 1871–1925, births 1871–1915, deaths 1889–1916, creed registers 1872–89; Raine Street Workhouse admission and discharge registers 1838–1921, creed registers 1864–1921, births 1854–75, deaths 1836–1918; Metropolitan Asylums Board register of patients 1907–27; Plashet School admission and discharge registers 1856–1925, lists pauper children 1859–1920, creed registers 1906–25; Mr Drouet's Home, Tooting, list of pauper children 1852–61.

Whitechapel Union, 1837–1925
It covered Holy Trinity Minories, Mile End New Town, Norton Folgate, Old Artillery Ground, St Botolph's Aldgate, St Katharine's by the Tower, Spitalfields, Tower Liberty and Tower, Whitechapel.

Whitechapel Workhouse was erected in 1842 in Vallance Road. This became the infirmary following the building of South Grove Workhouse (between what is now Southern Grove and Lincoln Street, next to the City Workhouse in Bow Road) in 1872.

LMA records: removal orders 1871–2, 1879–1924, lunatic admission book 1901–26, registers of lunatics 1838–1914; Baker's Row Infirmary admission and discharge registers 1853–1925, births 1902–25, deaths 1877–1916, creed registers 1915–26; Whitechapel Workhouse admission and discharge registers 1908–26, births 1905–26, deaths 1866–9, creed registers 1881–1925, registers of children 1871–1927, registers of deserted children 1889–1923, staff records 1857–1925.

Bethnal Green Poor Law Union, 1836–1930
It covered St Matthew's Bethnal Green parish.

This Union was created in 1836, taking over the parish workhouse (1777). In 1840 the Waterloo Road Workhouse was built and a second workhouse on Well Street in Hackney was used to house the 'respectable poor' (from 1890). The Union also managed the Cambridge Heath Road Infirmary and the Bethnal Green School for the Juvenile Poor in Leytonstone.

LMA records: case papers 1921–30, settlement exams 1839–1903 (gaps), lunatics 1922–35, settlement orders 1904–17, removal orders 1837–1916, lunatic orders 1925–35, lists of pauper lunatics 1897–1915, registers of lunatics 1857–1915 (gaps); Waterloo Road Workhouse admission and discharge registers 1919–35, creed registers 1869–1935, birth registers

1878–1926, deaths 1895–1935, registers of lost children 1897–1929, patients' records 1906–35; Well Street Workhouse creed registers 1891–1900; Infirmary (later Bethnal Green Hospital) creed registers 1900–18, registers of inmates 1900–15, history sheets children 1896–1906, registers of adoptions 1914–25, registers of apprentices 1928;

Leytonstone Children's Home admission and discharge 1915–37, creed registers 1876–1937, baptisms 1928–36, births 1901–14, deaths 1869–95, punishment books 1911–36.

TNA records: staff registers, 1838–66 at MH9/1.

Poplar Poor Law Union, 1836–1930
It covered Bromley, Bow and Poplar.

This Union, created in 1836, took over the Poplar High Street Workhouse. From 1871 only able-bodied men were taken in and put to hard labour; the aged and infirm were sent to the Stepney Union Workhouse and those in need of hospital care sent to the joint Poplar and Stepney Sick Asylum. The workhouse was forced to open for all classes of inmate in 1882 due to increased demand. In 1913, it was renamed the Poplar Institution.

The Poplar Union bought the Forest Gate School in 1897, which it used for training and as an overflow workhouse. The Union also managed a farm in Dunton, Essex (Laindon House) which housed unemployed men as farm labourers, with their families. The labour colony experiment ended in 1912, but the site was retained as a workhouse. In 1906, the Union constructed a cottage homes training school for children in Hutton, Essex.

LMA records: settlement exams 1885–97, removal orders 1874–1927, applications for relief 1893–1912, registers of relief to wives and children of interned aliens 1914–20, admission of imbeciles 1875–1903, lunatic reception orders 1851–1905, registers of lunatics 1857–86, reports on lunatics 1896–1902, visitors' books (lunatics) 1900–30, lists of pauper children 1850–75, 1884–1924, vaccination officers' lists of births 1872, registers of emigrants 1907–13; Poplar High Street Workhouse admission and discharge registers 1845–71, 1902–24, 1928–30, creed registers 1844–1940, births 1837–1914, baptisms 1881–1939, deaths 1860–1931; Wapping Branch Workhouse creed registers 1869–71; Dunton Farm Colony/Laindon House admission and disharge 1904–30, creed registers 1906–30, punishment book 1907–14, medical records 1909–31, applications 1912–31, inmates 1904–25; Well Street Hackney Workhouse creed register 1903;

Forest Gate Branch Workhouse creed registers 1908–12, deaths 1908–11, inmates 1908–15; Belmont Workhouse (Sutton) inmates 1908–22; Bow Institution inmates 1912–29; Poplar Training School/Hutton Schools, Forest Gate admission and discharge registers 1897–1932, creed registers 1899–1932, deaths 1869–99, lists of pauper children 1869–1903, punishment books 1913–16; Langley House Children's Home admission and discharge registers 1903–40, creed registers 1903–15, inmates 1929–40.

TNA records: staff registers 1837–67 at MH 9/13.

East London Poor Law Union, 1837–1930
This was formed in 1837, covering the parishes of St Botolph's Aldersgate, Aldgate and Bishopsgate and St Gile's Cripplegate. Its Homerton Workhouse was set up in 1852. In 1869 it merged with other City unions and became the City of London Union. The old City Workhouse in Bow Road (see illustration on p. 130) became its infirmary and re-opened as the Bow Institution in 1912.

LMA records: removal orders 1840–69; Bow Road Workhouse admission and discharge registers 1889–1910, deaths 1866–74; Bow Road Infirmary admission and discharge registers 1876–89, creed registers 1876–1914, deaths 1874–1930, lists of paupers 1904–11; Homerton Workhouse admission and discharge registers 1857–1902, creed registers 1876–1911, births 1865–1905, deaths 1865–1908; Lower Clapton Workhouse admission and discharge registers 1911, creed registers 1914–33, births 1914–25, deaths 1914–15; Lower Clapton Infirmary admission and discharge registers 1911–14; Thavies Inn Infirmary admission and discharge registers 1889–1902, 1917–32, creed registers 1895–1930, births 1889–1932, deaths 1889–1914, apprentices 1838–1928, lists of paupers 1870–1906; City of London Maternity Hospital baptisms 1813–1978, admission registers 1750–69, 1861–1948.

TNA records: staff registers 1841–67 at MH9/10.

Mile End Old Town Union, 1857–1925.
From 1857 the workhouse was in Bancroft Road.

LMA records: settlement exams 1860–75, 1894–1908, removal orders 1848–1922, lunatic reception orders 1851–1920, registers of lunatics 1875–1927, registers of imbeciles 1870–27, apprentice registers 1857–1924, indentures 1897–1924, infant deaths 1871–82; Mile End Workhouse Bancroft Road admission and discharge registers 1879–1926, creed registers 1883–1912; Mile End Infirmary admission and discharge registers 1883–1926, creed registers 1883–1915, births 1883–98, deaths 1883–1913; Bancroft Road School admission and discharge registers 1867–1900, creed registers 1877–99; Scattered Homes (small rural houses for children) admission and discharge registers 1900–28, creed registers 1899–1928, lists of pauper children 1912–26.

TNA records: staff registers 1857–66 at MH9/11.

Stepney Union, 1925–30
It covered Mile End Old Town Union, Whitechapel Union and Old Stepney/Limehouse Union.

LMA records: lists of paupers and registers of lunatics 1925–30; Bromley House admission and discharge registers 1926–9, creed registers 1926–31; South Grove Institution admission and discharge registers 1926–36, creed registers 1925–32; Grays Scattered Homes admission and discharge registers 1925–31, creed registers 1924–31; Stifford Homes admission and discharge registers 1924–31, creed registers 1921–31; staff records 1925–30.

Settlement and removals orders and appeals against removal can be found among the Middlesex Session Records, 1350–1889 LMA MJ/SP.

Further information about workhouses can be obtained from Peter Higginbotham at: www.workhouses.org.uk. Record listings are based on J. Gibson, Colin Rogers and Cliff Webb's *Poor Law Union Records 1. East England and East Anglia*, 2nd edn (FFHS, 2005).

Pauper Children Sent Abroad

Parishes occasionally got rid of their paupers, including children, by paying for them to be sent to the colonies. Notes of this may be found in vestry minutes and parish registers. From 1834, Poor Law unions were empowered to supply money, food and clothing for pauper families to go to the colonies and from 1850 they were empowered to offload children under 16. For some lists of emigrants among the Poor Law Commissioners Papers see MH 12 at TNA.

From the 1870s to 1914, numbers of poor children were sent off to Canada, US, Australia, Rhodesia and New Zealand. It is estimated that some 80,000 alone went to Canada. Many charities organised schemes, including the Salvation Army and Barnardo's (see below). The children's experiences are described in Roger Kershaw and Janet Sach's *New Lives for Old* (TNA, 2008), or visit www.britishhomechildren.org.

Records Online

The following records can be accessed via the Internet.

- Stepney Union Case Books, 1889–90. Six notebooks containing transcriptions of Stepney Union casebooks, 1889–90, have been digitised and are available online (indexed) at the Charles Booth Online Archive at: www.booth.lse.ac.uk>Stepney Union Casebooks. The volumes record detailed case histories of the inmates of Bromley and Stepney workhouses and of people who received outdoor relief from the union.

The following notes on Reuben Hart in Bromley Workhouse, a coal porter, 1889–90, give an idea of the type of information that can be uncovered.

Information from census: 1841 shows him to have been a poulterer's son of Newington. 1851 shows Reuben living with wife Mary and daughter Mary Ann Milson in Walworth. 1861 shows him living with wife Ann in Bermondsey and daughters Eliza and Ann. 1871 census shows him living at Triggs Cottages in Limehouse with wife Ann and children Eliza 13, Ann 10 and Reuben 6. In 1881 he and his wife Ann were living at 5 Gill Street, Limehouse. He describes himself as a general labourer born in Newington. The birth places of the children show that they have lived in Horsleydown and Bermondsey and Limehouse.

Union casebook entry: Stepney Union Casebooks Booth B/162 tells us that his wife died in 1884 (she would have been 55). Reuben was admitted to the workhouse and the cause of his pauperisation is given as 'drink and improvidence'. His living relatives are described:

> His daughter Ann born 1860, a prostitute, on the streets for a year, applied to the Union 11 November 1880, expecting to be confined shortly. She came out for a day on 21 December to see her dying brother. On 15 December 1883 her landlady, Mrs Eliza Moore, of 3, Union Place, came and asked for her admission and she was sent to the Sick Asylum suffering from syphilis. Her aunt Mrs Norton lives at 39 Pale Street. Stepney Green. Her one child, Elizabeth, is now in Dr Barnardo's. She is an associate of Margaret Cremer, Mary A Rudd & the McCarthys [well-known prostitutes].
>
> His daughter Eliza (32) is now married to a navvy called Howard of 1 Grosvenor Buildings.

His son Reuben (25) is a cigar maker turned carman married to Mary Ann, with two sons, Reuben (1886) and John (1887). They live in Barking Road.

General remarks.
Hart's wife applied to go in the workhouse in July 1878; she said her husband ill treated her – gave her only 4s 6d for six weeks, and had the doors and windows of their house/ lodging nailed up to keep her out because 'she told him he had carnal intercourse with his daughter, Ann'. She admitted to drinking a little but said 'It made her silly'. The Relieving Officer visited and the neighbours said the whole thing was the wife's fault because she drank; they, however, confirmed the report about the father and the daughter. Hart applied to go in the house in October 1887 – he was homeless and had no work. He went to stay with his son in Barking Road. He applied for re-admission and was referred to West Ham. In January 1889 he was passed from West Ham.

In the 1891 census Reuben is in the Lambeth Workhouse Infirmary.

- Poor Law records at Ancestry. Ancestry has digitised a number of LMA Poor Law records listed above; they are not indexed, but can be browsed online, i.e. you have to read through the registers to search for your ancestor. There is an ongoing programme of digitisation. Currently available are the following admission and discharge registers (from the boroughs of Poplar and Stepney only; Bethnal Green is not included):
  Bancroft Road School 1867–1900
  Bow and Thavies Inn Institution 1923–4
  Bromley House 1866–1929
  Grays Scattered Homes 1925–9
  Limehouse Children's Establishment 1838–73
  Mile End Infirmary 1883–1926
  Mile End Old Town Workhouse 1840–54
  Mile End Scattered Homes 1900–28
  Mile End Workhouse 1888–1926
  Plashet School 1856–1925
  Plashet School for Boys 1854–1920
  Raine Street Workhouse 1838–1921

Ratcliff Workhouse 1844–1908
Ratcliff Children Receiving Home Admission 1909–19
St George-in-the-East Infirmary 1871–1925
St George-in-the-East Infirmary Index 1874–1923
St George-in-the-East Workhouse 1790–1856
South Grove Institution Mile End Road 1912–25
South Grove Institution Mile End Road Index 1920–6
Stepney Union Infirmary 1913–16
Stifford Children's Homes 1902–21
Wapping Workhouse 1849–63
Whitechapel Infirmary 1910–23

Baptisms and births in the boroughs of Stepney and Poplar workhouses 1837–1906 can be searched at Ancestry's 'Births and Baptisms 1813–1906', indexed. Also, deaths and burials in the workhouses of Stepney 1836–1923 and Poplar 1860–1928.

Reference material of use includes:
www.workhouses.org.uk – an excellent, informative website
Simon Fowler, *Workhouse* (TNA, 2007)
W.J. Fishman, *East End 1888* (Five Leaves Publications, 1988) – for conditions in the Whitechapel Workhouse
Stephen Park, 'Records of the Stepney Board of Guardians', *Cockney Ancestor*, 32 (1986), 7–9; 33 (1986–7), 10; 34 (1987), 11
Stephen Park, 'Records of the Poplar Board of Guardians', *Cockney Ancestor* (1986), 8–11 (list)
J. Parr, *Labouring Children. British Immigrant Apprentices to Canada, 1869–1924* (Croom Helm, 1980).

Charities for the Poor

There is a bewildering array of charitable foundations that operated in the East End, many of which came under the auspices of the Charity Organisation Society (COS). The COS (later the Family Welfare Association) set up dispensaries and had relieving officers. From the 1870s, their activities largely replaced the state system of out relief in St George-in-the-East, Stepney and Whitechapel. The records are at LMA; search at TNA's Access to Archives (A2A) under COS. The list includes:

Salmon Lane Mission, Limehouse 1891–1952; Providence Row Night Refuge, Spitalfields 1872–96; East London Hospital for Children and Dispensary for Women 1868–1938 Glamis Road, Shadwell; Tower Hamlets Mission, 31 Mile End Road 1877–1922 (Frederick Charrington's Great Assembly Hall, where a free meal was offered if you attended a service); Homes for Working Boys in London 1876–1913, 30 Spital Square; Surgical Aid Society; Walter Austin's London Cottage Mission, 16 and 18 Conder Street, Limehouse Fields then 67 Salmon Lane, 1876–90; Royal Alfred Aged Seamen's Institute 1879–1939; Christian Community, Bethnal Green 1905–49; Barbican Mission to the Jews 1882–1942, Finsbury Square then 82 Whitechapel Road; Children's Country Holiday Fund 1884–1960; Seaside Camps for London Boys 1893–1938; Oxford House Bethnal Green (settlement) 1887–1961; St Martin's Mission, Bethnal Green 1892–1938; East End Mission, formerly Wesleyan Mission East 1894–1933, 1952, Stepney Central Hall, 583 Commercial Road; Seamen's Mission, Jeremiah Street, Poplar 1896–1940; Pearson's Fresh Air Fund 1895–1942 (holidays and outings for slum children); East End Mission to the Jews, 119 Leman Street 1896–1931; Toynbee Hall settlement (Toynbee Hall records are mainly lost).

Records of some parochial charities and those attached to chapels are at THLHLA; search TNA's Access to Archives>Tower Hamlets Charities.

For Barnardo's Homes children (first home founded in Stepney in 1867), go to: www.barnados.org.uk or write to Barnardo's at Tanners Lane, Barkingside, Ilford, Essex IG6 1 QG. They provide a family history service for a modest fee.

Salvation Army records are held at the Salvation Army Heritage Centre in South London (see Appendix 8), and may be researched on Tuesdays, Wednesdays and Thursdays by appointment. The archive provides a paid research service. Salvation Army records at LMA (1912–65) are closed until 2026.

Immigrants

As has been demonstrated, the East End has been a place of coming and going for hundreds of years. Most East End families are immigrants of one sort or another, drawn towards the great metropolis for work or asylum.

Coming into the East End from the countryside.

Since the sixteenth century, and probably before, young hopefuls have been coming into London to seek their fortune or save themselves from starvation. Many settled to the east where rents were (sometimes) cheaper and where trading restrictions were less severe than in the City. They came to work in the many trades that serviced the City, to take ship at Wapping and set sail for the New World and later to fulfil the enormous demand for labour that came with the building of the enclosed docks. Men who manned the coastal shipping trade might marry into the area, meeting girls on their frequent trips. In the early seventeenth century there was a colony of Newcastle collier boat men in Wapping, for instance.

People coming into the East End tend to come from Essex and East Anglia, although this is far from being the general rule. You may find immigrants from all over the British Isles. To trace these country East Enders back to their origins use the censuses (for the nineteenth and twentieth centuries), which provide a place of birth. Wills are the other recognised source for migrants as testators often leave something to family in their home village or to a home church or charity (see p. 82). The IGI (see p. 72) and any other countrywide indexes of births, marriages and deaths (as at Ancestry) will allow you to trace your family back to their country origins in a way that has never been possible before the present century. Young men often came to London to be apprenticed and the apprenticeship records (see p. 108) are a way of finding out where the family came from in the eighteenth century.

Irish/Roman Catholics

Irish East Enders are best sought among the usual range of records: census, GRO and parish records. They were Roman Catholic, mostly, but had to marry in the parish church until 1837 and were buried in the parish graveyard. From the Catholic Relief Acts of 1778 and 1791 a Catholic chapel might be legally registered as place of worship and from this date some church registers survive.

The Irish are a very important part of East End culture; they have been coming here for hundreds of years in search of work. In the late seventeenth century numbers came to join the French silk-weaving industry in Spitalfields; they came to find building work, often under-cutting the English brickies. They came to Stepney's riverside hamlets to work as ballast men and coal heavers, to work in the docks and at all manner of labouring and menial jobs. In 1816, there were said to be 14,000 in the parish of Shadwell alone.

Waves of starving immigrants arrived following the Great Famine of 1845. According to Mayhew (*London Labour and the London Poor* (1849–61)), the 'Irish Nests' in the East End were at Ratcliff Cross, Commercial Road, Limehouse Hole, Baker's Rents and Cooper's Gardens in Shoreditch, and at Flower and Dean Street, George Yard, Glasshouse Yard, Keate Street, Lambeth Street, Rosemary Lane, St George Street, Thrawl Street, Wentworth Street and Whitechapel High Street in Whitechapel and Spitalfields. There were Irish lodging houses at Mile End, Ratcliff Highway, Shadwell and Wapping. Paddy's Goose on Ratcliff Highway was reputedly the roughest pub in London, according to Charles Dickens junior: 'The uproarious rendezvous of half the tramps and thieves of London'.

A profligate, drunken and rowdy lot they were, or so it was said, very different from the Jews. George Sims, writing in 1911, compared the 'Jewish end' of Cable Street with its 'well-shod and comfortably clad' children with the 'Irish end' where he saw 'poorly clad women and ... barefoot, capless, coatless little Irish lads'.

Catholic Church Sources

Before 1850, the Catholic Church was based on missions rather than parishes and events from different places may be found in the same register. Many of these registers, kept by the priests, are now at the Westminster Diocesan Archives (WDA) with transcripts at the Catholic Central Library and SOG. See Michael Gandy's *Catholic Missions and Registers*, Vol. 1 (M. Gandy, 1993).

The following list details Catholic churches in Tower Hamlets. Registers are held by the churches. Those at the Westminster Diocesan Archive (WDA) are noted.

- Bethnal Green: Our Lady of the Assumption, Victoria Park Square; founded 1902.
- Bow: Our Lady and St Catherine of Sienna, Bow Road; founded 1868.
- Limehouse: Our Lady Immaculate, Commercial Road; founded 1881.
- Mile End: Guardian Angels, Mile End Road; baptisms 1869–90, marriages 1904–62 (see *Catholic Ancestor*, 9:6 (November 2003)).

- Poplar: St Edmund, West Ferry Road, Millwall; baptisms 1870–present, marriages 1875–present (not deposited). St Mary and St Joseph, Canton Street; baptisms 1818–present, marriages 1818–present (not deposited), transcripts baptisms and marriages 1818–56 WDA, marriages and baptisms 1818–56 EoLFHS CD-ROM.
- Spitalfields: St Anne, Underwood Road; index to baptisms 1848–1909, baptism registers 1848–1920, confirmations 1856–91, index to marriages 1851–1934, marriages 1851–90 (see *Catholic Ancestor* 6:6 (1997)).
- St George-in-the-East: Virginia Street chapel; baptisms 1789–1800, 1832–56 WDA (see *Catholic Ancestor* 8:1 (February 2000), for an introduction to nineteenth-century baptisms), baptisms 1832–40 EoLFHS CD-ROM. The chapel was burnt down in the anti-Catholic Gordon Riots of 1780.
- Stepney: St Boniface German Church, Adler Street, Commercial Road; baptisms 1809–present, marriages 1864–present, copies baptisms 1809–1950, marriages 1864–1968 at AGFHS. St Mary and St Michael, Commercial Road; baptisms 1856–93, marriages 1856–99; WDA, baptisms 1893–present and marriages 1899–present not deposited (formerly in Virginia Street, see under St George-in-the-East). Holy Name and Our Lady of the Sacred Heart, Bow Common Lane; founded 1892.
- Wapping: St Patrick, Dundee Street; baptisms 1871–present (none 1853–65), marriages 1877–present (not deposited). The English Martyrs, Prescot Street; founded 1876.

Before Catholic chapels were made legal London/Irish Catholics might sometimes use the Catholic Chapels Royal and embassy chapels. Betty Boulter of Whitechapel, who ran off with an Irish soldier in 1684, married him in the Spanish Embassy Chapel in Wild Street, or so she said (Jane Cox, *Hatred Pursued Beyond the Grave* (HMSO, 1993)). The records of these chapels are listed in Vol. 1 of Michael Gandy's *Catholic Missions and Registers*.

A useful research tool is *Catholic Marriage and Baptism Indexes, eighteenth century–1870s*, compiled by Anstruther (CD-ROM from IHGS); entries are mainly from London and Essex.

Poor Law Records

The records of the Poor Law unions (see p. 131) abound with Irish names; the vicar of Wapping's St Peter's London Docks (the first

Anglican Mission Church to the East End poor) reported in 1883 that all his parishioners were on poor relief, most of them the 'lowest type of Irish'. The index to admissions and discharges for St George-in-the-East Infirmary (accessed at LMA) for August 1881–3 lists under 'Kelly':

> Susan Kelly 19 (pregnant), Edward Kelly 35 (rheumatism), Edward Kelly 73 (debility), Catherine Kelly 30 (bronchitis), Mary Kelly 60 (mental), John Kelly 30 (leg ulcer), Margaret Kelly 40 (finger ulcer and lead poisoning*), Louisa Kelly 63, Ann Kelly 30 (injury to face), William Kelly 56, William Kelly 57 (paralysis), Timothy Kelly 26 (bronchitis), Ann Kelly 24 (dermatitis), William Kelly 19 (bronchitis), Maria Kelly 21 (chest), Timothy Kelly 23 (bubos), Mary Kelly 70.

*The 'Uncommercial Traveller' (in Dickens's book of the same name) met a 'poor craythur' lying in a 'horrible brown heap' on the floor of an Irish home in St George-in-the-East in 1860. 'Sure 'tis the lead mills' said her hostess. Lead poisoning caused ulcers and paralysis, but it paid 18 pence a day.

Records of Persecution

In the sixteenth and seventeenth centuries, and in periods of anti-Popish behaviour thereafter, Roman Catholics might be prosecuted for not attending their Anglican parish church. These individuals were known as 'recusants' and names may be found among the records of the Sessions and among State Papers and Exchequer records at TNA (described in Amanda Bevan's *Tracing your Ancestors in the National Archives* (TNA, 2006)). See also, *Jacobean Recusant Rolls for Middlesex 1603–25*, ed. J.J. La Rocca (Catholic Record Society Publications Record Series, Vol. 76).

Reference material of use includes:
TNA's website www.movinghere.org.uk/galleries/roots/irish
www.IrishOrigins.com (the Origins network)
www.irishfamilyresearch.co.uk.
John Grenham, *Tracing your Irish Ancestors*, 3rd edn (Genealogical Publishing Company, 2005)
Ian Maxwell, *Tracing Your Northern Irish Ancestors* (Pen & Sword, 2010)
R. Swift and Sheridan Gilley (eds), *The Irish in Britain* (Pinter, 1989)
Michael Gandy, *Catholic Family History: A Bibliography of Local Sources* (M. Gandy, 1996)
Michael Gandy, *Tracing Catholic Ancestors* (PRO, 2001).

Scots and Welsh

Welsh dairymen abound in the records and numbers of Scots came to work in the docks and in the shipyards of Poplar. In the 1850s, many Scots came to Scott Russell's yard in Millwall to work on the construction of Brunel's *Great Eastern*. They built their own Presbyterian chapel, St Paul's, in West Ferry Road (1859), known as 'the Scotch church' (now a theatre).

The registers of the eighteenth-century Scottish (Presbyterian) church St Andrew in Broad Street, St George-in-the-East (moved to Mile End Old Town) are at TNA (RG 4: access via The Genealogist).

The following are useful reference books:

A Dictionary of Scottish Immigrants into England and Wales (Anglo Scottish Family History Society, 1984)

Ian Maxwell, *Tracing your Scottish Ancestors* (Pen & Sword, 2009).

Immigrants from Abroad

There was always a mix in the East End with people from the Low Countries and Germany coming in from the Middle Ages. There were Dutch breweries in St Katharine's in the fifteenth century; the government located 285 aliens in the precinct in 1583. In Shakespeare's day it was the most concentrated immigrant area, where in Ben Jonson's *The Devil is an Ass*, Vice, 'Iniquity', flew to 'drink with the Dutch'.

The first phase of religious refugees arrived in the late sixteenth century when continental Protestants, French, Dutch, Walloons and Flemings came into the north of the borough in considerable numbers to join the silk-weaving trade, following the massacre of Protestants on St Bartholmew's Day in 1572 and the sack of Antwerp in 1585. They were followed a hundred years later by another wave (see p. 149).

As the port of London expanded immigrants arrived from anywhere in the world where Britain traded. Some of them came as sailors on merchant vessels, and, for a variety of reasons, remained; there were 'blackamoors' or 'moors' from Africa (many brought in by the slave ships), Chinese and Indians. Many of the latter came as sailors on East India Company vessels; in 1813, there were said to be 500 Chinamen in the company's barracks at King David's Fort. The Chinese would later make their home in Limehouse (established there by the 1880s), famous

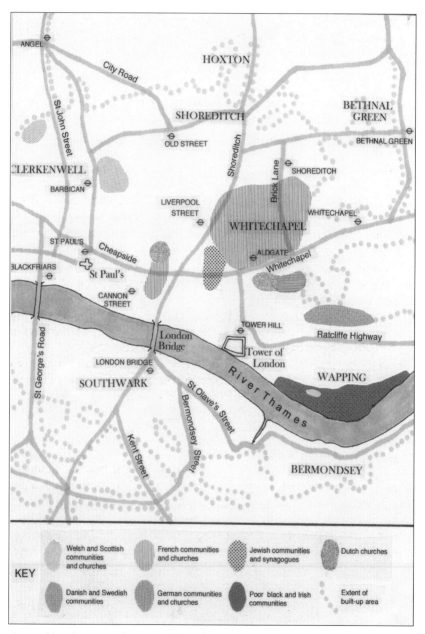

Areas of immigrant settlement in the eighteenth century. Drawn by Jane Seal

for its opium dens, laundries and restaurants. By 1911, Limehouse and Pennyfields were known as 'Chinatown'. Scandinavians came with the timber and some stayed, establishing churches in Wapping – the Danish Church in Wellclose Square (1696–1869) and the Swedish Church in Princes' Square (from 1728; no records survive). Strong trading links with Portugal brought numbers into the East End from the sixteenth century; those who stayed might attach themselves to the Catholic Virginia Street chapel in Wapping. For Portuguese Jews, see pp. 155–7.

From the late nineteenth century Somali seamen were to be found in the Cable Street area, with mass immigration in the 1980s. Goans were employed on East India Company ships and some settled from the mid-nineteenth century: one Shadwell Street was known as 'Tiger Bay'. Immigrants from the British West Indies came in great numbers after the Second World War. The arrival from Pakistan/Bangladesh is a recent phenomenon. Although there were Asian seamen around from the eighteenth century (called Lascars), it was not until the 1950s, following partition, and the 1970s, after the creation of the state of Bangladesh, that mass immigration began. These days one-third of the population of Tower Hamlets hails from the Indian sub-continent, a far higher proportion than the Jews ever constituted.

Most of the immigrants were absorbed into the population and traces of them will be found in the usual range of sources. Some changed their names officially and some went through the process of denization or naturalisation.

Sources for Immigrants

There is no general source or list of aliens coming into the country; what there is you will find described in TNA's 'Research Guide: Immigrants'. The passenger lists at TNA start in 1878 and only cover immigrants from non-European countries.

Some immigrants went through the legal processes of naturalisation or denization; the vast majority did not. Some went through the legal formalities of changing their names; most did not. Relevant records are available from the following sources:

- Naturalisation and denization: records 1509–1800 are published by the Huguenot Society of Great Britain. For the post-1800 period you will have to go to TNA (see information leaflet cited above).

- Change of name: see Phillimore and Fry's *Index to Change of Name 1760–1900* (Genealogical Publishing Co., 1968). After that go to TNA or consult lists in the *London Gazette*. See TNA's 'Legal Records Information 32: Change of Name'.

Ancestry has access to the following records:

- Aliens Entry Books 1794–1921 (correspondence about naturalisation: not in any way comprehensive, browse only). Records at TNA at HO 5.
- Lists of Aliens Arrival 1810–11, 1826–69 (not comprehensive, browse only). From various TNA sources.
- Passenger lists (incoming) from 1878 – from places outside Europe only. Indexed. Original records at TNA.

The following reference material is useful:

R. Kershaw and M. Pearsall, *Immigrants and Aliens*, TNA Reader Guide (2004)

R. and E. Kirk, *Return of Aliens Dwelling in the City and Suburbs of London Henry VIII to James I* (Huguenot Society, 1900–8)

'Black Caribbean Community Archives in the London Metropolitan Archives', LMA information leaflet 21

The Black and Asian presence in Tower Hamlets, a collection of cuttings, 1707–1823 (THHOL and THLHLA)

G. Grannum, *Tracing your West Indian Ancestors* (TNA, 2002)

www.movinghere.org.

Huguenots

The French weaving legacy is evident in Spitalfields still, with names like French Place and Loom Court and Huguenot weavers' houses still standing in Fournier Street and Princelet Street. A French-sounding name in an East End family probably indicates Huguenot ancestry, although the name may have been altered over the years.

'Huguenot' was the nickname given to French and Walloon Protestants who fled religious persecution in the sixteenth and seventeenth centuries. The first wave came to the East End after the massacre of St Bartholomew in 1572 and many joined the already established weaving industry. A third of the names on the list of Spitalfields residents in the 1641

Protestation Returns are French or Dutch and the hamlet (of Stepney) was populous enough to have its own churchwarden, a Frenchman. The newcomers established their own Calvinist churches in Threadneedle Street and at the Savoy.

A second and greater wave of immigration came in 1685 when Louis XIV withdrew the toleration edict issued by his grandfather in 1598. Between 50,000 and 80,000 refugees are said to have come to London. Many of them came from Tours and Lyons and were skilled weavers. The main area of settlement was in Spitalfields (with another in Soho) spreading out to Bethnal Green. A terrific boost was given to the silk-weaving trade and textile workers were drawn to east London from all over the country and from Ireland. Houses had to be hastily erected for the newcomers who were flooding in and a 'new town' was created for them. This was christened 'Mile End New Town', a mere 2 miles in circumference, lying to the east of Brick Lane, an 'estate' of closely packed, jerry built houses. In July 1690, the new town came into being and was constituted a separate hamlet of Stepney parish, having its own parish officers and Poor Law officers. George Wheler, a local landowner, bought a wooden building to serve as a chapel of ease for the new town; it was opened for worship, with the Reverend Mr Milbourne officiating, on Christmas Day 1692. By 1792 there were 620 houses, most of which were 3 storeys high with 15ft frontages. Birds sang from ornamental cages in these houses (the Frenchmen were very fond of them) and the air hummed with the clack of looms.

The vicar of Whitechapel called the new French Huguenot immigrants 'the very offal of the earth'; in fact, they came from all walks of life. Masters of the weaving craft tended to live in the City, although some had houses in Spital Square. Weaver town became so swollen, that fifty years after the Frenchmen came, the hamlet of Spitalfields would become its own parish. Mile End New Town would become the poor industrial area of Stepney parish. Sleepy, select Bethnal Green would be changed beyond recognition.

Huguenot chapels in Spitalfields were L'Eglise Neuve, the daughter church of Threadneedle Street, in Church Street, La Patente in Brown's Lane, St Jean (in St John Street), Crispin Street, Perle Street, Wheeler Street, Bell Lane, Eglise de Marche and the Artillery. There were two further chapels in Bethnal Green referred to in 1711 (no records survive). Even after the establishment of these churches, many families still used

Protestation Returns for Petticoat Lane, 1641–2. Huguenots were sometimes given rude names – see third entry, Charles Lepoxon. Parliamentary Archives

the Threadneedle Street church. Some married in their Anglican parish church and some married in the Fleet (see p. 76).

In the 1820s and 1830s, a great depression hit the silk industry and times were hard in Bethnal Green, Spitalfields and Mile End New Town. A House of Commons Committee reported in 1831–2 that there were 100,000 people in these hamlets, of whom half were involved in the weaving industry and 17,000 were loom weavers. The final death blow came to the industry in 1860 when a treaty with France allowed the import of French silk. According to Booth's researcher, reporting in the 1890s, they were 'a respectable set of men ...' but 'curious, cantankerous and warped' and obsessed with their trade (LSE Booth: B 350, p. 134). In 1931, there were still two weaving firms in Bethnal Green; the robes for George VI's coronation were made from silk made by Messrs Warner and Sons, who had moved to Braintree from Spitalfields some forty years earlier.

After a few generations the Frenchmen lost their foreign identity and became absorbed into the indigenous population. Many were successful and moved out of the area, many into Essex.

Records

Baptisms, Marriages and Burials

Huguenots married and baptised in their own Calvinist chapels and in parish churches. They were buried in dissenters' burial grounds (see p. 121) or in parish churchyards. Thus, Samuel Beuzeville, Minister of St Jean's Church, was buried in the churchyard of St Dunstan's Stepney in 1782.

The first place to look for Huguenot ancestors is in the publications of the Huguenot Society and/or the indexed entries to their registers at The Genealogist (go to 'Nonconformist records'); original records at TNA (RG 4). They may also be found in parish registers. The registers of St Dunstan's Stepney, for instance, have marriages, baptisms and burials for many French Spitalfields weavers.

The Huguenot Society of Great Britain and Ireland (founded in 1885) has a library in London (open to the public by appointment and on payment of a small fee). It has published a magnificent and comprehensive series of proceedings which make the search for Huguenot ancestry much easier than most areas of genealogical research, allowing you to find your East End ancestors and, in some cases, take them back to their French origins.

Huguenot houses in Spitalfields. Yvonne Hughes

The registers of the Huguenot chapels, and much more relating to their community, have been published by the Society (original registers at TNA; also available online at The Genealogist); see a list of their publications in LMA's information leaflet 24. The records include:

- Registers of the Threadneedle Street church and the chapel of the Spitalfields Hospital (later Founder's Hall Chapel) 1599–1840.
- Records of relief to refugees from the above 1681–7.
- Records of the French Hospital 1718–1957.
- Repertoire General 1689–1742: register entries from La Patente, Wheeler Street, Le Marche, Bell Lane, Crispin Street.
- Register of the Artillery church 1691–1786.
- Register of L'Eglise Neuve 1753–1809.
- Register of the Pearl Street church 1698–1701.
- Register of La Patente 1689–1785.
- Register of St Jean 1687–1751.

The churches organised a poor relief system and the full records of this operation may be consulted at the Huguenot Library; do an Internet search 'Tracing your poor Huguenot Ancestors' to find the relevant manuscript references.

The twice-yearly publication *Huguenot Families* has a number of articles relating to specific families and also some useful source-based items: issue 2: 'Huguenot Burials in Bishopsgate 1803–12'; issue 5: 'Huguenot Apprentices in Livery Companies'; issue 12: 'Huguenot Marriages at Shadwell, Bromley and Shoreditch 1740–1757'; issue 13 'Bethnal Green Settlement Examinations 1839–1861'.

The following are examples of entries from Huguenot registers:

> Louis Lemay was baptised at the Crispin Street Chapel 14 November 1703, born 6 November 1703, son of David and Susanne; godparents Abraham Chedieu and Louise Alain.

Many East End Huguenots patronised the 'mother church' in Threadneedle Street:

> Philip Lebrun, son of Jean and Marie of Spicer Street, Stepney, was baptised at Threadneedle Street 24 January 1702.

Numbers of Huguenot couples married at the Fleet (see p. 76):

> Francis Lemay, Stepney weaver married Ann Druett of Westminster 13 April 1712.

Other Records

- Wills (see p. 82). The French community in Spitafields was close knit and it is well worth checking through will indexes and reading any likely wills. For example, the will of Margaret Dubois, a wealthy Spitalfields spinster with South Sea Company stock, mentions:

  > Her sister, Magdalen Martin, her niece Susan Lemery, daughter of Lewis Lemery master silk weaver of Spitalfields, her niece Margaret de Niort, wife of Francis Niort, master silk weaver of Spitalfields, her great niece Margaret Lemery, her cousin Margaret Lobley, her late cousin (with children) Daniel Cartier and her brother

John Dubois in Carolina. Witnesses: Matthew Padrewissen
& James Gautier.

See also the 1724 probate inventory for Thomas Short, Stepney
weaver, on p. 85 (not a Huguenot, but ancestor of the author).

- Tax lists (see pp. 106 and 115). The records of the Four Shillings in
  the Pound Aid (at LMA (CLRO); access at: www.british-history.
  ac.uk/source.aspx?pubid=26) shows (among others) the following
  wealthy Frenchmen in 'Petty Coate Lane': Raphael Duboyce, with
  a £12 house (annual rent) and stock valued at £200, James Duboyce
  with stock of £200, Francis Poussett with a £27 house and stock
  of £300.
- Livery Company records (see p. 111).

The following reference material is useful:
www.cyndislist.com/huguenot/htm   for   worldwide   Huguenot
   families, bibliographies and sources
Robin Gwynn, *The Huguenots of London* (Alpha Press, 2001)
N. Currer-Briggs and Royston Gambier, *Huguenot Ancestry* (Phillimore,
   1985).

Jews

Most people with ancestry from the East London Jewish community are
descendants of the immigrants who came from the Russian Empire,
to escape from the pogroms following the assassination of the Tsar
in March 1881. There were Russians, Lithuanians, Germans, Austro-
Hungarians, but overwhelmingly they were Poles. Lord Rothschild
remarked, 'We now have a new Poland on our hands in East London'.
However, Jews were living in the East End from the seventeenth
century, although in the 1730s there were only about 6,000 Jews in the
whole country, so it was a small community.

The 'Jewish East End' lasted until the 1960s.

There are no general lists of aliens entering the country, therefore for
researching East End Jewish family history the censuses of 1891–1911
are the prime source, and will tell you where your ancestors came from
(see p. 66). Thence you can go to the foreign archive sources and the
many Jewish websites. Specifically Jewish sources are described in

Rosemary Wenzerul's books (see below) and there is an immensely useful list of foreign contacts.

Researching Jewish ancestors can be difficult and it would be worthwhile joining the Jewish Genealogical Society of Great Britain (JGSGB). One of the problems is names. Before the early nineteenth century European Jews were known by their first name and father's given name, *ben* for 'son of' and *bat* for 'daughter of'. When they arrived in Britain they might take the name of the town they had come from (like Hamburger) or their occupation (like Schneider – tailor.) Only a handful went through the formal processes of name change (see 'Jewish Name Variations' at: www.jewishgen.org. or Ancestry).

Before the 1880s

When Cromwell allowed the Jews back into the country in 1656 it was predominantly Portuguese and Spanish Jews of the Sephardim, wealthy and respected middle-class merchants and manufacturers, who came. They were soon followed by the poorer Ashkenazi Jews from Holland, Germany, Russia and Turkey who tended to join the already established trade in second-hand stuffs and stolen goods. Jewish hawkers and peddlars were known for their trickery. They settled on the eastern side of the City and in Whitechapel, in Goodmans' Fields, Wellclose Square and Petticoat Lane. A steady stream of immigrants came; by the 1850s there were between 30,000 and 40,000 Jews in the country.

Synagogue, Marriage and Burial Records

Jews were allowed to marry in synagogues or private houses, so the records of marriages pre-1837 are to be found among Jewish not parish records, along with records of births and circumcisions. Jews also had their own separate burial grounds. Many Jewish births and marriages are on the IGI (see p. 72).

The main 'Dutch' or Ashkenazi synagogues were the Great Synagogue in Duke's Place Aldgate, the New Synagogue in Bishopsgate (there was also the Hambro in Fenchurch Street). Registers of births and marriages from the Great (from 1791–1879) can be viewed at LDS libraries or found in H. and M. Lewin's *Marriage Records of the Great Synagogue, 1791–1885* (privately printed, 1904). New Synagogue marriages 1791–1823 are on CD-ROM, see www.eclipse.co/exeshul/susser/newsyn. htm, and at LDS. The Synagogue Scribes website at:

www.synangoguescribes.com/sources.html has ketubah book entries (marriage contracts) from the New 1819–32, and some circumcision records.

The Spanish/Portugese (Sephardic) synagogue was (and is) at Bevis Marks in Aldgate. Its early records are published: abstracts of marriage contracts (Ketubot) to 1901 in *Bevis Marks Records Pt 2*, ed. L.D. Barnett (OUP, 1940); the circumcision registers of Isaac and Abraham de Paiba 1715–75, records of circumcision 1679–1699, marriages 1679–89 and some female births 1679–99 in *Bevis Marks Records Pt 4*, compiled by M. Roderigues-Pereira (The Congregation, Jewish Historical Society of England, London, 1991); birth registers 1767–1881, circumcision registers 1767–85, 1803–20, 1815–27 and 1855–69, Jewish births in College of Arms register 1707–63 in *Bevis Marks Records Pt 5*, ed. M. Roderigues-Pereira and Chloe Loewe (The Congregation, London, 1993); the burial register of the Novo (new) Cemetery 1733–1918 in *Bevis Marks Records Pt 6*, ed. M. Roderigues-Pereira and Chloe Loewe (The Congregation, London, 1997).

Permission of the Congregation is needed to consult the original records of the Sephardic Congregation at LMA, and include the records that have been published, and others, as listed at AIM25 (Google 'Spanish and Portuguese Jews' Congregation'). For permission, apply in writing to the Honorary Archivist and Chief Executive of the Spanish and Portuguese Jews' Congregation, 2 Ashworth Road, London W9 1JY.

The Sephardic cemeteries were: the Velho (old) behind 253 Mile End Road (registers at the United Synagogue from 1657) and the Nuevo Beth Caim (the New) opened 1725; records 1733–1918 published in Bevis Marks Synagogue Records Pt VI, 1733–1918. The Ashkenazi cemeteries were: Alderney Road, opened 1696; records with United Synagogue, MIs are transcribed in Bernard Susser (ed.)'s *Alderney Road Jewish Cemetery* (United Synagogues, 1997), list at THLHLA. Brady Street cemetery, opened by the New Synagogue in 1761; records with United Synagogue.

For more about these and other East End synagogues see web. ukonline.co.uk/Laurence.rigal/Stepney/oldeastend/old_sites.htm.

Other Records

- 1841–71 censuses and GRO (see pp. 55–72).
- For a list of Jews in London and Metropolitan Middlesex 1693–4 see the Synagogue Scribes website at: www.synagoguescribes.com/.

The list is taken from the abstraction of the tax records made by the Centre for Metropolitan History at: www.british-history.ac.uk/source.aspx?pubid=26 (records at LMA, formerly CLRO).

- A database of some 18,000 Jews (countrywide) based on the 1851 census is at: www.jgsgb.org.uk.
- A database of London Jews 1790–1860 is at: www.jewishgen.org.
- Change of name and naturalisation records (see p. 148).
- Directories – many Jews had shops and were in trade (see p. 100).
- Wills (see p. 82).
- Land Tax records, eighteenth century (see p. 106).

To get an idea of life in eighteenth-century London Jewry (and for a good laugh), read Israel Zangwill's *The King of the Schnorrers*.

From the 1880s

The new immigrants settled in the western side of the borough, mainly in Whitechapel and Spitalfields, spreading east to St George-in-the-East, Stepney and then to Bow. Few were to be found in the riverside hamlets; 'No Jews allowed down Wapping'. Most were absorbed into the local 'rag trade' and the Jewish sweat shops became notorious. In 1888, there were 1,015 tailoring workshops in Whitechapel. Others became costers, getting themselves a stall and selling whatever they could. The top East End Jewish occupations in 1903 were:

Tailoring	25,698
Bakers	6,334
Hawkers, costers	5,372
Cabinet makers	4,815
Boot and shoe makers	4,770
Hairdressers	3,355
Dressmakers	3,068
Hat and cap makers	2,022
Textile dealers	1,825

Royal Commission on Alien Immigration cd 1741, cited in W.J. Fishman, *East End Jewish Radicals 1875–1914* (Duckworth, 1975).

There were said to be about 30,000 Jews in the East End in the 1880s; the Whitechapel/Spitalfields ghetto was a place of solid, sodden poverty, with families living 3,000 to the acre, as opposed to 800 in the Gentile parts. It was, however, a law-abiding community, with no drunkenness or licentiousness, families clinging tight together and a strong work ethic. Henry Walker wrote in 1896: 'The fact that the invading race gradually settle down and hold their own, superceding the lower class of Londoners, is full of significance'. Many families 'made it' and moved away; there was a gradual shift to north London, notably, Golders Green, Finchley, Hendon and Stamford Hill, and out east to Ilford, Leyton, Epping, Woodford and Chigwell.

Home for Aged Jews, Stepney Green, 1898. From T.R. Way, *Reliques of Old London Suburbs* (George Bell, 1989)

Records

There are two excellent LMA guides which you can download from their website: information leaflet 24, 'Jewish Genealogy', and no. 20, 'Records of the Anglo Jewish Community at LMA'.

Synagogue records are problematical as many have been lost and most are difficult to access. Use the national records first (GRO and census). THLHLA has records of the Great Spitalfields Synagogue 1909–47 and of the Princes (later Princelet Street) Synagogue in Spitalfields 1884–1988. The latter collection includes a variety of marriage records spanning 1877–1944. For tracing Jewish marriage records you will find the JGSGB's website most useful at: www.jgsbg.org.uk/engmarr.shtml.

The most useful sources are:

- Census and GRO (see pp. 55–72).
- Marriage authorisation indexes (like licences) from the United Synagogue website (www.theus.org.uk) 1845–1908 (includes the East London Synagogue (Stepney), the New and the Great (Bishopsgate and Aldgate), and Sandys Row). The certificates have to be purchased.
- Marriage notice books for Stepney from 1926 and Bethnal Green 1837–78 and 1920–65 are at THLHLA. They give names and addresses, age, length of residence in UK and intended place of marriage.
- Records of the Poor Jews' Temporary Shelter in Leman Street (Whitechapel) – reception centre for immigrants from 1885 to 1914. No records pre-1896; database (via http://chrysalis.its.uct.ac.za) of records 1896–1914 maintained by the University of Leicester. Records at LMA (permission needed). Many thousands of Jewish immigrants came through the shelter; entries give names and ages, place of birth, destination and port of departure.
- Records of the Jews' Free School in Bell Lane, Spitalfields. Records at LMA 1868–1900. The great Jews' Free School, founded in 1821, which grew out of the religion school of the Great Synagogue, founded in 1732, grew to be one of the largest schools in Europe. The admission and discharge registers (and much else besides – headmaster's books listing staff, school magazines etc.) for the period 1868–1939 are at the LMA (LMA 4046/C/01) and for the period 1868–1900 have been digitised and can be read free at www.movinghere.org.uk. The school was bombed in the Second

World War and moved to Camden in 1858 and is now in Kenton. See G. Black, *The History of the Jews' Free School, London since 1732* (Tymsder Publishing, 1998).

- School records – there were a number of Jewish schools in the area. See Cliff Webb's *An Index of London Schools and their Records*, 3rd edn (SOG, 2007). Many Jewish children attended local board or LCC schools (see pp. 91–9).
- Bevis Marks (Sephardic Synagogue) published records (see above).
- Marriages at Sandys Row Synagogue in Wentworth Street 1894–1928 at: www.jgsgb.org.uk/SandysRowSynagogueMarriages.htm.
- Records of Princelet Street Synagogue, off Brick Lane, 1884–1988. Marriages and burial society records at THLHLA. The synagogue was originally set up by Jacob Davidson, a Polish immigrant and boot maker in 1869. An astonishing survival, it is now a museum and quite untouched, one of the very best places to get a feel for Victorian Jewry. See EoLFHS CD-ROM's 'Marriages at Princelet Street 1897–1907'. THLHLA also has some subscription books for the Great Spitalfields Synagogue 1909–47 and membership lists for the Philpot Street Sephardic Synagogue 1938–9.
- *Jewish Chronicle.* Search for obituaries and marriage notices, for example:

> Abrahams 10 Jan 1868. On 8th January at 2 Magdalen Row, Great Prescott St, by the Rev Artom, assisted by Rev D Piza, Mr M Abrahams of 3, Sydney Square, Commercial Rd, to Sylvia, second daughter of ML Green.

Read the paper and consult its indexes at BL. Some marriage entries to 1869 are at: www.jeffreymaynard.com.
- United Synagogue Burial Society register 1872–1912 (they will search for a fee).
- Directories at THLHLA (1910–48) have many advertisements for Jewish shops etc.
- Naturalisation and denization records (see p. 147).
- Poor Law union records (see p. 128). There was a separate charitable Board of Guardians for Jews (records held by Southampton University), but the problem of poor relief was enormous and shared by the local Poor Law unions. The Mile End Scattered Homes were used for Jewish children; records at LMA 1900–28.

- Records of various Jewish Organisations at LMA. See the section of their catalogue 'Jewish Organisations'. Records include admission books for The Home for Aged Jews (now Nightingales) 1914–33. It was at 37–9 Stepney Green 1894–1907. It combined the Hand in Hand Asylum for Decayed Tradesmen (1843 Dukes Place, 1950 Jewry Street, 1854–78 Wellclose Square), the Widows' Home Asylum (1843 Mitre Street then Duke's Place, from 1857–67 Prescott Street, 1880 moved to Hackney) and the Jewish Workhouse, founded 1871 at 123 Wentworth Street.

The following reference material is useful:

The LMA information leaflets (nos 24 and 20, cited above) are really clear and ideal for beginners

Rosemary Wenzerul, *Tracing your Jewish Ancestors* (Pen & Sword, 2008)

Rosemary Wenzerul, *Jewish Ancestors* (JGSGB, 2006)

W.J. Fishman, *East End Jewish Radicals 1875–1914* (Duckworth, 1975) – this is the best book for informing yourself, in general terms, about Jewish immigration into the East End

Cecil Roth, *A History of the Jews in England* (OUP, 1941) – a good overview

For reminiscence books and novels, see p. 229 below.

Websites are numerous and changing:

www.jewishgen.org – worldwide database

www.jgsgb.org.uk/ – website of the Jewish Genealogical Society of Great Britain

www.synagoguescribes.com/ – especially good for London Jewry

The Knowles Collection from FamilySearch includes thousands of London Jews in a database building on the work of the late Isobel Mordy

www.movinghere.org – TNA site for immigrants

There are many more – see Rosemary Wenzerul's books.

Websites giving information about East End Jewry are: http://web.ukonline.co.uk/lawrence.rigal/stepney/oldeastend/old_sites .htm – lists synagogues and cemeteries

http://olamgadol.pwp.blueyonder.co.uk – pictures, histories etc.

It is useful to visit the Princelet Street Synagogue in Spitalfields, now the Museum of Immigration, and the Museum of Jewish Life in Finchley.

Dutch

The term 'Doche' or Dutch was often used to describe Germans as well as people from the Low Countries, Flanders and Holland. Walloons came from Belgium. See also Huguenots (p. 148).

Many Dutch Jews came into the East End from the seventeenth century, but immigrants from the Low Countries had been a strong presence there since the Middle Ages (see pp. 21–2), many engaged in the brewing trade, weaving and printing. Religious refugees came from the sixteenth century, followed by numbers of immigrants after the Glorious Revolution of 1689 when a Dutch King, William III, took the English throne.

They had their own church in Austin Friars in the City. Numbers of the sixteenth-century refugees settled in the precinct of St Katherine's, which was free from City restrictions and a place much favoured by arrivals from abroad, being close to where immigrant ships docked. The 1572 Return of Aliens listed for St Katharine's: 828 Dutch, 169 French, 8 Danes, 5 Poles, 2 Spaniards, 1 Italian and 12 Scots; there were 30 Dutch brewhouses. Strype, writing in 1720, noted 'a churchyard for poor Flemings who came over under Elizabeth' (*A Survey of the Cities of London and Westminster* (London, 1720)).

Records

East End Dutch and Walloons are to found among the records of the Dutch Church at Austin Friars. See W.J.C. Moens's *The marriage and baptismal registers, 1571–1874 and monumental inscriptions of the Dutch Reformed Church, Austin Friars, London* (1884; amended version at TNA) and J.H. Hessels (ed.)'s *The registers of the attestations or certificates of membership, confessions of guilt, certificates, betrothals, publications of banns etc. preserved in the Dutch Reformed Church, Austin Friars, London 1568–1872* (The Consistory, 1892). Records of the Church of St Katharine's by the Tower are described in Appendix 2.

D. Ormond's *The Dutch in London* (HMSO, 1973) is a useful source of information.

Germans

If you are researching a German name in the East End, the chances are that the family are of Jewish stock. However, before the mass immigration of the 1880s there were a number of Germans in Whitechapel and Wapping-Stepney (St George-in-the-East). The Anglo German Family History Society has many useful publications, lists of names being researched and offers expertise.

German merchants and sailors had been coming to London since the Middle Ages; their church was at the Savoy. From the eighteenth century, the main single concentration was in the 'Little Germany' part of Whitechapel, around Commercial Road and in St George-in-the East. Most worked in the sugar refineries and sugar bakeries.

Sugar had been refined in the East End since the sixteenth century and in the eighteenth the refiners, desperate for labour, started recruiting in Germany. Ranks of poor Germans, many from Hanover, came to live in increasingly overcrowded conditions and to make good money from the gruelling work in the great 'boiling houses'. In 1829, the new curate at St George, William Quekett, arriving to start his new job (in what he had mistakenly thought was St George's Hanover Square) was horrified at the slum he had come to. In 1875, it was claimed that you could count about fifteen refineries from the tower of the church. At its peak, the German Lutheran population of Whitechapel was about 16,000.

The sugar bakers' church was St George's German Lutheran Church in Alie Street, founded in 1762 by Dietrich Beckmann, a rich local refiner. It is still there.

St Paul's, the German Evangelical Reformed Church (Calvinist) established in 1697 by Protestant refugees, mainly from the Palatinate, was consecrated in the Savoy in 1771, but moved to the East End, opening in 1819 in Hooper Square, Leman Street, Whitechapel. It was replaced in 1886–7 by a church built in Goulston Street, Whitechapel. The church had a new influx of parishioners in the 1930s, as refugees fled Hitler's Germany. It was bombed in 1941.

A church for German Catholic immigrants was established in Adler Street, Commercial Road.

Records

- St Paul's German Evangelical Reformed Church. Registers are at THLHLA. Alphabetical abstracts produced by the Anglo-German Family History Society can be inspected at LMA; also available on CD-ROM are: baptisms 1824–1940; marriages 1858–1938; burials 1832–1940.

- St George's German Lutheran Church, Alie Street. AGFHS CD-ROMs of: baptisms 1763–1895; burials 1818–53; marriages 1825–96.
- St Boniface's German Church (Catholic), Adler Street, Commercial Road. Baptisms 1809–present; marriages 1864–present; copies (baptisms 1809–1950, marriages 1864–1968) at AGFHS.
- Registers of relief to interned aliens 1914–20, Bethnal Green Union at LMA.
- Directories (see p. 100) for sugar refineries.

The following sources are useful:

J. Farrell, 'The German Community in 19th Century East London', *East London Record*, 13 (1990)

H. Deicke, 'A Short History of the German Evangelical Reformed Church' (1907; typescript at LMA)

'German Lutheran St George's Church', *Cockney Ancestor*, 34 (Spring 1987)

www.agfhs.org.uk – website of the Anglo German Family History Society

LMA information leaflet 23 'The German Community in London'

www.stgite.org.ul/germanchurches.html – the St George-in-the-East website, which has a full description (with pictures) of the German churches and information about the history of the community

'Sugar Refiners and Sugar Bakers' at: www.home.clara.net/mawer/intro.html – information on the sugar and baking communities

Tom Almeroth-Williams, 'A Sticky Business', *Ancestors* 55 (May 2007).

Emigrants

Since the slum days began, East Enders who had the wherewithal have been moving out, especially since the Second World War. Many went east to the leafier suburbs and new towns of Essex. The Jewish community tended to favour north London. To trace their movements use anything that has countrywide indexes, such as census, PPR and PCC wills, and GRO indexes.

Since the sixteenth century many have taken ship and left for the New World. In the eighteenth and nineteenth centuries many East Enders were deported to Australia. For pauper children sent abroad in the nineteenth and twentieth centuries (mainly to Canada), see p. 136.

Emigrants to North America and the West Indies

In Elizabethan times great expeditions to the New World set off from Blackwall and Limehouse and Stepney lads were aboard these ships. Records show that a high proportion of the early American settlers were from the East End.* When the *Mayflower* set sail from Blackwall in 1620, it took on board twenty-five people, many from what historian Charles Banks described as the 'pilgrim heart of London' (*The English Ancestry and Homes of the Pilgrim Fathers* (Grafton Press, 1929)), from Aldgate, Whitechapel and Shoreditch. The ship sailed down to Southampton and then to Plymouth, where it picked up the rest of the Pilgrim Fathers, Puritan refugees, mainly from the north of England, who had fled to Holland in 1608. Tired of the struggle with poverty in Leyden and the unhealthy influence of the Dutch youth on their children, they too were off to make a new life. They arrived at Cape Cod on 11 November and the rest is history.

The following year the *Fortune* sailed to the embryonic colony in New England, taking more pilgrims. On board this vessel were at least two Stepney men. One was Thomas Prence/Prince, a carriage-maker's son, who was to become Governor of Massachusetts. His family had come to London from Gloucestershire and the boy grew up in Ratcliff. The other was William Bassett, a gunsmith from Bethnal Green.

In 1720, in Shakespeare Walk in Shadwell (named after a local rope-making family) Jane Randolph was born. Her father, Isham Randolph, a seamen and a colonial agent in Virginia, took his family and settled in Virginia where he named his estate 'Shadwell'. Jane married a man called Jefferson and her son, Thomas, became President of the United States.

From the first days of exploration and colonisation in North America, thousands of people, desperate or adventurous, left British shores to chance their luck as indentured servants. Their passage would be paid for by their master (often a West Indian plantation owner) and, in return, they would agree to work for a term of years. At the end of their time they might be given a grant of land and a cash payment. In the

* *American Wills and Administrations in the Prerogative Court of Canterbury, 1610–1857* (PCC). The London and Middlesex section in the index shows a high incidence of East End immigrants: references to Bethnal Green 6, Ratcliff 8, Limehouse 14, Wapping 27, Whitechapel 21, Shoreditch 5, St Katharine's 6, Shadwell 28, Stepney 100, St Botolph's Aldgate 18, St Botolph's Bishopsgate 12. For Holborn there are 21, for Clerkenwell 5 and Islington 10 (access at Ancestry).

space of only 150 years Middlesex provided about 15,000 labourers for the American colonies. Before the American colonies declared themselves independent in 1776, British convicts might be sent there to penal colonies.

Sources

There is a wide and diverse range of records, mainly held at TNA and described in the three research guides listed below, but the first port of call in tracking down an emigrant should be the magnificent compilations made by P.W. Coldham, drawn from these records. Copies are at SOG. They include details of many thousands of sailors, religious refugees, indentured servants and convicts:

- *The Complete Book of Emigrants, 1607–1660; The Complete Book of Emigrants, 1661–1699; The Complete Book of Emigrants, 1700–1750; The Complete Book of Emigrants, 1751–1776; The Complete Book of Emigrants in Bondage, 1614–1775; Supplement to The Complete Book of Emigrants in Bondage, 1614–1775.*
- *American Migrations 1765–1799.* The lives, times and families of colonial Americans who remained loyal to the British Crown before, during and after the Revolutionary War, as related in their own words and through their correspondence (access at Ancestry). Potted biographies of people claiming compensation from the British goverrment for loss of land and property as a result of action taken against Loyalists before, during and after the Revolutionary War. (TNA AO 12 and 13.)
- *Emigrants from England to the American Colonies, 1773–1776.*
- *Emigrants in Chains. A Social History of Forced Emigration to the Americas of Felons, Destitute Children, Political and Religious Non-Conformists, Vagabonds, Beggars and Other Undesirables, 1607–1776.*
- *English Adventurers and Emigrants, 1609–1660. Abstracts of Examinations in the High Court of Admiralty with Reference to Colonial America* (originals at TNA HCA).
- *English Estates of American Colonists. American Wills and Administrations in the Prerogative Court of Canterbury, 1610–1699* (PCC).
- *English Estates of American Colonists. American Wills and Administrations in the Prerogative Court of Canterbury, 1700–1799* (PCC).
- *English Estates of American Settlers. American Wills and Administrations in the Prerogative Court of Canterbury, 1800–1858* (PCC).
- *American Wills Proved in London, 1611–1775* (PCC; access at Ancestry).

The Coldham PCC volumes summarise wills that can be read in full at: www.nationalarchives.gov.uk/documentsonline>wills. The grants of administration may not, but the original records of these add nothing to the Coldham entries.

Also refer to TNA research guides *Emigrants; Transportation to America and the West Indies 1615–1777* and *Amerian and West India Colonies*. The oldest and most venerable of genealogical societies, the New England Historic Genealogical Society, has a useful website at: www.newenglandancestors.org.

Emigrants to Australia

Convicts were deported to Australian penal colonies from 1787 to 1868, and there has been a steady stream of free emigrants over the years, peaking in the decades following the Second World War.

Among the 'First Fleeters' to Australia, taken in the first eleven convict ships in the spring of 1787, were a number of East Enders. They included: silk winder and prostitute Mary Harrison of Catherine Wheel Alley (off Petticoat Lane), who, with her mate, threw acid over a woman who they thought was encroaching on their patch, Ann Fowles, a Wapping hawker who stole clothes from her fellow lodger in Old Gravel Lane, and Jane Langley, the swarthy whore (and apprentice embroiderer) from East Smithfield, who stole money from a client in the Brown Bear. (See Mollie Gillen, *The Founders of Australia: a biographical dictionary of the First Fleet* (Library of Australian History, 1989).) Some served their term and settled; some returned home; many died in transit.

Records of Convicts

- The transportation registers 1791–1868 (TNA HO 11; access via Ancestry) list all deportees with place of conviction (no exact addresses), crime and length of sentence.
- The criminal registers (TNA HO 26 for London and Middlesex; access via Ancestry) have much more detail than the transportation registers (see sample below).
- The 1828 NSW census, available in M.R. Sainty and K.A. Johnson (eds)'s *Census of New South Wales, 1828* (Library of Australian History, 1980). It can also be accessed at: www.ancestry.com.au.

- Convicts musters, pardons and lists 1757–1859: TNA HO 10 (access at: www.ancestry.com.au).
- Trials of deportees may be found among the Old Bailey Proceedings at: www.oldbaileyonline.org (also at LMA).

The following record of an Old Bailey trial was taken from Oldbaileyonline:

11 September 1799 John James (44) and William Lycett (55), were tried for stealing cash from a Stepney resident Mary Shackle, just near Aldgate Bars.

Mary was walking along the Whitechapel Road, returning to her house near Stepney village, from a shopping expedition to buy raisin wine from her grocer's. William Lycett engaged her in conversation on 'country matters'; they went into the White Horse at Mile End Turnpike, and his accomplice conned her into coughing up £20 for a diamond pin, for which they 'found' a receipt of 150 guineas. He suggested that it might be a good present for her daughter in law who was expecting her twelfth child.

Lycett and James were both condemned to seven years transportation. Lycett, it appears from earlier proceedings was a serious criminal; he had once run the Hole in the Wall in Chancery Lane and had already been deported (presumably to America) thirteen years previously. He was said to have married a wealthy woman.

The transportation register (TNA HO/11/1) shows that Lycett sailed for New South Wales on the *Royal Admiral*, departing in March 1800. No entry can be found in the name search for his fellow thief, John James.

The criminal registers were searched for the two men. John James has an entry which describes him; fair complexion, brown hair, grey eyes. It says he was 40 years of age, a Covent Garden buckle maker, that his fellow thief was William Lycett. He 'stole the sum of £20 and upwards from Mary Shackle by dropping her diamond cross'. It also says that he died in Newgate – hence no entry in the Transportation Register!

The name search for Lycett in the Criminal Registers (HO 26) at Ancestry was unproductive; a page seems to be missing from the register or the film. Lycett made it to Australia, as is evident from his appearance in the convict musters (HO 10). In 1825, aged 80, he was in an asylum there.

The following sources are useful:

TNA research guide *Transportation to Australia 1787–1868* – this has a good bibliography of published material

Mollie Gillen, *The Founders of Australia: a biographical dictionary of the First Fleet* (Library of Australian History, 1989)

David T. Hawkings, *Bound for Australia* (Chichester, 1987).

Voluntary Emigrants

The following notes will assist in tracing voluntary emigrants:

- For people leaving the country from 1890 see the outward bound passenger lists (TNA BT 27; access at Findmypast.co.uk). These records (indexed) give name, age, port of departure, destination and residence (destinations outside Europe only).
- www.coraweb.com.au provides a way into the most useful Australian websites.
- Assisted passage. Over many years people wishing to emigrate to Australia were offered cheap fares or 'assisted passage'. A one-eyed fish-basket maker interviewed by Walter Austin in 1884 (*One Dinner a Week*) reckoned that state-assisted emigration would never solve the problem of East End poverty:

> It's like this way. The man there goes away, the more there comes to fill the gaps. See here now, Sir. Last month about five hundred was shipped off ... Well, thinks I, a good riddance. There'll be fewer mouths to fill, and fewer hands to work here now. But the last week there come about a thousand from abroad, an' they all landed at the docks, an' here they seem to stick, and mostly Polish Jews they are.

Reference to individuals who went to Australia under the terms of the Poor Law Act of 1834 may be found among the Ministry of Health Poor Law Union Papers at TNA (ref. MH 12). These are arranged alphabetically under county and union but are difficult to use.

A useful and readily accessible source are the *Assisted Immigrant Passenger Lists 1828–1896* held by the State Archive of New South Wales (access at Ancestry), which give a good amount of detail about each family or individual. The following example is taken from these lists, accessed via Ancestry:

> Thomas Short, a carman ('schoolmaster on board'), aged 34, from Stepney, an Independent (Congregationalist) arrived in Australia in 1865 aboard the *Himalaya*. The entry says he can read and write. His parents are: father William, living in Walthamstow, mother, Elizabeth, dead. Two brothers: Benjamin, an agent in Sydney, and William at the Commercial Banking Company.
>
> His wife, Elizabeth, 34, of Dover, Kent. Parents William (dead), mother Elizabeth living in Mile End. She has no siblings, is an Independent and can read and write.
>
> Son, William is 12 and can read and write.

A click or two reveals (from the 1861 and 1851 censuses) that Thomas Short's father was a sugar baker from St George-in-the-East.

Criminals

There were a good many criminals around in the East End, from William Kidd and other pirates who were strung up at Execution Dock in Wapping to Jack the Ripper and the Kray twins.

Minor crimes and misdemeanours, along with a good deal of business concerning pauper settlement, the issue of pub licences and other matters were dealt with by magistrates at Hicks Hall, the Middlesex Sessions House in Clerkenwell (1549–1889), while more serious cases went to the Old Bailey. In 1889, the County of London Sessions were established.

The records of trials and proceedings (pre-1834) are mainly held at LMA in various series, as described in LMA's information leaflets 30 and 40 ('A Brief Guide to Middlesex Sessions Records' and 'Sessions Records in the City of London and Southwark').

The Central Criminal Court was set up in 1834 and the court records, along with prison records, are at TNA, and are described in the research

Letter from Captain Kidd to the Admiralty from Newgate Prison. He refers to this two 'Negro children', presumably slaves. TNA ADM 1/2004

guides *Tracing 19th and 20th Century Criminals* and *Old Bailey and Central Criminal Court: Criminal Trials*. TNA records include:

- Criminal registers London and Middlesex 1791–1849 (HO 26; access at Ancestry).
- Calendar of Old Bailey prisoners 1855–1949 (CRIM 9/1-95).
- Lists of prisoners in Newgate 1782–1853 (HO 77/1-61).
- Transportation registers 1787–1867 (HO 11; access free at: www. slq.gld.gov.au/info/th/convicts, also at Ancestry). For information about deportees to the colonies, see above.

A selection of Middlesex Session records (1689–1709) can be inspected at British History Online. Old Bailey Proceedings 1674–1913 (trials written up for public consumption) have been made available online at: www.oldbaileyonline.org, with links to associated sources. This is a valuable and easily accessible source but is not completely comprehensive.

See also:

- Published Middlesex sessions records for 1549–1688 in J.C. Jeaffreson (ed.)'s *Middlesex County Records* (1886–92); for 1612–1709 see W. le Hardy's *Calendar to the Sessions Records*. Sessions records 1612–89 (selective) are at British History Online.
- LMA: indexed typescript calendars of Sessions Rolls and Books for 1607–12 and 1638–1751. A. Knapp and W. Baldwin's *Newgate Calendar* (4 vols, 1824–8) describes 'notorious' cases 1700–1825.
- Reports of trials in local and national newspapers (at THLHLA and/or the BL Newspaper Library).

The following publications are useful:
R. Paley and S. Fowler, *Family Skeletons; exploring the lives of our disreputable ancestors* (TNA, 2005)
S. Wade, *Tracing your Criminal Ancestors* (Pen & Sword, 2009)
David Hawkings, *Criminal Ancestors* (Sutton, 1992 and 1996).

Jack the Ripper books and websites are legion, but the following books are recommended:
Donald Rumbelow, *The Complete Jack the Ripper* (Penguin, 1988)
Paul Begg, Martin Fido and Keith Skinner, *The Jack the Ripper A to Z* (Trafalgar Square Publishing, 1991, rev. edn 1996)
Philip Sugden, *The Complete History of Jack the Ripper* (Carroll & Graf, 1994).

Visits to the Captain Kidd, a pub near Execution Dock in Wapping High Street, and the Blind Beggar, in the Mile End Road, where the Krays shot George Cornell in 1966, are recommended. Taking a Jack the Ripper or Kray Twins Walk, with Louis London Walks, is enlightening.

Notables

For well-known people connected with the borough, see *The Tower Hamlets Connection* (London Borough of Tower Hamlets, 1996). From 1731 to 1868, the *Gentleman's Magazine* contained brief biographical notes on prominent men and women (Guildhall, BL, SOG).

For famous people, see the *Dictionary of National Biography* and *Who was Who?*

Chapter 6

OCCUPATIONAL GROUPS

For a bibliography of some books relating to East End occupations, see Appendix 7. See also, sections on apprentices (p. 108) and livery companies (p. 111).

Dockers

Nineteenth-century dockers were overwhelmingly casual labourers and you are unlikely to find anything much about these individuals in specifically occupational sources; they are best sought in census returns.

For about 150 years, from the early nineteenth century, the docks were by far the biggest East End employers and you may well find docking ancestors in the census returns, if you don't know about them already.

The docks were first built during the Napoleonic Wars and created, initially, a permanent, sober, responsible workforce. In 1802, West India Dock wages were fixed at 5½d an hour or 3s 6d a day, high wages occasioned by wartime scarcity of labour. Then the silk-weaving industry collapsed (in the 1830s), leaving some 30,000 unemployed weavers. Mayhew, writing mid-century, said that the docks

> constitute ... a house colony to Spitalfields ... we find men of every calling labouring at the docks. There are decayed and bankrupt master builders, master butchers, publicans, grocers, old soldiers, old sailors, Polish refugees, broken down gentlemen, discharged lawyers' clerks, suspended government clerks, almsmen, pensioners, servants, thieves – indeed everyone who wants a loaf and is willing to work for it.

Sidney Short in the shop he ran with his sister Frances in Roman Road, Bow, c. 1925. 'Oil and colour' shops were a common feature in the East End. Author's Collection

By the mid-1860s the great days of Poplar ship building were over, as was the boom in the London building trade and the heyday of the sugar-baking industry. In 1866–7, 10,000 out of 40, 000 in St George-in-the-East were out of work. From this point on, the East End's poverty problem is one of a labour surplus and casual dock work – queuing up at the dock gates for 5 pence a day was virtually the only work open to the unskilled.

Records

The men who loaded and unloaded ships used to be known as 'fellowship porters'. The records of the Society of Fellowship Porters (1604–1871; the society was not disbanded until 1894) include membership lists 1673–1869..

For the period 1803–1909, that is to say from the opening of the first enclosed docks in the East End until the Port of London Authority took over the running of the docks, the vast majority of dock workers were casual labourers. They were employed on a daily or half-daily basis by the various dock companies, such as the West India Dock Co., Millwall Dock Co. etc., and you are most unlikely to find any record of their employment. If, however, your ancestor was a regular employee, a skilled worker, like a cooper (barrel maker), sampler, clerk, foreman or dock master, or was a dock policeman, then there probably will be some mention of him in the records of the company concerned. These are kept in the archive at the Museum in Docklands.

For the post-1909 period, the Museum in Docklands has record cards for permanently employed manual staff who would have left the service by the 1960s. This includes permanent labourers, electricians, clerical staff, dredger and salvage crews, policemen and workers in the canteens.

These records can be most informative, supplying places and docks worked in, sick records, characters, physical descriptions, referees, name of father, address, date of birth, a break down of previous employment, details of previous employers, promotions, with comments, such as 'very mediocre', 'too late in life to change now'.

The staff at the Museum will do a search for you and then you can go and look at the original record if you make an appointment. For contact details, see Appendix 8.

A sample from a dock-company staff register held at the Museum:

> The staff register for the East and West India Dock Company (1802–1893) lists salaried staff e.g. Thomas Blackwell 1st class cooper August 1832–1860 35s a week. Foreman cooper at 56 in 1865 earning £105; H C Forbes, taken on as a clerk in 1864 aged 15 years, stayed still 1869; Thomas Collett a 'preferable labourer' from March 1841. Promoted to wharfinger 1853 at £90. d. 11 Feb. 1857, William Stannadr, constable from 1852–1854 (28s per week). Dismissed for intoxication 10 Nov 1854.

List of donations to widows may include labourers: C. Sullivan died in 1854 when a bag of sugar fell on him; his widow got £20. G. Marquand, a watchman for one year, died when the Eastern Dock sluice gate fell on him.

The records of the various unions are listed (with places of deposit) in John Bennett and Alistair Tough's *Trade Union and Related Records*, ed. Richard Storey (University of Warwick, 1991). And see www.union ancestors.co.uk.

The following publications are useful:

Survey of London, vols 43 and 44 (Poplar, Blackwall and the Isle of Dogs), ed. Stephen Porter (Royal Commission on Historical Monuments of England, Athlone Press, 1994); available at: www.british-history.ac.uk/surveyoflondon – provides a detailed and scholarly description of the docks

H. Mayhew, *London Labour and the London Poor* (1851)

A.E. Jeffery, *The History of Scruttons: shipbrokers and ship owners 1802–1926; stevedores, master porters and cargo superintendants 1890–1967* (privately published, 1971) – includes list of 'dock staff'

A. Bazzone, 'Another Police Force of East London', *Cockney Ancestor*, 43 (1989) – brief notes on records of Dock Company Police Forces.

Seamen

> *'He who sails upon the sea*
> *Is a parishioner of Stepney'*

Stepney's riverside hamlets became known as 'sailortown' in the eighteenth century and if your ancestors came from this part, then the chances of their being seafarers are quite high, right up until the opening years of the twentieth century. They are called 'mariners' in the earlier records.

From the sixteenth century ships were fitted out and got ready for voyages in Blackwall, Wapping and Limehouse; here they were victualled (loaded up with food and drink for the sailors) and manned. 'Jack tars' were press-ganged or recruited in the alehouses along the river bank, while sea captains bought fine houses for themselves in Limehouse and Wapping-Stepney; Bligh of the *Bounty* and Captain Cook both lived in Wapping for periods of time. The Highway was famous for its sailors' lodging houses and slop shops in the eighteenth and nineteenth centuries.

Such was the overwhelming seafaring presence in Stepney parish that St Dunstan's Church became known as 'the Church of the High Seas' and the notion arose that all baptisms at sea were registered in Stepney church registers. This practice seems to have started as a deliberate piece of antiquarianism by a Victorian rector, Edwyn Hoskyns, and there are a smattering of baptisms at sea in St Dunstan's registers from 1888.

Trinity House, originally established in Deptford, in 1514, perhaps having its origins in a medieval Trinity Guild, was a body of great influence which extended its activities to all matters of navigation in coastal waters and provided shelter and pensions for seamen and their families. In the early years of the century, certainly by 1610, Trinity House acquired a house in Stepney, probably in Whitehorse Street, where they held meetings.

The East India Company, founded in 1600, traded in ivory, pearls, diamonds, calicoes and spices from the East Indies and India, even venturing as far as Japan. Sailors pressed for government service were

Meridian House, built 1801–2 for the chaplain to the East India Company almshouses. A rare survival from the past, it is situated in Poplar High Street. Yvonne Hughes

the 'left overs', the men not good enough for the company's ships. It was the largest commercial operation in London; its great ships – 'mobile maritime fortresses' – dominated the river. The company's presence in Stepney was overwhelming, where its shipyards and warehouses were. It gave direct or indirect and lucrative employment to numbers of men and its leading officers, merchants and ship builders, particularly the latter, had houses built for themselves in Limehouse, Blackwall and Poplar. The company built houses for seamen in Blackwall in 1614 and it provided generously for the relief of local women whose husbands had been wounded or killed in their employ.

Records of the East India Company

These records are held by the BL; there are no overall indexes. East India Company directories and registers include lists of masters and mates. About 9,700 ships' logs survive (1605–1856), and include crew lists. The records of the 'Poplar Fund' have useful information about the inmates of the company's almshouses in Poplar and sailors and widows in receipt of relief. See p. 209 for records of the East India Company chapel.

The following books and websites are useful:

I.A. Baxter, *India Office Library and Records; a brief guide to biographical sources* (British Library, 1990)

I.A. Baxter, 'Records of the Poplar Pension Fund', *East London Record*, 8 (1985) – for nineteenth-century company pensioners in the Poplar almshouses

A. Farrington, *A Biographical Index of East India Company Maritime Service Officers 1600–1834* (British Library, 1999)

Derek Morris, 'Mile End Old Town Residents and the East India Company', *East London Record*, 9 (1986) – details East India Company grandees living in Mile End

www.barnettmaritime.co.uk/mainheic.htm – summarises the history of the company and itemises categories of records at BL

www.fibis.org – the Families of British India Society website.

It is worthwhile going to look at Meridian House in Poplar High Street, built 1801–2 for the chaplain to the (adjoining) East India Company almshouses, and St Matthias's Church in Woodstock Terrace (formerly the East India Company Chapel). (See photographs on pp. 177 and 179.)

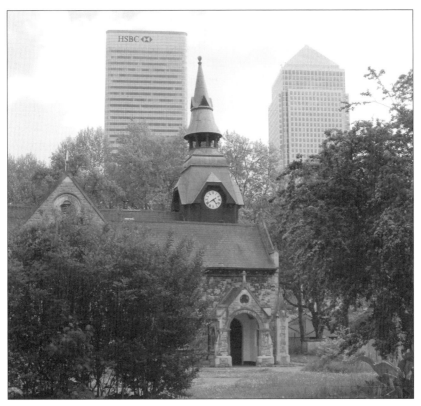

St Matthias's Church, Poplar, formerly the East India Company Chapel. Yvonne Hughes

Sailors' Records (General)

Most records are held at TNA.

Until the mid-nineteenth century there was no such thing as 'joining the Navy', except for officers. The Royal Navy and private companies or individuals recruited from the same pool of labour, and for the port of London this was mainly in the East End.

Thus, one Obadiah Mitchell might have been recruited in the Black Boy and Trumpet in Wapping by the captain of a naval vessel who was going to fight with Nelson at Trafalgar. Once the campaign was over he would have been paid off and might have joined the crew of an East Indiaman. When not serving aboard a naval or merchant vessel, sailors might ply for hire as watermen (for records of watermen, see below, p. 183).

Records of sailors before 1853 are patchy and difficult to find; officers are much easier to trace than men and you can do this at TNA, using the published *Navy Lists*.

A good starting point for East End sailors in general are the PCC wills, which can be accessed online through TNA's website or viewed at Kew. Sailors employed by the state were required to make wills to ensure that their back pay or bounty was paid to their next of kin. East End sailors' wills are to be found in great profusion from the seventeenth to nineteenth centuries at TNA and they are available online. There are two main TNA collections: wills and administration grants registered in the church probate court, the Prerogative Court of Canterbury (TNA code PCC, to 1858) and the wills kept in the registry at the Admiralty (TNA code ADM 48 1786–1882; registers of seamens' wills ADM 142 1862–1909). Grants of administration (made to many sailors' widows) are not available online, but can be viewed at Kew. Sailors' wills for the parish of St Botolph's Aldgate also exist in great profusion among the records of the Archdeaconry Court of London (originals at LMA/Guildhall, access at Origins) and for the rest of the area in the will archive of the London Commissary Court (see p. 83).

For Elizabethan and Jacobean 'sea dogs' there are numerous references to individuals among the accounts of exploration published by the Hakluyt Society, like William Ivie of Stepney who called his shipmate a 'copper nosed rascal'. W.H. Frere's *Memorials of Stepney Parish; Vestry Minutes 1579–1662* (Billing, 1890–1) contains potted biographies of the leading local mariners. East End sailors pepper the pages of the voluminous records of the High Court of Admiralty at TNA (code HCA). These records are very difficult to read and interpret and there are no general indexes; some have been abstracted and published in P.W. Coldham's *English Adventurers and Emigrants, 1609–1660, Abstracts of Examinations in the High Court of Admiralty with Reference to Colonial America*. See also, G.G. Harris (ed.)'s *Trinity House Transactions 1609–1635* (London Record Society, 1983).

For the period 1666–*c*. 1730 it is well worth looking to see if a sailor left a probate inventory of his belongings – just an old sea chest perhaps. These probate inventories (TNA codes PROB 4 and 5), associated with PCC wills and grants of administration (in cases on intestacy), can be located by doing a name search of TNA's catalogue online. To read the document you will have to go to Kew.

Sailors and their widows in receipt of pensions and old sailors housed in the Royal Hospital at Greenwich may be located among the

The sign board of the Widow's Son, or Bun House, in Devons Road, Bow. The story attached to this pub originated in 1824, when sailors still lived in the area. A woman laid the table with hot cross buns, awaiting the return of her son on Good Friday, but he never came as his ship had gone down. She kept the table laid with hot cross buns until she died. A pub was built on the site in 1848 and successive landlords kept the tradition alive. On Good Friday each year a naval man adds another bun to the collection that hangs behind the bar.

Greenwich records at TNA. For lists of available records (from 1704), see TNA in-depth guides *Military Records*, nos 60 and 61, which can be downloaded from TNA's website.

Many ordinary East End seafarers were also licensed watermen and it may well be possible to track them down in the easily accessible records of the Watermens' and Lightermens' Company (see p. 184).

Service records of both Royal Navy men and merchant seamen are in TNA and from the mid-nineteenth century are full and informative, often giving personal details of the men, including physical descriptions. For a full and proper search it is best to go to TNA at Kew. Beforehand it might be prudent to read some of the in-depth research guides on TNA's website, listed under 'Royal Navy', such as *Records of Ratings Military Records Information 31.*

If your ancestor served in the Royal Navy between 1853 and 1923 you could make a start online. You can search and download 600,000 service records for most of the ratings who joined the Royal Navy between 1853 and 1923 in the Registers of Seamen's Services (ADM 188) and the Continuous Service Engagement Books (ADM 139), for £3.50 an item. These records can tell you when and where your sailor was born, what he looked like, his occupation and the ships he served on. Details of service are recorded up to 1928. The indexes are free. The entry for Henry Ralph Bean (ADM 139/45), for example, shows:

He was born on 19 April 1826 in Wapping, he volunteered for continuous service engagement, signing on for 12 years and joining HMS *President* as an able seaman on 9 August 1853. The ships he had served on since 1847 are listed. He is described as 5ft 4 inches, of swarthy complexion, with dark brown hair, hazel eyes and an anchor tattoo on his left hand.

A search of the census and deaths at Ancestry shows that our tattooed old salt, after being pensioned off, became 'discipline officer' at Sunbury Industrial School. At the age of 64 he was a casual in the customs service and died at West Ham in 1906.

The government took little interest in merchant seamen (those serving on cargo vessels etc.) before 1835, and there are unlikely to be any government records relating to them before this date. A useful source for the period 1754–1854 (for all sorts of mariners) are the petitions of distressed mariners and their relatives received by Trinity House, calendared in *The Trinity House Petitions: a calendar of the records of the Corporation of Trinity House, London* (SOG, 1987). The original petitions are at LMA and on microfilm at SOG. They may be accessed via Origins, along with merchant seamen's apprenticeship indentures

Trinity almshouses, Mile End Road, eighteenth century. They still stand today.
St Dunstan's Church Archives

from Trinity House, 1780 and 1818–45. Other Trinity House sources are described in LMA information leaflet 51, 'Records of the Corporation of Trinity House' (download from LMA's website).

Medals awarded to merchant seamen during the Second World War can be located online through TNA's website; the records cover the period 1946–2002 and give information about the seaman's service and usually provide date and place of birth.

From 1835 there is good range of records relating to merchant seamen at TNA; download in-depth research guides from the website, starting with *Merchant Seamen: Records of the RGSS, Domestic Records Information 110*.

An index of gifts to Stepney seamen's widows in 1860 is available at THAOL.

The following publications are useful:
Bruno Pappalardo, *Tracing Your Naval Ancestors* (TNA, 2003)
C. and M. Watts, *My Ancestor was a Merchant Seamen* (SOG, 2002)
TNA in-depth research guides – there are a number relating to the Royal and Merchant Navy at: www.nationalarchives.org.uk; go to 'records', then 'research guides', then to 'Royal Navy' and 'Merchant Seamen'.

Visits to the Museum in Docklands, to see a recreation of eighteenth-century 'sailortown', and the National Maritime Museum in Greenwich are recommended.

Watermen and Lightermen

Plentiful records are extant for these men, who plied for passenger hire and took the cargoes of merchant vessels to shore in their barges from Wapping, Limehouse, St Katharine's, Shadwell and Ratcliff. The trades often continue through several generations of a family. The Navy recruited and pressed from the community of watermen.

Before there were Hackney carriages (from the end of the sixteenth century), and for some time afterwards, watermen were the 'taxi drivers' of London and the Thames the main highway. They lived in the East End's riverside hamlets, and in Greenwich, Southwark, Westminster and Chiswick. Like their modern counterparts, they apparently enjoyed topical gossip, 'Evermore telling strange news, most commonly lies' (Sir Thomas Overbury, *Characters* (1614–16)). An Elizabethan statute authorised Trinity House to license sailors between voyages to ply as watermen, to keep them from 'folly and idleness' and to prevent 'evil and ignorant persons who robbed and spoiled of their [passengers'] goods, and also drowned them'. The Watermen's Company was set up in 1566 and still flourishes today.

Lightermen joined the Watermen's Company in 1700, having, formerly, been associated with the Woodmongers' Company. They unloaded the cargoes of ships and carried them into port by lighters (barges). Gaffer Hexham in Charles Dickens's *Our Mutual Friend* was one such. He rowed about in the river round Limehouse Hole, in the hope of helping undermanned vessels and hauling out dead bodies to sell. It is doubtful if the likes of Hexham ever registered with the Company!

Records

The records of the Watermen's and Lightermen's Company are at LMA/Guildhall for the period 1688 to 1908; later records are housed at Watermen's Hall.

A search of the binding books (MS 6289, 1688–1908) and the affidavit books (MS 6291, 1759–1897) together will give you name, date and place of baptism, date an apprenticeship starts, name of master and date of becoming free. The company books contain reference to some 20 per cent of individual members of the company (MS 6301-6305, from 1801). A privately compiled index of bindings, apprenticeship affidavits and contract licences from 1692–1949 is available to buy on CD-ROM or fiche from its compiler R.J. Cottrell. The index is at LMA and Mr Cottrell will also do paid searches; contact him at: RJCindex@aol.com or 19 Bellevue Road, Bexleyheath, Kent DA6 8ND.

MID has an index of barge owners (Association of Barge Owners) 1900–9, 1915 and 1955, and a register of barge owners 1890–1910 (4 vols).

Trinity House licensed some old ex-mariners as watermen; register for 1829–64; LMA Guildhall MS 30335 (index at the Enquiry Desk).

Some watermen joined the Shipwrights' Company, see p. 187.

The following publications and websites are useful:
LMA information leaflet 18 'Records of the Watermen and Lightermen'
www.parishregisters.com – the Docklands Ancestors' site, which lists a
    number of useful publications
www.watermenshall.org – website of the Company of Watermen and
    Lightermen

James Legon, *My Ancestors were Thames Watermen*, 2nd edn (SOG, 2008) – an excellent guide.

Soldiers

There is a vast military archive at TNA and numerous books on the subject of Army ancestry. The records of East End soldiers are much the same as those from anywhere else. As noted above (p. 42), there was much resistance to conscription in the First World War and details of men who avoided joining the Army, and their reasons for being 'excused', may be found in local newspapers.

The Tower Hamlets Militia

The Tower Hamlets Militia, a civilian force or 'citizen army' (also known as 'trained bands'), was first raised in the sixteenth century and garrisoned at the Tower. In 1641 there were *c*. 600 of them drawn from the hamlets of St Katharine's, East Smithfield, Whitechapel, Wapping, Ratcliff, Limehouse, Blackwall, Spitalfields, Norton Folgate, Mile End, Bethnal Green, Bromley and Old Ford, together with Hackney and the Shoreditch hamlets of Halliwell and Hoxton.

The modern militia originated with the Militia Act of 1757, whereby county regiments were raised, officers appointed by the Lord Lieutenant (in the case of the East End the Constable of the Tower) and men chosen by ballot. The Yeomanry (cavalry) was used as a police force. Eventually the militia evolved into the Territorial Army.

Records

- Tower Hamlets muster rolls 1644: TNA SP 28/121A. See www.traynedbands.org.uk/content.php?content=men for details of Tower Hamlets militia men in 1644.
- Militia Enrolment Lists 1817–53 1st Tower Hamlets: TNA WO 68/ 432 and pay lists for the same; WO 68/437.
- County Regimental Returns, East London (names without location in county): TNA WO 13/1353-70 (1796–1820); WO 13/1419-44 (1781– 1876); for 1st and 2nd Tower Hamlets 1805–16: WO 13/2561-2.
- Records of the Constable of the Tower: TNA WO 94.

For Huguenots in the trained bands of London, see *Proceedings of the Huguenot Society* 15. A summary history of the Tower Hamlets Militia can be found at: www.traynedbandes.org.uk/content.php?content=bef.

The Army

Tracing soldiers from the East End (or anywhere else) is best achieved, in the main, by visiting TNA. Consult Simon Fowler's excellent guide, *Tracing your Army Ancestors* (Pen & Sword, 2006) and download the research guides with reference to 'military' from TNA's website.

Service records (those that have survived) for the First World War can be accessed at Ancestry (or you can go to TNA). Other records available at Ancestry for the First World War are pensions records, medal roll card index (campaign medals), National Roll of the Great War, *Soldiers died in the Great War*. War diaries for the First World War are also at TNA; they are described in TNA's research guide *British Army Campaign Records*.

For service records of men who served in the Second World War, apply to the Ministry of Defence's Army Personnel Centre (see p. 234; they charge a fee). War diaries for the Second World War are available at Kew, with a selection at TNA's 'documents online'.

For casualties from both world wars, the Commonwealth War Graves Commission's 'Debt of Honour Register' supplies details and is at: www.cwgc.org. The following sample is taken from this source:

> Albert Edward Short* of the 7th Battalion Gordon Highlanders, private, aged 19 d. 26 June 1918; son of George Francis Short of Gladstone Street, Hathern Loughborough, grave ref. VB10 at Chambrecy British Cemetery.

The website will also tell you how to find the grave.

Albert Short appears in *Soldiers Killed in the Great War* (Ancestry and TNA); his entry on the *Campaign Medal Roll indexes* (TNA and Ancestry) adds nothing to the above, except to say that the Gordon Highlanders were also the 14th London Regiment. There are no service records for him as two-thirds of these records were destroyed in the Blitz. The war diary for his battalion was found by searching TNA's catalogue under 'Gordon Highlanders 7'; the reference for the diary is WO 95/2882. This gives details of the engagements his unit was involved in, but ordinary soldiers are rarely mentioned.

According to a note found among family papers, Albert died during the French advance west of Rheims, dying of wounds inflicted by a

---

* See Albert Short in the pedigree on p. 57. He came from the branch of the Short family who did well for themselves and moved away, the youngest child of George, who took over the running of his aunt's coffee shop in Bethnal Green.

shell. A note from his school magazine says he was of a 'frank and open disposition'. He joined up in 1917 aged 18. His commanding officer said he was 'a great favourite and a thorough gentleman'.

Policemen

Staff records of the Metropolitan police (incomplete) from 1830 are at TNA (code MEPO). They are described in *Research Guide: Domestic Records Information 52*, which can be downloaded from TNA's website.

The docks employed their own police and the staff records are to be found with those of other dock employees (see pp. 173–6).

For information on the records of the River Police (now the Marine Policing Unit), established in 1789, apply in writing to the Thames Police Museum in Wapping (see Appendix 8 for details).

The following reference material is useful:
Police History Society Journal
S. Wade, *Tracing Your Police Ancestors* (Pen & Sword, 2009).

Ship Builders

Ships were built in Ratcliff in Medieval times. With the setting up of the Royal Docks at Woolwich and Deptford (1513), the main centre for the construction of ships moved to the south bank of the river, although there were still yards in Limehouse. The most famous East End shipwrights in the seventeenth century were the Pett family of Limehouse. For information about sixteenth and seventeenth-century shipwrights in Stepney, the footnotes to W.H. Frere's *Memorials of Stepney Parish; Vestry Minutes 1579–1662* (Billing, 1890–1) are a most useful source.

In Stepney's maritime hamlets of Ratcliff, Shadwell, Wapping and Limehouse there were, and continued to be, numbers of small workshops where masts, anchors, sails and ropes were made; hence Cable Street. Here lived ships' carpenters, blacksmiths, fitters and chandlers. There are no special occupational sources for any of these; you may find them among the apprenticeship records and, later, directories (see p. 99). East Indiamen were built and fitted at Blackwall from the seventeenth century.

In the nineteenth century, Poplar became a most important shipbuilding centre. There was open land (at Millwall) and it was near the docks, and by 1848 there were thirty-eight ship-building firms, as well

The Alfred, *built by Richard and George Green. It was launched at Blackwall Yard on 8 April 1845 and towed to the East India Dock for fitting. It was used for Indian and Australian trade.* Private Collection

as iron founders, blacksmiths, sail makers and rope makers. Workers came in from Scotland, Ireland, Wales and Italy. Brunel's *Great Eastern*, the largest ship of its day (launched in 1858), was built in John Scott Russell's shipyard, bringing in vast numbers of Scottish workers. At its height in the 1860s the ship-building industry in Poplar employed some 15,000 men and boys. The boom time came to an end in the late 1860s when many builders moved their operations to the Clyde; some firms diversified and stayed put until the 1920s.

Scruttons remained until 1926. Other firms of note were Yarrows (which started in 1863 and moved north in 1906), Dudgeons, Ash, Stewart's and Samuda's, Green and Siley Weirt Ltd, the London Graving Dock, Badger's and Rye Arc.

Records

The main source is the records of the Worshipful Company of Ship-wrights *c.* 1595–1998. There is a huge archive of these records at the

Guildhall Library. The company's first hall (1605) was in Ratcliff, and moved to Tower Hill in 1794. There are registers of freedoms from 1660 and apprentices from 1659. See MS 04597-611, 10397-8, 31608 and 32968-8A. Also, see Hakluyt Society publications. C.H. Ridge (ed.)'s *Records of the Worshipful Company of Shipwrights – a Digest List of Freemen and Apprentices 1428–1858* (2 vols, Phillimore, 1939–46) refers to lots of related trades, for example, watermen.

For individual firms consult directories (see p. 99). Also, search at the NRA at: www.nationalarchives.gov.uk/nra under 'corporate names' or 'personal names' or go to www.a2a.org.uk and search under 'London' and 'ship builders'. The latter notes, among other things, many references to shipwrights' yards among the Sun Insurance Company registers (1800–39; records at LMA).

The following publications are useful:

W.H. Frere's, *Memorials of Stepney Parish; Vestry Minutes 1579–1662* (Billing, 1890–1)

L.A. Ritchie, *The Shipbuilding Industry: a Guide to Historical Records* (Manchester University Press, 1992)

An Outline History of the Isle of Dogs (Island History Trust, 1987)

A.E. Jeffery, *The History of Scruttons: shipbrokers and ship owners 1802–1926; stevedores, master porters and cargo superintendants 1890–1967* (A.E. Jeffery, 1971)

A. Burton, *Tracing your Shipbuilding Ancestors* (Pen & Sword, 2010) – this provides good background information.

Match Girls

These tough East End girls, as 'smart as paint', deserve a section of their own. Their strike at the Bryant and May's match factory in Bow in 1888 was a landmark in the history of the trade-union movement. My great aunt, Esther Daniels, was one of the many women who contracted the deadly disease of 'phossyjaw' from contact with phosphorous in the factory.

Sources

Staff and other records for the factory (1840–1978) are held by the Hackney Archives Department. A strike-fund register, which gives details of all the women who took part in the strike, is held by the

London Metropolitan University and online at: www.unionhistory.info. A great deal of information about the match girls and their strike can be found at THHOL. See also, Reg Beer's *The Match Girls Strike, 1888* (National Museum of Labour History, 1983).

The Bryant and May factory in Fairfield Road, Bow is still there, transformed into elegant flats called the Bow Quarter. A statue of

The Bow Quarter, formerly Bryant and May's match factory. Yvonne Hughes

Statue of W.E. Gladstone in Bow, erected 'with the blood of the match girls'. Yvonne Hughes

W.E. Gladstone, paid for by factory owner, Theodor Bryant, stands in the middle of the road by Bow church. The locals said it had been erected 'with the blood of the match girls'.

Clergy

Men of the cloth, many of whom did amazing social work in the East End from the mid-nineteenth century to the Blitz) are usually fairly easy to trace. Some are very well known, see p. 172. The main sources are:

- The Revd G. Hennessy's *Novum Repertorium Ecclesiasticum Parochiale Londinense* (1898) and Richard Newcourt's *Repertorium Ecclesiasticum Parochiale Londinense* (2 vols, 1708–10) list London clergy (Church of England) from earliest times.
- *Crockford's Clerical Directory* from 1858, *Clergy List* from 1842, *Clerical Guide* 1817–36 (Church of England), supplying outline biographies.
- Most Anglican clergy had degrees from Oxford or Cambridge so should have entries in the published *Alumni Oxonienses* and *Alumni Cantabrigienses*.
- The Clergy of the Church of England database at: www.theclergy database.org.uk. This is a developing database that aims to provide information about the careers of all clergymen before 1855.
- For famous East End clergy, see THHOL and Harold Finch's *The Tower Hamlets Connection* (London Borough of Tower Hamlets, 1996) and K. Leech's 'Anglo-Catholic Socialist Clergy in East London 1870–1970', *East London Record* 12 (1989).
- Roman Catholic priests are listed in *The Catholic Directory*, from 1850.
- For Methodist ministers, see O.A. Beckerlegge's *United Methodist Ministers and their Circuits, 1797–1932* (Epworth Press, 1968). For Baptist ministers, see *The Baptist Handbook* (Baptist Union of Great Britain and Ireland, 1861–1972). Dr Williams's Library in Bloomsbury has a wealth of material relating to Congregational and other Nonconformist ministers.
- For rabbis, see pp. 154–61.
- For all of the above, look among the records of their church or chapel (see Appendices 2 and 3).

- Being 'the only gentlemen' in the East End (from the mid-nineteenth century), they are more than likely to have left wills (see p. 82).
- LMA information leaflet 'Sources for tracing Clergy and Church Officials' and S.A. Raymond's *London and Middlesex, a genealogical Bibliography*, 2nd edn (FFHS, 1998).

Prostitutes

Many thousands of girls and women took to the streets in the East End, and from the sixteenth century the mariner community provided good pickings. In the 1871 census for Shadwell's Albert Square practically all the heads of household are brothel keepers. Charles Booth's researcher (1889) reported that in Wapping prostitutes were 'of a sturdy kind and there are no bullies who live off the earnings of women'. They 'plied for hire ... in the Old Ford Road and Roman Road ... the Polish Jews are the worst. They won't leave you alone.' (www.boothlse.ac.uk). Jack London saw women in Spitalfields prepared to sell themselves for two or three pence or a loaf of stale bread (*The People of the Abyss* (Macmillan, 1903)).

Many had a 'day job' in the rag trade, while some were 'flower girls' in the spring and prostitutes in the winter.

Records

- Census. They may be described as 'fallen women'.
- Legal prosecutions. Many appear in the Old Bailey records and numbers were deported (see pp. 167 and 170–2).
- Parish registers sometimes make mention of them. St Dunstan's register for 25 January 1602: 'A whore died of the pocks against the sugar house'.

The following publications and websites are informative:

J.R. Walkowitz, *City of Dreadful Delight* (Virago, 1992)

H. Mayhew and B. Hemyng, *The Prostitute Class Generally* (BL, n.d.)

R. Paley and S. Fowler, *Skeletons; Exploring the Lives of Our Disreputable Ancestors* (TNA, 2005)

www.booth.lse.ac.uk – reports on East End prostitutes in 1889 (no names).

Railway Workers

Records of porters, engine drivers, station masters, engineers and the rest may be found at TNA, which has some records of railway companies before nationalisation (code RAIL).

The East End companies were the London & Blackwall Cable Railway (1840 trains hauled by cable; 1848 steam engines introduced), the Eastern Counties Railway, the Great Eastern Railway, the East & West India Docks & Birmingham Junction Railway (later North London Railway; online list of staff via TNA's website) the East London Railway Co. (1865), the Metropolitan and the Metropolitan & District Railway 1878, and the London, Tilbury and Southend Railway. For a description of where the lines ran, see *Victoria County History of Middlesex*, Vol. 11 (online at: www.british.history.ac.uk/report.aspx?compid=22732).

For a full list of staff records, download TNA's research guide *Railways: Staff Records*. There are records for the following: Eastern Counties 1851–7; Great Eastern 1855–1930; North London 1854–1920; London, Tilbury and Southend 1871–1923.

For staff records post-nationalisation (1948–94), apply to: BRB (Residuary Ltd), Whittles House, 14, Pentonville Road, London N19HF; tel: 020 7904 5079; www.brb.gov.uk.

The following books are useful:

D. Hawkings, *Railway Ancestors* (Sutton, 1995)

F. Hardy, *My Ancestor was a Railway Worker* (SOG, 2009) – for background information.

Chapter 7

THE SECOND WORLD WAR – THE BLITZ

East Enders' heroism in the Blitz is legendary and stories are often told of how they got through the terrors and the loss by cultivating an air of apathy, hiding their pain with Cockney understatement.

'Black Saturday', 7 September 1940, when the 'poor old docks copped it' was the most concentrated assault on Britain since the Spanish Armada, with Stepney, especially Wapping, bearing the brunt. The planes covered 800 square miles of sky and the glow of the burning warehouses could be seen a hundred or more miles away. After Black Saturday the raids went on, night after night, until the following May; the East End was bombed by an average of 200 planes nightly for 57 nights in succession, with 788 high-explosive bombs falling on Stepney alone. By 11 November 1940 four out of ten houses in Stepney had been damaged. It was a world of wailing sirens at dusk, hustling down to the public shelters, into the crypts of churches and Stepney Green, Mile End and Bank Underground stations, waving goodbye to children sent off to the country for safety, fire watching and making the best of it all. Whole streets disappeared and evacuation reduced the population of the borough of Stepney from 200,000 to 80,000. The Bethnal Green Tube shelter disaster of 3 March 1943 saw 173 people crushed to death in a panic with no enemy action involved.

On 13 June 1944 the first German flying bomb hit London and blew up the LNER at Bow Viaduct. Night and day the 'huge dragons' came with light in their tails. The last bomb to fall on London hit Hughes Mansions in Vallance Road on 27 March 1945 (see below). On 8 May 1945 Germany collapsed; what church bells were left rang out and the women of Stepney threw up their skirts to reveal hastily put together red, white and blue knickers, and did 'Knees up Mother Brown'.

Sources

- The Commonwealth War Graves Commission has lists of civilian casualties from the Second World War. These can be searched online at: www.cwgc.org. The following is an example of the type of detail that can be uncovered:

  > Blanche Cohen aged 17 of 58 Hughes Mansions, Vallance Road died on 27 March 1945.

- Evacuees are very difficult to trace. See LMA's leaflet 'The Evacuation of Children from the County of London during the Second World War 1939–1945' and R. Samways (ed.)'s *We Think You Ought to Go* (GLRO, 1995).
- THLHLA has a collection of photographs, a map of Bethnal Green showing air-raid incidents and other material.

The following books are useful:

Sean Dettman, *The Bethnal Green Tube Shelter Disaster – A Stairway to Heaven* (Brentwood, 2010)

R. Taylor and C. Lloyd, *The East End at War* (Sutton, 2007)

W. Spencer, *Family History in the War* (TNA, 2007).

Simon Fowler, *Tracing Your Second World War Ancestors* (Countryside Books, 2007).

Chapter 8

THE STREET/HOUSE THEY LIVED IN

Having found out from the census or other sources where your family lived in the past, you may want to find out more about the house and street they lived in. There are good collections of photographs at THLHLA and LMA.

You may want to go and see the street or house, if it has survived the Blitz and slum clearance. Some street names have changed, some streets have disappeared altogether and, in some, the numbering of the

Lacey Street, Bow, c. 1911. This street no longer exists. The arrow marks the house (no. 29) where Sidney and Lil Short set up home in 1907. See p. 70. THLHLA

houses has been altered. Using the sources listed below, in combination with a modern A to Z and a map from an appropriate date, you will be able to locate the street and the house or tenement, if still standing.

- For the renaming of London Streets, refer to: www.maps.hunthouse. net/streets/street_Name_Ch.
- To check if the numbering has been changed, consult *LCC List of Streets and Places* (1901; revised 1912, 1929 and 1955). Changes before 1860 are not noted. Copies of this work are held behind the staff desks at LMA and THLHAL.
- There is a very useful (free) index of streets at GenDocs>'Victorian London Street Index'. For example:

  > Hague Street All Saints, BETHNAL GREEN (1862)
  > Hague Street, Bethnal Green E2 (1997)
  > Hague Street, Bethnal Green Road, BETHNAL GREEN (1871)

- For a description of the street *c*. 1889 you could go to: www.booth. lse.ac.uk and consult Charles Booth's survey. The areas covered are Shoreditch, Bethnal Green, St George-in-the-East, Stepney, Mile End Old Town, Poplar and Hackney (original material in the library of the London School of Economics). For example:

  > On the East side of Old Ford Road, Summer Street, Spring Street and Autumn Street. Summer and Spring Street are the resort of prostitutes and a low class of labourers' [B346 pp. 64–5; my grandmother lived in Spring Street!]

- If your ancestor's house was standing *c*. 1910, you will, almost certainly, be able to find a description of it at TNA. The Board of Inland Revenue Valuation Office Field Books (IR 58) list every single property in the country in 1910–14, describing its rooms etc. Go to the Map Room, on the first floor at Kew, and ask how to find your ancestor's house. There are a parallel set of records at THLHLA called the Domesday Books.

If your family were property owners, a search of the the following sources may be profitable:

- Deeds. For property owners or leaseholders (including builders' leases) search the Deeds Registry at LMA (see LMA information leaflet 38, 'The Middlesex Deeds Registry 1709–1932') or consult the card index of local deeds at THLHLA.

- Records of properties insured (private and commercial) may be researched at LMA (information leaflet 48, 'Fire Insurance Records'); for policies issued by the Sun Insurance Company 1800–39, go to: www.nationalarchive.gov.uk/a2a. See D. Morris's 'The Benefits of Insurance; House History in MEOT', *Ancestors* 13 (2003).

Chapter 9

MAPS

There are collections of maps at THLHLA, LMA and TNA. In addition, many are published and there is access to maps on numerous websites. Refer to the following:

- A wonderful online source is the collection of maps of Tower Hamlets at: www.mernick.co.uk/elhs/mapgallery.htm.
- Parish maps can be viewed on the EoLFHS and GENUKI websites.
- *Old Ordnance Survey Maps*, Godfrey Editions (with historical notes on areas); London Sheets: 52 (Bethnal Green and Bow 1894), 63 (Whitechapel and Spitalfields 1913) 65 (Poplar 1894), 77 (Bermondsey and Wapping 1894). These are cheap and available from book shops or online at: www.alangodfreymaps.co.uk.
- The London Topographical Society's A to Z series of London: *Georgian, Victorian and Edwardian London*. This is worth buying – from the Guildhall Library book shop or order from the Society at: www.topsoc.org.
- List of maps in Stuart Raymond's *London and Middlesex, A Genealogical Bibliography* (FFHS, 1994).

Appendix 1

THE BOROUGH AND ADMINISTRATIVE UNITS

To check whether the place you are interested in is in Tower Hamlets, go to LMA's website at: www.cityoflondon.gov.uk/lma>London Generations>Guide to Areas in Greater London Boroughs. See maps on pp. 16, 17, 59, 69 and 73.

The London Borough of Tower Hamlets is an area of 7.6 square miles to the east of the City, most of it formerly in the ancient county of Middlesex, in the Hundred (county sub-division) of Ossulton. The hundreds of Middlesex were probably created in early Saxon times. Ossulton wraps round London to the east and north; its name derives from Oswulf's stone, the hundred's meeting place, which was probably in South Street, off Park Lane.

The name Tower Hamlets seems to have been first used in the sixteenth century when the Constable of the Tower was Lord Lieutenant of Tower Hamlets and commanded the bands of the Tower Hamlets Militia. The name was used in 1832 for the parliamentary borough that was created, incorporating Stepney, Whitechapel, Hackney and Shoreditch. Hackney was taken out of the borough in 1868.

Modern Tower Hamlets is bordered by Hackney to the northwest, the River Lea and Newham to the east, the Thames to the south and the City of London to the west.

For some purposes it has always been accounted part of London; for others, before 1889 (except the areas covered by the parishes of St Botolph's Aldgate, St Botolph's Bishopsgate and Holy Trinity Minories, which were in the City of London), as part of Middlesex.

Shoreditch is in the borough of Hackney and is not considered in this book. Neither are the riverside suburbs on the south of the Thames, now part of 'Docklands' (Southwark and Bermondsey). These were formerly in the county of Surrey and are now in the London Borough of Southwark.

The borough of Tower Hamlets comprises:

- Most of the ancient parish of Stepney, including its hamlets (see p. 204 and map on p. 73).
- The ancient parish of St Leonard Bromley.
- Some areas bordering on the City, including the Tower, Tower Hill, the precinct of St Katharine's, the Liberties of East Smithfield and Norton Folgate, the parishes of St Botolph's Aldgate (part, including the Old Artillery Ground) and Holy Trinity Minories, St Botolph's Bishopsgate (part). The Portsoken was the ancient name of the strip of land running from Bishopsgate down to the river, including the precinct of St Katherine's, East Smithfield, the parishes of St Botolph's, Aldgate and Holy Trinity Minories, incorporating part of what is now Spitalfields, Whitechapel and Wapping. Its eastern boundary was Nightingale Lane, now Thomas More Street.

Until the 1830s local-government activity was at parish level and the parish vestries ran affairs. Our ancestors had rights of settlement in the parish of their birth; so they were eligible for poor relief if they fell on hard times. In 1834, with the reform of the Poor Law, parishes were grouped into Poor Law unions and a Board of Guardians appointed. These unions were the basis for the registration districts which were used for census taking and the central registration of births, marriages and deaths. In 1855, the Metropolitan Board of Works was created with responsibility for sanitary matter over an area that became known as the Metropolis.

In 1889 the County of London was formed and the following metropolitan boroughs created in the East End:

- Stepney (incorporating Whitechapel).
- Bethnal Green.
- Poplar.

In 1965 a new large London Borough of Tower Hamlets was created, merging Stepney, Bethnal Green and Poplar.

For research purpose you will need to be able to identify the different places, by borough, registration district and parish. The main archive for East End research, the London Metropolitan Archive (now incorporating records from the Guildhall Library), arranges its records by modern borough.

Registration Districts (From 1837)

These are administrative divisions used for census and registration of births, marriages and deaths. You will need to know about these to search GRO and census indexes. For the East End they are:

- Bethnal Green 1837–1966 (then Poplar and Bethnal Green).
- London East 1838–70 (then 'London City' (for St Botolph's Aldgate and St Botolph's Bishopsgate)).
- Limehouse taken from Stepney 1921.
- Mile End Old Town 1857–1926, otherwise part of Stepney.
- Poplar, including Bow and Bromley, 1837–1966 (then Poplar and Bethnal Green).
- Stepney 1837–1921, including Limehouse, Ratcliff, Wapping, Mile End Old Town.
- St George-in-the-East 1837–1926 (then Stepney).
- Whitechapel 1837–1926 (then Stepney), including Holy Trinity Minories, Goodmans' Fields, Mile End New Town, Norton Folgate, Old Artillery Ground, Old Tower Without, Spitalfields, St Botolph's Aldgate, St Katharine's by the Tower, Tower of London.

Civil parishes, local-government units were formed in the mid-nineteenth century, usually based on the ancient or mother parish. These should not be confused with the ecclesiastical parish. For example, a search of the 1901 census return for the Shorts of Cardigan Road, Bow show the family living in the ecclesiastical parish of St Stephen and the civil parish of St Mary Stratford Bow. Bow church (still there in the middle of the road at Bow Flyover) was the parish church for the area from 1719; the parish of St Stephen, Tredegar Road, was carved out of the old parish in 1858. The church was destroyed by enemy bombing in 1941 and the parish combined with that of St Paul, St Stephen's Road after the Second World War. Hopefully, it is among the records of

St Stephen's Church where the baptisms and marriages of the Shorts will be found for this period (see pp. 56–7).

Poor Law Unions

From 1834 the country was divided into unions (combinations of parishes), see map on p. 129. You will need to know something about these for searching for ancestors who might have spent some time in the workhouse, as many thousands did in the late nineteenth-century East End. See www.institiutions.org.uk for more about the unions.

Parishes

You will need to know about these mainly for researching before census and GRO registration, when the parish was the basic unit of local government and you have to search for your ancestors among parish registers of baptisms, marriages and burials. See p. 72.

Before the mid-nineteenth century there were seventeen parishes in the area; thereafter there were a great number, and for these refer to Appendix 2, the map of parishes in 1819 and maps of parishes in Stepney, Poplar and Bethnal Green taken from Stanford's 1903 map and accessed at GENUKI (pp. 69 and 73).

From the Middle Ages Stepney parish was divided into hamlets.

Stepney's Hamlets

Stepney parish in the early days was enormous and encompassed most of what is now Tower Hamlets. As the name suggests, it was divided into 'hamlets', some of which were really small towns in themselves; by the mid-sixteenth century the hamlets had their own chapels or altars within the church. The hamlets elected their own churchwardens from this time and, with the introduction of the Poor Law in the early seventeenth century, the appointment of Poor Law officials, the raising of poor rate and, later, the establishment of workhouses was done on a hamlet basis. Most of the hamlets eventually acquired parish status, which means they had their own records of baptisms, marriages and burials. Ratcliff finally disappeared, as did Mile End New Town. The others remain as districts within the London Borough of Tower Hamlets.

The hamlets were:

- Ratcliff; absorbed into Limehouse in the nineteenth century.
- Whitechapel (previously called Aldgate Street); parish 1338.
- Mile End (called 'Old Town' after the creation of Mile End New Town); various nineteenth-century parishes created; own metropolitan vestry 1855.
- Mile End New Town; created seventeenth century.
- Shadwell; seventeenth-century 'new town', parish 1669.
- Poplar, Blackwall and Stepney Marsh (Isle of Dogs); parish 1817.
- Bethnal Green; parish 1745.
- Limehouse; parish 1730.
- Spitalfields; parish 1729.
- Stratford Bow and Old Ford; church built 1311, parish 1719.
- Wapping was in two parts: Wapping-Whitechapel (the strip along the river bank) which acquired its own chapel in 1617, made parochial in 1694, and Wapping-Stepney which became St George-in-the-East.

Ecclesiastical Arrangements (For Wills)

The East End was in the diocese of London and the Archdeaconry of Middlesex. Wills went for probate to church courts before 1858, to the bishop's or archbishop's court. Wills from Aldgate were proved by the Archdeacon of London. For more about this, see pp. 83–5. The diocesan boundaries are thought to have been based on the ancient Kingdom of the East Saxons, and stayed the same from 604 to 1845.

Appendix 2

PARISH REGISTERS

Parish boundary maps from 1877 are available at EoLFH's website at: www.eolfhs.org.uk>parish information>(name of parish)>parish map. See also the Docklands Ancestors' website at: www.parishregister.com.

Entries from LMA registers may be found in Ancestry's databases 'London England Marriages and Banns 1754–1921', 'Births and Baptisms 1813–1906' and 'Deaths and Burials 1813–1980'. Earlier entries have been digitised but not indexed, as indicated.

For a complete list of LMA's Tower Hamlets' register holdings, with call number and dates, go to: www.parishregister.com and scroll down to 'Tower Hamlets Parish Registers'.

These are the abbreviations used below:

b	burials
Boyd	marriage index
Browse at Ancestry	indicates that the registers (or part of them) have been digitized at: www. ancestry.co.uk, but there are no indexes or transcripts at the time of publication
c	christenings
Challen	series of transcripts made by W.H. Challen at LMA
conf	confirmations
Docklands Ancestors	indexes and transcriptions of baptisms at: www.parishregister.com (fee) or buy CD-ROMs
Docklands Ancestors	Series (as above). Also at Findmypast

LDS	This indicates that the records have been filmed by the Mormons and can be read at an LDS library. They may be on the IGI; they may be incomplete
m	marriages
pop	population
PR	parish registers
Webb, Cliff	Webb's published transcripts and indexes of marriages (to 1837).

The 'Mother Parishes' – For Research Pre-1837

See map of parishes in 1819 on p. 73. Many churches were built and new parishes created from the mid-nineteenth century. They are not as vital to research as those listed below.

Stepney

St Dunstan's and All Saints' Stepney, Stepney High Street; still there. An Anglo- Saxon foundation; building fifteenth century, much restored.

The mother church for almost the whole area, a huge parish, one of the largest in the country, until its major division in the mid-eighteenth century. At its peak at the beginning of the eighteenth century it served a population of 86,000, had 10 churchwardens and encompassed the 9 hamlets of Bethnal Green, Bow with Old Ford,* Limehouse, Mile End Old Town, Mile End New Town, Poplar with Blackwall, Ratcliff, Spitalfields and Wapping-Stepney. Until 1754 it was also a 'marriage centre' (see p. 77). Numerous mariners and weavers; it was known as the 'Church of the High Seas'.

By virtue of the size of the parish, its proximity to London and the numbers of emigrants who left from here for the New World, its registers are among the UK's most important genealogical sources for the sixteenth to eighteenth centuries.

PR at LMA: c 1568–1958, m 1568–1962, b 1568–1929. IGI, Boyd (1568–1754). Transcript and index of marriages 1568–1719 T. Colyer-Fergusson. Docklands Ancestors: 1568–1608, 1730–1848. Browse at Ancestry 1538–1815. Excellent series of published vestry minutes 1579–1662: W.H. Frere's *Memorial of Stepney Parish; Vestry Minutes 1579–1662* (Billing, 1890–1).

* Bow, although only a chapelry of Stepney until 1719, maintained its own registers (see below).

Bromley

St Mary's Bromley, St Leonard's, Bromley High Street; 610 acres. Twelfth-century foundation, monastic in origin, serving Bromley village. Population 1801: 4,493; 1861: 48,611.

PR at LMA: c 1622–1960, m 1622–1960, b 1622–1866. Bishops' transcripts 1639 MS 10,108A. Webb. Challen 1624–1749. Browse at Ancestry 1622–1812. Vestry minutes 1722–1825 THLHLA.

Whitechapel

St Mary's Matfelon/Whitechapel, Whitechapel High Street; 170 acres. Fourteenth-century foundation; destroyed in Blitz. Population 1801: 23,666; 1871: 34,454. Includes Wapping Whitechapel (strip of Wapping by the river) until 1612. Range of craftsmen and traders from the Middle Ages. Large Jewish presence from 1880s (see Jews, p. 154).

PR at LMA: c 1558–1940, m 1558–1940, b 1558–1857. Boyd 1616–25. Transcript and index of registers 1813–31 (LMA typescript). Docklands Ancestors 1768–1865. Browse at Ancestry 1558–1818. LDS 1558–1940.

Bow

St Mary's Stratford-Bow/Bow; 565 acres. The church (still there in the middle of the road) served the village on the west side of Bow Bridge from 1311, as a chaplery of Stepney, although, unusually, it conducted its own baptisms, marriages and burials. Parish from 1719. Many bakers. Population 1801: 2,181, 1861: 26,055.

PR LMA: c 1538–1956, m 1539–1968, b 1538–1862. Webb 15. Browse at Ancestry 1538–1812. Docklands Ancestors 1771–1831.

Wapping (see also St George-in-the-East)

St John's Wapping, Wapping High Street; 41 acres. Originally part of Stepney parish; Whitechapel parish from fourteenth century; church built 1617, parish 1694. Population 1801: 5,889; 1861: 3,410 (had its heart torn out by the building of docks). Many sailors.

PR LMA: c 1618–1940, m 1620–1940, b 1620–1881. Transcripts baps 1617–65, baptism extracts 1666–97, marriages and burials 1620–65. Challen 38. Docklands Ancestors 1618–1855. Browse at Ancestry 1617–1812.

Shadwell

St Paul's Shadwell, The Highway; still there; 68 acres. Originally part of Stepney parish and the Manor of the Dean and Chapter of St Paul's;

church built for a 'new town' development in 1656, parish 1669. Many sailors and marine craftsmen. Popularion 1801: 8,828; 1861: 8,230.

PR LMA: c 1670–1927, m 1671–1934, b 1670–1903. Bishops' transcripts baptisms 1663, burials 1663–4 MS 10,952. Marriages 1671–1754. Challen 13; Boyd. Docklands Ancestors 1712–1881. Browse at Ancestry 1670–1812. LDS 1680–1823.

Poplar and the Isle of Dogs

This includes Blackwall and the Isle of Dogs; also Cubitt Town and Millwall, which were developed in the mid-nineteenth century as ship-building centres; thereafter engineering works and food-processing plants.

All Saints', Poplar, East India Dock Road, and the Poplar Chapel (East India Company; now St Matthias's Church, Woodstock Terrace (see below)); 1,158 acres. Population 1801: 4,493; 1861: 48,611.

Poplar was a hamlet of Stepney until 1817, a settlement strung across the peninsula of the Isle of Dogs (Stepney Marsh). It had its own chapel-of-ease, St Mary in the Marsh, which was lost in the Great Flood of 1448. The East India Company dominated the hamlet from the early seventeenth century and the company's chapel (Poplar Chapel) served as a quasi-parish church.This chapel was consecrated as the Church of St Matthias in 1867. The parish church, All Saints', was built in 1821–3 and the Poplar Chapel registers transferred to the new church. The old building was then renamed St Matthias's and a new set of registers started. Both churches are still there.

PR at LMA (they include the records of the Poplar Chapel): c 1728–1985, m 1711–1989, b 1802–1917, burial order book 1824–38. Poplar Chapel marriages 1711–54. Challen 52. Transcripts 1584–1799, by J.S. Burn (LDS index). Docklands Ancestors 1813–72. Browse at Ancestry 1788–99.

St George-in-the-East

This was Wapping-Stepney until 1729; nicknamed 'St George-in-the-Dirt' in the nineteenth century).

St George-in-the-East, Cannon Street Road; 244 acres. Fine Hawksmoor church; still there. Originally hamlet of Stepney; parish 1729. 'Sailortown' in the eighteenth century; described as one of London's worst slum parishes in the nineteenth century. Many Irish. Population 1801: 21,170, 1861: 48,052.

PR at LMA: c 1729–1928, m 1729–1966, b 1729–1875. Docklands Ancestors 1729–1877. EoLFHS 1729–1848. IGI (some). Browse at Ancestry 1729–1812. LDS. Parish Chest records at THLHLA.

Limehouse

St Anne's Limehouse, Commercial Road; 244 acres. Hawksmoor church; still there. Originally hamlet of Stepney; parish 1730. Lime burners from Middle Ages, sixteenth–seventeenth centuries seamen and shipwrights. From *c.* 1890 Chinatown. Population 1801: 4,678; 1861: 29,919.

PR at LMA: c 1730–1955, m 1731–1968, b 1730–1897. Docklands Ancestors 1783–1877. Browse at Ancestry 1730–1821.

Spitalfields

Christ Church Spitalfields, Commercial Street; 73 acres. Hawksmoor church; still there. Area developed sixteenth–seventeenth centuries; a hamlet of Stepney; parish 1729. Large Huguenot presence from 1685 (see Huguenots, p. 148). Many weavers. Very poor slum late nineteenth century. Population 1801: 15,091; 1861: 20,783.

PR at LMA: c 1729–1961, m 1729–1998, b 1729–1859. Browse at Ancestry 1729–48. LDS 1729–1916. Challen transcripts 1730–1832. Docklands Ancestors 1729–95, 1819–43.

Wheeler Chapel, Spital Square, Norton Folgate. Opened 1692. Rebuilt and consecrated as St Mary Spital in 1842. Served Norton Folgate and Mile End New Town (NB most MENT c, m, b are in St Dunstan's registers). Many weavers and brewers.

PR at LMA (with records of St Mary Spital): c 1743–1911, m 1720–1911. Browse at Ancestry 1720–1824. LDS 1720–1875. Challen transcripts Wheeler Chapel 1720–52.

Bethnal Green

St Matthew's Bethnal Green; 755 acres; church still there. Population 1801: 22,310; 1861: 120,104. Originally a hamlet of Stepney; parish 1743. A country village before the influx of weavers late seventeenth century. It was given its own place of worship because of the rise in population and the 'Increase of Dissoluteness of Morals and a Disregard for Religion'. One of the worst slum areas in the nineteenth century. By mid-century twelve churches had been built there; according to Bishop Winnington-Ingram, they were thoughtlessly and fruitlessly 'flung down among the population'.

PR at LMA: c 1746–1993, m 1746–1987, b 1746–1877. Browse at Ancestry 1746–1812. IGI. Vestry minutes 1747–1875 THLHLA. Challen transcript 1746–1938.

Aldgate

Holy Trinity Minories, Haydon Square, Aldgate. Originally the chapel of the convent of Poor Clares, made into parish church at the Dissolution of the Monasteries, in 1539. Destroyed 1666, rebuilt 1706, bombed 1940. Parish united to St Botolph's Aldgate 1893. Parish 4 acres. Population 1801: 644; 1861: 449. As a 'peculiar' exempt from Diocesan visitation, it became a popular marriage venue *c.* 1644–*c.* 1725. Marriages from all over London may be found in the registers for this period.

PR at LMA: c 1563–1897, m 1579–1898, banns 1754–1898, b 1566–1852. Partial index to baptisms 1563–1875 IGI. Marriages 1676–1754: EoLFHS CD-ROM and on fiche at LMA. Browse at Ancestry (listed under 'Stepney' not 'Tower Hamlets') 1563–1812. LDS.

For later baptisms and marriages registers, see St Botolph's Aldgate.

St Botolph's Aldgate, Aldgate High Street; 38.7 acres. Destroyed 1666, rebuilt 1741. Still there. Includes Houndsditch and East Smithfield. A large, poor urban parish. Famous for bellfounding and armaments manufacture from the Middle Ages. Numbers of artisans and sailors. Area of Jewish settlement from seventeeth century. Population 1801: 8,689; 1861: 8,433.

PR at LMA: c 1558–1927, m 1558–1695, 1711–1945, banns 1653–8, 1754–1846, b 1558–1695, 1711–1853. Later baptisms and marriage registers retained by incumbent. Vestry minutes 1826–1900 THLHLA. Partial index to baptisms and marriages on IGI. Browse at Ancestry 1558–1812 (listed under 'City').

The parish archive (now at LMA) is especially rich in early records; described in detail in *City of London Parish Registers*, Guildhall Research Guide 4, 6th edn (1990). The parish clerk's memoranda books (1583–98), and the memoranda and vestry minutes (1616–71) (LDS) give a very lively account of events. For example:

> Burial in August 1617 of Goodwife Scraggs, a cutler's wife from East Smithfield;

'She was a woman of Antiquitie
And kept a house of Iniquity'.

See T.R. Forbes, *Chronicle from Aldgate* (Yale University Press, 1911 and 1971*).*

Bishopsgate

St Botolph's Bishopsgate EC2; 44.5 acres. Medieval foundation; damaged 1666, rebuilt 1725. Parish outside City walls includes liberties of Norton Folgate and the Old Artillery Ground; united with All Hallows' London Wall 1954. Population 1801: 10,314; 1861: 6,107. Houses of wealthy merchants sixteenth century; numbers of recusants, Huguenots from 1685.

PR at LMA: c 1558–1898, m 1558–1958, banns 1653–60, 1833–1950, marriage licences 1848–73, b 1558–1849. Later baptisms and marriages registers held by incumbent. Rent roll for 1787–1852 at Bishopsgate Institute. Partial index to baptisms and marriages 1558–1862 on IGI. Indexed transcripts: Challen c 1558–1690, m 1558–1754, b 1558–1752. Typscript at LMA: c, m, b 1639–40, m 1800–37, b 1800–53. Registers 1558–1753 available on CD-ROM (www.GenealogySupplies.com). Browse at Ancestry 1558–1812.

Precinct of St Katharine's by the Tower

St Katharine's by the Tower; 14 acres. Church removed to Regent's Park in 1825, following the construction of St Katharine's Dock and the clearance of the area (petitions and names of inhabitants who lost their homes among parliamentary papers at Parliamentary Archives). Population 1801: 2,652; 1861: 241. Rough liberty sixteenth–seventeenth centuries with many immigrants from Low Countries. Many Dutch breweries; sailors, watermen and lightermen.

PR at LMA: c 1584–1946, m 1584–1924, b 1584–1854. Harleian Society: c, m, b 1584–1695, marriages to 1726; marriages in Boyd 1584–1625. Browse at Ancestry 1581–1812 (lised under 'City').

Tower of London

Royal Chapel of St John. In the White Tower of the Tower of London, built *c*. 1080. PR held by the Chaplain at The Green, Tower of London, EC3N 4AB.

Parish Registers – From *c.* 1837

LMA and Ancestry's databases: 'London England Marriages and Banns 1754–1921', 'Births and Baptisms 1813–1906', 'Deaths and Burials 1813–1980'. (For mother churches, see above.)

The churches are grouped by area in EoLFHS parish information. Dates given below indicate the span of the records; there may be gaps. See the maps of parishes in Stepney, Poplar and Bethnal Green at GENUKI (taken from Stanford's 1903 map on p. 69).

All Hallows' Poplar, East India Dock Road 1880–1947; All Hallows', Devons Road, Bromley 1875–1972; All Saints' MENT, Buxton Street 1840–1951 (Docklands Ancestors 1840–80; LDS 1840–75); Christ Church Poplar, Manchester Road, Isle of Dogs 1876–1998 (Docklands Ancestors 1876–1904); Christ Church, Jamaica Street 1877–1941; Christ Church, Watney Street, St George-in-the-East 1842–1947 (Docklands Ancestors 1842–60); East London Mission to the Jews, Commercial Road 1892–8; Holy Trinity Bethnal Green, Old Nicol Street 1867–1923; Holy Trinity Mile End, Morgan Street 1841–1972 (Docklands Ancestors 1841–84); St Andrew's Bethnal Green, Viaduct Street 1843–1957 (LDS 1843–75); St Andrew's Poplar 1900–48; St Anthony's Stepney, Globe Road 1879–1936; St Augustine's, Settle Street, Stepney 1879–1948; St Bartholomew's Bethnal Green, Coventry Road 1844–1949; St Barnabas's Bethnal Green 1870–1917; St Benet's, Mile End Road 1929–51*; St Faith's, Shandy Street, Stepney 1891–1945; St Frideswide's, Follett Street, Poplar 1888–1947; St Gabriel's, Chrisp Street, Poplar 1869–1947; St James the Great's Bethnal Green, Bethnal Green Road (known as 'The Red Church') 1844–1981; St James the Less's Bethnal Green, St James' Avenue 1843–1956; St James's Ratcliff, Butcher Row 1840–1940 (Docklands Ancestors 1841–1913); St John the Evangelist's, Golding Street, St George-in-the-East 1870–1948 (LDS 1853–82; church combined with St Peter's London Docks in 1951); St John's Bethnal Green 1837–1931; St John's Cubitt Town, East Ferry Road, Isle of Dogs 1872–1964 (Docklands Ancestors 1887–1902); St John's Limehouse Fields, Halley Street 1853–1955; St Jude's Bethnal Green, Old Bethnal Green Road 1846–1951; St Jude's Whitechapel, Commercial Street 1848–1923; St Luke's, Burdett Road, Stepney 1869–1958; St Luke's Millwall, West Ferry Road, Isle of Dogs 1864–1964 (Docklands Ancestors 1864–87); St Mark's, Goodman's Fields, Stepney 1840–1926; St Mark's, Victoria Park, Cadogan Terrace, Old Ford 1869–1955; St Mary Spital Square, Norton Folgate 1720–1911

(LDS 1720–1875); St Mary's, Cable Street, St George-in-the East 1850–1959; St Matthew's, Limehouse Fields, Salmon Lane, Stepney 1871–1954; St Matthew's, Pell Street, St George-in-the-East 1859–91; St Matthias's Bethnal Green, Cheshire Street 1842–1958; St Matthias's Poplar, Woodstock Terrace 1867–1976; St Michael and All Angels's, St Leonard's Road, Bromley 1862–1975; St Nicholas's Blackwall, chapel-of-ease, Blackwall Stairs, Poplar 1900–41, m 1967; St Olave's Mile End New Town, Hanbury Street 1875–1914; St Paul's Bethnal Green, Virginia Street 1867–1947; St Paul's, Bow Common, Stepney 1858–1936; St Paul's, Dock Street, Stepney 1848–1982; St Paul's Old Ford, St Stephen's Road 1878–1966; St Peter's Bethnal Green, St Peter's Avenue 1843–1914; St Peter's Limehouse, Garford Street 1866–1967 (Docklands Ancestors 1866–1903); St Peter's London Docks, Wapping Lane, St George-in-the-East 1857–1945 (Docklands Ancestors 1878–1933; church combined with St John the Evangelist's 1951); St Peter's MEOT, Cephas Street 1839–1957 (LDS 1839–75); St Philip's, Swanfield Street, Bethnal Green 1842–1952; St Philip's, Newark Street, Stepney 1838–1979 (LDS 1838–75); St Saviour's, Northumbria Street, Poplar 1874–1964; St Saviour and the Cross's, Wellclose Square, Stepney 1857–68; St Simon Zealotes's Bethnal Green, Morpeth Street 1847–1951; St Stephen's Tredegar Road, Old Ford 1880–1980; St Stephen's, Commercial Street, Spitalfields 1861–1930; St Thomas's, Arbour Square, Stepney 1840–1942 (Docklands Ancestors 1840–76; LDS 1840–1900); St Thomas's, Baroness Road, Bethnal Green 1848–1919.

*Not at Ancestry.

Appendix 3

NONCONFORMIST CHAPEL REGISTERS

Tower Hamlets Nonconformist Chapel Registers, Pre-1837

For Huguenot churches, see pp. 148–53; for Roman Catholic churches, see pp. 141–4. Abbreviations used:

TNA	original registers at The National Archives (access at The Genealogist)
LDS	filmed by Mormons, available at LDS centres/IGI
THLHLA	indicates there is a microfilm copy of the registers at Tower Hamlets Local History Library and Archives (unless otherwise stated).

Beulah Chapel (Baptist), Commercial Road, St George-in-the East, formerly Church Lane, Whitechapel: births 1787–1816, 1831–7. TNA. THLHLA. LDS.

Bethnal Green Independent/Congregational Church, Cambridge Road: births and baptisms 1704–55, 1771–1836, 1845–58. TNA. THLHLA. LDS.

Bishopsgate Presbyterian, Hand Alley, later Broad Street: 1705–89. TNA. LDS.

Broad Street Chapel/Independent Meeting House, New Broad Street, Bishopsgate: 1727–1837. TNA. LDS.

Brunswick Wesleyan Chapel, Limehouse: births, baptisms and burials 1831–7. TNA. THLHLA. LDS.

Bull Lane Chapel: see Stepney Meeting.

Church of Christ, Nightingale Lane, East Smithfields (Independent): 1715–62. LMA (Guildhall MS 01777).

Church Street Wesleyan Chapel, Spitalfields: baptisms 1814–37. TNA. THLHLA.

Coverley Fields Chapel, Mile End New Town (Independent): baptisms 1782–1831, burials 1815–54. TNA. Baptisms only at THLHLA.

Cubitt Town Primitive Methodist Church: baptisms (indexed) 1865–1947, original records at THLHLA. EoLFHS CD-ROM for marriages 1833–61.

Ebenezer Chapel, Shadwell (Independent): births, baptisms and burials 1822–37. TNA. THLHLA. LDS.

Gibraltar Chapel, Bethnal Green: burials (index only) 1793–1804, 1809–37; burials 1809–37. TNA. THLHLA.

Globe Fields Wesleyan Methodist Chapel, Mile End Old Town: burials 1820–57. TNA. THLHLA.

Great Ayliff (Alie) Street Chapel, Whitechapel: baptisms 1756–80, 1783–1817, burials 1783–94. TNA. THLHLA.

Hale Street Wesleyan Chapel, Poplar: births and baptisms 1712–1837. TNA. THLHLA.

Hope Street Chapel, Spitalfields (Independent): baptisms 1830–5. TNA. LDS. THLHLA.

John Knox Church, Oxford Street, Stepney (Presbyterian): baptisms 1844–1985, marriages 1957–73. TNA and THLHLA. 1844–1939 at LDS.

Little Alie Street Baptist Church: membership 1753–1837, original document at THLHLA. LDS.

Little Prescott Street Chapel, Goodman's Fields, Whitechapel (Baptist): births 1786–1803. The Meeting originated in Wapping c. 1633, then moved to James Street, Stepney. TNA. LDS. THLHLA.

Mile End New Town Independent Chapel: burials 1815–54. TNA. LDS. THLHLA.

Mile End Old Town Latimer Chapel, Bridge Street, formerly Mile End Road (Independent): births and baptisms 1825–37. TNA. THLHLA: communion attendances 1909–67 and records of East London Mission 1893–1934.

Mill Yard Baptist Chapel, Goodman's Fields, Whitechapel (founded c. 1600): burials 1732–1837. TNA. LDS. THLHLA.

Mulberry Gardens Chapel, Pell Street, St George-in-the-East: see Pell Street Chapel.

Nightingale Lane: see Church of Christ.

Old Ford Baptist Chapel: burials 1814–37. TNA. LDS.

Old Gravel Lane Independent Chapel, St George-in-the-East: admissions 1704–77, baptisms 1704–1837, burials 1737–1837 and 1762, 1785 and 1795. TNA. THLHLA. LDS.

Parliament Court Catholic and Apostolic Church (Irvingite, a 'Pentecostal' sect), Old Artillery Ground, Bishopsgate: baptisms 1829–40. TNA. Pamphlet at THLHLA.

Pell Street Chapel, St George-in-the-East (formerly Nightingale Lane, Wapping; Countess of Huntingdon's Connexion, united with Old Gravel Lane, Independent): TNA and LDS 1736–1829 and 1784–1937. THLHLA film 1736–1829. LDS 1736–1829.

Queen Street Chapel, Ratcliff Cross (Independent): admissions 1698–1728, 1777–91, baptisms 1741–74, 1777–1831, 1760–4, births and baptisms 1835–7, burials 1822. TNA. THLHLA.

Rose Lane Chapel, Ratcliff (Independent), united with Queen Street Chapel in 1834: births and baptisms 1785–1837, burials 1786–1833. TNA. THLHLA.

St George's German Lutheran Chapel, Alie Street, Whitechapel: baptisms 1763–1897, marriages 1825–96, burials 1799–1853, original documents at THLHLA; LDS film. Index of baptisms 1763–1895 and burials 1818–53 in *Anglo German Family History Society Record Series 2* (microform, 1997), available at LMA.

St George's Wesleyan Chapel, New Road, St George-in-the-East: births and baptisms 1812–37. TNA. THLHLA.

St Paul's German Reformed Church, Goodman's Fields Whitechapel: baptisms 1824–1940, marriages 1858–1938, burials 1821–53, 1925–40. Original documents at THLHLA; alphabetical abstracts at LMA. LDS.

Scotch Church, Broad Street, St George-in-the-East (moved to Vincent Street, Mile End Old Town): 1741–1824 TNA. LDS to 1840.

Sion Chapel, Union Street, Mile End Old Town (Lady Huntingdon's Connexion): 1791–1837 TNA. LDS. THLHLA births and baptisms 1791–1802.

Shadwell Independent: see Ebenezer Chapel.

Somerset Street, Goodman's Fields, Whitechapel (Prebyterian): 1756–1826. TNA. LDS.

Stepney Meeting House/Bull Lane Independent Chapel. The oldest Independent/Congregational chapel in the world, 1644. Meeting House built 1674. Ministers: Matthew Mead 1671–99, Revd J. Galpin 1700–12, Thomas Mitchell 1713–20, J. Hubbard 1721–43, Samuel Brewer 1746–96, George Ford 1796–1821, Joseph Fletcher 1822–46, John Kennedy 1846. Baptisms 1644–1834 (TNA; film at THLHLA), baptisms 1822–45, 1847–1940, 1971–86 (original documents at THLHLA), marriages 1646–77 (TNA; film at THLHLA), transcript marriages 1918–74 at THLHLA, burials 1780–1837 (TNA; film at THLHLA), burials 1780–1853 (original documents at THLHLA). LDS 1644–1827.

Union Chapel, Bow Lane, Poplar: births and baptisms 1812–37. TNA. THLHLA.

Universal Baptist Church, Parliament Court, Artillery Street, Bishops-gate: births 1789–1811 TNA. Indexed transcript, pamphlet at THLHLA.

Virginia Chapel, Bethnal Green (Independent): baptisms 1825–37. TNA. THLHLA film and indexed transcripts (pamphlet).

Whites Row Chapel, Spitalfields: births and baptisms 1756–71 and 1828, 1775–1837. TNA. THLHLA. LDS.

Wycliffe Chapel (Independent), Cannon Street Road, St George-in-the-East (afterwards in Commercial Road, Whitechapel): births and baptisms 1784–1837. TNA. THLHLA. LDS.

Nonconformist Chapel Registers, Post-1837

These are at LMA unless otherwise specified. They are scheduled for digitisation by Ancestry; see the website for progress to date. See EoLFS's 'parish information' for details of chapel records, arranged by area.

Benledi Street School Methodist Chapel, Poplar
Bethnal Green Circuit
Bow Circuit
Bow Common Wesleyan Methodist Church, Bow, Poplar
Bow Road Wesleyan Methodist Church
Bromley by Bow Congregational Church, Bruce Road, Poplar
Bruce Road Central Hall, Poplar
Brunswick Hall Congregational, Whitechapel Road, Stepney
Brunswick Methodist Chapel, Three Colt Street, Limehouse
Burdett Road Congregational Church, Stepney
Cable Street Methodist Chapel, Stepney
Cannon Street Road Congregational Church, Stepney
Chrisp Street Methodist Church, Bromley, Poplar
Coverdale Chapel (Independent), Limehouse 1849–57: baptisms, records at TNA (LDS)
Driffield Road Methodist Church, Bow, Poplar
East London Tabernacle (Baptist): marriages 1923–42, records at THLHLA
Edinburgh Castle Methodist Chapel, Rhodeswell Road, Mile End, Stepney
Emery Hall, Augusta Street, Stepney
German Evangelical Reformed St Paul's Church, Hooper Square, Stepney

Harley Street Congregational Chapel, Bow, Poplar

John Knox Presbyterian Church, Stepney Way, Stepney

Latimer Chapel (Congregational) now in Ernest Street, Mile End: records of East London Mission 1893–1934. THLHLA

Lycett Memorial Methodist Chapel, White Horse Lane, Stepney

Lighthouse Baptist Church, Bromley by Bow: infant dedications, marriages and funerals 1962–7 at THLHLA

Manchester Road Methodist Church, Cubitt Town, Poplar

Maria Street Methodist Church, Millwall, Poplar

Milwall Methodist Church, Poplar

Mitre Street Schools, Poplar

New Road Congregational Meeting House, Stepney

North Bow Primitive Methodist Church, Driffield Road, Poplar

Old Ford Methodist Church, Poplar 1871–1925

Old Mahogany Bar Methodist Church, Poplar

Poplar Methodist Chapel

Poplar Presbyterian Church, Plimsoll Street, East India Dock Road

Poplar Wesleyan Mission, Woodstock Road, Poplar

Queen Victoria's Seamen's Rest, Poplar

St George's East Chapel, Cable Street

Seamen's Mission Circuit, Poplar

Sidney Street Congregational Chapel, Bethnal Green

Sion Congregational Church, Whitechapel Road

Spitalfields Methodist Church, Stepney

Stepney Green Methodist Church and East End Mission

Tredegar Road Methodist Church, Bow, Poplar

Trinity Congregational Church, Poplar: baptisms 1842–1922, 1945–71, marriages 1842–72, burials 1842–54 and 1863, attendance 1850–1903, membership 1951–75. THLHLA

Victoria Park Baptist Church: membership 1868–84, communicants 1931–40. Original records at THLHLA

Victoria Park Congregational Church, Approach Road, Bethnal Green

White's Row Chapel, Stepney

Whitechapel Methodist Mission, Stepney

Whitechapel Road Working Lads' Institute, Stepney

Wycliffe Congregational Church, Philpot Street, Stepney

The records of the Armenian Apostolic Church of St Sarkis 1922–87 (Spitalfields) have been filmed by LDS.

Appendix 4

MARRIAGE VENUES FOR EAST ENDERS

The following records are from the seventeenth century to 1754. In addition, see Tony Benton's *Irregular Marriage in London* (SOG, 1993).

- Fleet registers and notebooks. Original records at TNA (ref. RG 7) 1667–1754. See TNA Research Guide *Legal Records 37*. The registers have been digitised, transcribed and indexed and are available in their totality at The Genealogist. Partial index only IGI and Boyd.
- Holy Trinity Minories. See Appendix 2.
- Keith's Mayfair Chapel. Original registers 1719–54 split between TNA (RG 7) and St George's Hanover Square parish. Printed transcripts Harleian Society, Vol. 15; indexed by Boyd.
- St Benet Paul's Wharf. Original registers Guildhall (LMA) 1619–1754. Browse at Ancestry. Transcripts and indexes 1618–1837 Harleian Society, vols 39 and 40. 1619–1754 indexed in Boyd. Partial index IGI.
- St Botolph's Aldgate. See Appendix 2.
- St Dunstan's Stepney. See Appendix 2.
- St Gregory's by St Paul's. Original registers Guildhall (LMA) 1559–1754 (no marriages 1641–50 during church rebuilding); indexed in Boyd; transcript 1559–1837 typescript W.H. Challen, Vol. 11. Browse registers at Ancestry. Licences 1687–1837 (with St Mary Magdalene's, Old Fish Street) held at College of Arms, Queen Victoria Street EC4V 4BT. Partial index (and to baptisms) IGI.
- St James's, Duke's Place. Original registers Guildhall (LMA) 1664–1754 (gaps); indexed in Boyd. Allegations MS, 10,091. Printed transcripts 1665–1837: W.P.W. Phillimore and G.A. Cokayne's

Marriages at St James Duke's Place, London (1900–2). Browse registers at Ancestry. 1664–1812. Some entries on IGI.

- St Katharine's by the Tower. See Appendix 2.
- St Mary Magdalene's, Old Fish Street. Original registers Guildhall (LMA) 1539–1639 (index and transcript C.R. Webb, Vol. 40), 1664–1754 (transcripts W.H. Challen, Vol. 10, indexed by Boyd). Browse registers at Ancestry 1539–1812. Some entries on IGI. Licences held by College of Arms 1687–1837.
- St Pancras's. Original registers LMA 1660–1754; indexed in Boyd; transcripts 1660–1754 W.H. Challen, Vol. 22; browse at Ancestry.

Appendix 5

SUMMARY LIST OF RECORDS AT TOWER HAMLETS LOCAL HISTORY LIBRARY AND ARCHIVES

See also TNA's Access to Archives website at: www.nationalarchives. gov.uk/a2a.

- Census. Microfilm copies of 1841–1911 and MS volumes of 1821 and 1831 for Poplar, with name indexes.
- Parishes. Church registers are deposited at LMA; THLHLA has copies of some. It also holds a variety of other parish and local authority records: Poplar from 1705–1902, Bromley 1650–1928, Metropolitan Borough of Bethnal Green 1877–1965, Spitalfields 1627–1875, Holy Trinity Minories 1687–1895, Limehouse Board of Works 1855–1901, St Matthew's Bethnal Green 1722–1900, Hamlet of MEOT 1697–1900, Norton Folgate 1654–1900, Old Artillery Ground 1729–1885, Poplar Board of Works 1855–1900, Metropolitan Borough of Poplar 1894–1966, Hamlet of Ratcliff 1762–1921, St Anne's Limehouse, 1724–1880, St Botolph's Aldgate 1826–1900, St Dunstan's Stepney 1730–1805 (2 items only; a great deal at LMA), St George-in-the-East 1717–1905 (497 items), St John's at Wapping 1781–1922, Precinct of St Katharine's by the Tower 1844–59, Metropolitan Borough of Stepney 1900–71, St Mary's Stratford Bow 1719–1961 (Bow Apprenticeship register for 1803 is indexed at Tower Hamlets Archives online, see websites), St Mary's Whitechapel 1771–1961, St Paul's Shadwell 1811–1900, Whitechapel Board of Works 1855–1901.

- Poor relief. For records relating to this, see pp. 126–38. For a description of the parish material go to: www.nationalarchives. gov.uk/a2a.
- Chapel registers. Listed in Appendix 2.
- School records. Ben Jonson School, Stepney 1945–78 (earlier records at LMA), Bonner Primary School, Bethnal Green 1876–1969, Central Foundation Girls 1800–1984, George Green School, Poplar 1883–1976, Guardian Angels Roman Catholic School, Mile End 1874–1992, Hamlet of Ratcliff (Greencoat School) 1710–1970, MEOT Charity School (minute books) 1771–1809, Middlesex Society's Charity School, St George-in-the-East (minutes) 1806–19, Olga Primary School, Bethnal Green c. 1875–1982, Poplar and Blackwall National School 1804–31, St Matthias's Church of England School, Poplar 1879–1983, St Matthew's National School, Bethnal Green 1852–79.
- International Genealogical Index (IGI).
- London Commercial Directories. Microfilm copies of Guildhall Library's collection 1667–1888. Original directories 1790–1980s. Small local directories for Bow, Stratford, Mile End Road, Poplar, Limehouse and Stepney 1866, for Bow, Bromley and Old Ford 1867, for Hackney, including part of Bethnal Green, 1872 and 1888.
- Electoral registers. Parliamentary Borough of Tower Hamlets 1901–15 (Stepney and Poplar, not Bethnal Green), Bethnal Green Metropolitan Borough 1901–64, Poplar Metropolitan Borough, Stepney Metropolitan Borough 1918–64, London Borough of Tower Hamlets 1965–present.
- Rate book, land tax books etc. Rate books for Poplar, Bromley, Bow and Bethnal Green from the eighteenth century (gaps); very few for Stepney area. For online indexes to rate books for Bow 1820, Limehouse 1767, Spitalfields 1700, Poor Rate Bromley 1821 go to: www.ideastore.co.uk/en/containers/universal/arch (Tower Hamlets Archives online), EoLFHS CD-ROMs include: Tower Hamlet Rate Books (Vol. 1), Bethnal Green Church Rates 1743, Bethnal Green Rate 1850–1, Bow Poor Rate 1837, Bow Rate April 1851, Bromley Church Rate June 1861, Bromley Land Tax 1750, Old Artillery Ground Drainage Rate 1861, Poplar Church Rate June 1851, Shadwell Poor Rate 1725, St George-in-the-East Land Tax 1801, Wapping Watch Rate 1800, Wapping Church Rate 1875, Whitechapel Watch Rate 1800 and 1805, Settlement examinations:

Bromley 1778–91, Old Artillery Ground 1792–1826. For Land Tax records held at THLH and LMA, see pp. 106–8.

- Archive collection. This comprises about 7,000 property deeds and other miscellaneous items, indexed by name and place. It is very useful; see Access to Archives.

- Local newspapers. *Tower Hamlets Independent*, later *East London Advertiser*, 1866–present, *East London Observer* 1857–1944, *Eastern Argus* 1877–1912, *East End News* 1869–1963, *Eastern Post* 1868–1938, *Jewish Chronicle* 1841–present. Also some more recent newspapers, including some Bengali publications. Many of the newspapers are microfilm copies of those held at the British Library Newspaper Library.

- Hoppers. For some East Enders who went to Kent 'hopping', see the records of the Red House, Stepney and the Little Hoppers Hospital at Paddock Wood.

- A good collection of photographs of the area and maps. See digital collection at www.ideastore.co.uk/en/articles/information_digital_gallery.

Appendix 6

MEDIEVAL ANCESTORS – SOME SOURCES

- See p. 117 for manor court records.
- Wills from the fourteenth century. See wills and and death duties, pp. 82–9. The Commissary Court Wills (Bishop's Court) start in 1374 and the Prerogative Court of Canterbury (Archbishop's Court) in 1383. The former is a very rich source for East London; some of the testators are quite humble folk made good. City of London wills enrolled in the Court of Hustings (a City probate court, 1258–1688) can be searched at British History Online at: www.british-history. ac.uk for City men with property in the East End, as can other City records, such as the *Calendars of Letter Books*. These sources may be used for people living in Aldgate and Bishopsgate.
- *Victoria County History of Middlesex*, Vol. 11 (www.british.history. ac.uk/report.aspx?compid=22732) provides a very detailed account of major Stepney land holders, from Domesday (1086) onwards.
- www.medievalgenealogy.org.uk is a most useful website.
- Calendars of Chancery and other medieval government records held at TNA. These magnificent publications record the dealings of the Crown with individuals in various ways and are available at good reference libraries. Dip into their indexes if you are serious about searching for medieval ancestors. For a complete list of volumes available go to: www.medievalgenealogy.org.uk>public records. One of the traditional sources for tracing families back this far are the documents known as *Inquisitions post Mortem*. These tell you who a man's heir was and what property he held, but they only apply to tenants-in-chief, that is to say people who were direct

land holders from the Crown. The calendars summarise the original entries: *Calendar of Miscellaneous Inquisitions Henry III to Henry VII* (London, 1916–68), *Calendar of Inquisitions post Mortem, Henry III to Henry VI and Henry VII* (London, 1898–2004), *List of Inquisitions Post Mortem, Henry V to Richard III; Inquisitions ad quod damnum and Miscellaneous Inquisitions, Henry VII–Charles I* (List and Index Society, 1998). See M. McGuiness's 'Inquisitions post Mortem', *Amateur Historian*, Vol. vi (1963–5), 235–41.

- TNA's online catalogue. A name search of this may throw up your medieval ancestor. For a guide to which records are available in the catalogue go to: www.medievalgenealogy.org.uk>links.

Appendix 7

SELECT BIBLIOGRAPHY

East End Occupations

- GenDoc's glossary of occupations.
- Stuart Raymond, *Londoners' Occupations, A Genealogical Guide*, 2nd edn (FFHS, 2001).
- For a description of many of the different trades, see C. Booth, *Labour and Life of the People in London*, series 2 *Industry* (5 vols, Macmillan, 1903).
- Trade-union records with place of deposit are listed in John Bennett and Alistair Tough, *Trade Union and Related Records*, ed. Richard Storey (University of Warwick, 1991). See also S. Fowler, *Sources for Labour History* (PRO, 1995).
- MS diaries of Elijah Goff, coal merchant of St George-in-the-East, 1788–99, THLHLA.
- MS of R.W. Carr, sailmaker of Stepney 1857–9, THLHLA.
- From the Middles Ages brewing was a prominent East End occupation; there was a famous brewery at the Hermitage at Wapping; numerous Dutch breweries at St Katharine's and many in Bow. The best known are the Trumans's Black Eagle brewery in Spitalfields from 1669 and Charrington's vast Anchor Brewery in Mile End, from 1743. These and many others are described in *Victoria County History of Middlesex* (online at: www.british.history. ac.uk). For brewing and pubs, see S. Fowler, *Researching Brewing and Publican Ancestors* (FFHS, 2009) and LMA's information leaflet 'Records of Licensed Victuallers'. Pubs are probably best sought in directories and there may be advertisements in local papers (see pp. 100 and 104). For a very long list of East End victuallers

(inn and ale-house keepers, with their houses named) prosecuted in the Laudian purges of 1632–41, see LMA Guildhall MS 9064/18, 19 and 21. For brewers, see L. Richmond and A. Turton, *The Brewing Industry: A Guide to Historical Records* (Studies in Business Archives, 1990).

- B. Howlett, 'Records of Nurses and Nursing in the LMA', *Genealogists' Magazine*, 26 (1999). For wet nurses (children were often sent out to nurses in Stepney), see G. Clark in *Local Historian*, 19 (1989) and *Genealogists' Magazine*, 23 (1989).
- Women worked as stall holders, bar maids, prostitutes, spinners and thowsters of silk and seamstresses (at home and in sweat shops). A list of 1888 includes brush makers, button makers, cigarette makers, electric-light fitters, fur workers, India rubber-stamp machinists, magic-lantern slide makers, perfumers, portmanteau makers, spectacle makers, surgical instrument makers and tie makers (Margaret Harkness, 'Girl Labour in the City', *Justice*, 3 March 1888, cited Fishman, *East End 1888* (Five Leaves Publications, 1988)).
- A.D. Tyssen, 'The History of the Whitechapel Bell Foundry', *Transactions of the London & Middlesex Archaeological Society*, n.s. 5 (1929). Bells were made in the area from medieval times and still are. You can visit the Whitechapel Bell Foundry, but book well in advance.
- Oliver J. Leonard, 'The East London Furniture Industry', *East London Papers*, 4 (2) (1961) – nineteenth-century trade.
- D.E. Gratwick, MS history of Bow, 1925, THLHLA – for china factory workers, eighteenth century.
- E.G. Easton, *The Metropolitan Dairymen's Directory and Handbook of Reference for 1886* (Office of the Cowkeeper and Dairyman's Journal, 1886). There were many Welsh dairymen in the East End.
- *An Outline History of the Isle of Dogs* (Island History Trust, 1987). After the collapse of ship building in the 1860s a number of engineering firms were established on the Isle of Dogs. Islanders made gasholders and bridges, boilers, engine parts, tanks, valves, pipes, propellers, tubes, chains, wire ropes, sacks and tarpaulins, prams and mangles, paint, varnishes and chemicals.
- Francis Buckley, *Old London Glasshouses* (Stevens and Sons, 1915) – many names (Ratcliff).

- Howard L. Blackmore, *A Dictionary of London Gunmakers 1350–1850* (Phaidon Christie, 1986) – guns were made in Whitechapel and Aldgate from the sixteenth century.

General Books on the Old East End

- Picture books are numerous; one of the best is W.J. Fishman, *The Streets of East London* (Duckworth, 1979 and 2006).
- For the seventeenth century, see the *Diary of Samuel Pepys*.
- For the eighteenth-century Jewry, see Israel Zangwill, *The King of the Schnorrers* (1894), a novel, and Derek Morris, *Mile End Old Town, 1740–80* (London, 2002).
- For the early nineteenth century (St George-in-the-East), see T.A. Critchley and P.D. James, *The Maul and the Pear Tree: the Ratcliff Highway Murders, 1811* (Faber and Faber, 1971), a novel.
- For the 1830s–60s, refer to the works of Charles Dickens, especially *The Uncommercial Traveller* and *Our Mutual Friend* (Limehouse).
- For Stepney in the 1840s, Mrs J.H. Riddell, *The Race for Wealth* (1866), a novel.
- For the 1850s and 1860s, Henry Mayhew, *London Labour and the London Poor* (1849–61).
- For the 1880s and 1890s, Arthur Morrison, *A Child of the Jago* (1896), a novel set in Spitafields, Shoreditch and Bethnal Green; Arthur Morrison, *The Hole in the Wall* (1902), a novel set in 1890s Wapping; W.J. Fishman, *East End 1888* (Five Leaves Publications, 1988), for workhouses and the sweated industries, especially in Whitechapel.
- For Whitechapel and the Jewish East End, 1880s and 1890, Jerry White, *Rothschild Buildings, Life in an East End Tenement Block 1887–1920* (Pimlico, 2003); W.J. Fishman *East End Jewish Radicals, 1875–1914* (Duckworth, 1975); Israel Zangwill, *Children of the Ghetto* (1893); and for Jewish East End in general, Ed Glinert, *East End Chronicles* (Allen Lane, 2005).
- For Wapping, 1886–1915, Walter Jones, *Tender Grace; Wapping Letters and Diaries*, ed. Madge Darby (3 vols, History of Wapping Trust, 1991–4).
- For Whitechapel in the 1890s, innumerable books on 'Jack the Ripper' (see p. 172).
- For the interwar period, Jewish sweat shops and St George-in-the-East at this time, Willy Goldman's *East End, My Cradle* (Faber

and Faber, 1940), Grace Foakes, *My Part of the River* (Shepheard-Walwyn Publishers, 1972); Stepney, John Blake, *Memories of Old Poplar* (Stepney Books Publications, 1977 and 1982).
- For the 1950s, Jennifer Worth, *Call the Midwife* (Merton Books, 2002), for Stepney, Michael Young and Peter Willmott, *Family and Kinship in East London* (Institute of Community Studies, 1957), Bethnal Green.
- For the First and Second World Wars, R. Taylor and C. Lloyd, *The East End at War* (Sutton, 2007).

Appendix 8

ORGANISATIONS

For more details of archives and libraries, see TNA's ARCHON directory or J. Foster and J. Sheppard (eds)'s *British Archives: a Guide to Archive Resources in the United Kingdom*, 4th edn (Palgrave Macmillan, 2002).

- Anglo German Family History Society: www.agfhs.org.uk.
- Association of Genealogists and Researchers in Archives: www.agra.org.uk; Acting Secretary, AGRA, 120 North Gate, Newark on Trent, Notts NG24 1HJ.
- Bishopsgate Institute: library at 230 Bishopsgate EC2M 4QH; library@bishopsgate.org.uk.
- British and Foreign Schools Archives Centre: West London Institute of Higher Education, Borough Road, Isleworth TW7 5DU.
- British Library (BL): www.bl.uk; 96 Euston Road, London NW1 2DB.
- British Library Newspaper Library: Colindale Avenue, London NW9 5HE.
- British Telecom Archives: 268–70 High Holborn, London WC1V 7EE; 020 7440 4220; archives@bt.com. Search rooms open Tuesday and Thursday, 10 am–4 pm.
- Catholic Education Council: 42 Cromwell Road London SW7 2DJ.
- Catholic Family History Society: www.catholic-history.org.uk/cfhs; Michael Gandy, 3 Church Crescent, Whetstone, London N20 0JR.
- Catholic National Library: www.catholic-history.org.uk; St Michael's Abbey, Farnborough, Hants GU 14 7NQ; 01252 543818.
- Commonwealth War Graves Commission: www.cwgc.org; 2 Marlow Road, Maidenhead, Berks SL6 7DX; 01628 634221.

- Dr Williams's Library: www.dwlib.co.uk/visiting.html; 14 Gordon Square London WC1H OAG.
- East London History Society: www.mernick.org.uk/elhs/elhs.htm; Philip Mernick, 42 Campbell Road, Bow, London E3 4DT.
- East of London Family History Society: www.eolfhs.org; Ian Whaley, 46 Brights Avenue, Rainham, Essex RM13 9NW. Journal is *Cockney Ancestor*. The places covered are: Hackney (Clapton, Dalston, Hackney, Haggerston, Homerton, Hoxton, Kingsland, Shoreditch and Stoke Newington), Tower Hamlets, Newham, Redbridge (Barkingside, Chadwell Heath, part of Chigwell, Clayhall, Cranbrook, Fairlop, Fullwell Cross, Gants Hill Cross, Goodmayes, Hainault, Ilford, Little Heath, Newbury Park, Redbridge, Seven Kings, Snaresbrook, South Woodford, Woodford Bridge and Woodford Green), Barking and Dagenham (Barking, Becontree, part of Chadwell Heath, Dagenham Village, Rush Green and Upney), Havering (Chadwell Heath, Collier Row, Corbets Tey, Cranham, Elm Park, Emerson Park, Gidea Park, Havering-atte-Bower, Harold Hill, Harold Wood, Hornchurch, Rainham, Romford, Upminster and Wennington).
- Church of England Record Centre: 15 Galleywall Road SE16 3PB; 020 7898 1030; archive@c-of-e.org.uk. Book, open Monday–Friday, 10 am–5 pm.
- College of Arms: www.college-of-arms.gov.uk; Queen Victoria Street EC4V BT.
- Docklands History Group: www.docklandshistorygroup.org.uk; info@ docklandshistorygroup.org.uk.
- Friends House: www.quaker.org.uk/library; 173–7 Euston Road NW1 2BJ; 020 7663 1135. Archives of the Religious Society of Friends (Quakers). Library open Tuesday–Friday, 10 am–5 pm.
- General Register Office GRO: www.gro/gov.uk/gro/certificates; Certificate Section, PO Box 2, Southport PR8 2JD; 0845 6037788.
- Guildhall Library: Aldermanbury, London EC2V 7HH; guildhall.library@cityoflondon.gov.uk. The manuscripts formerly held at the Guildhall have almost all been transferred to LMA q.v. For more information go to: http://.history.ac.uk/gh.
- Hackney Archives Department: 43 de Beauvoir Road, London N1 5SQ; 020 7241 2886; archives@hackney.gov.uk.
- House of Lords Record Office: see the Parliamentary Archives.
- Huguenot Society of Great Britain and Ireland: www.huguenotsociety.org.uk; Hon. Sec., PO Box 3067, Warlingham CR6 0AN;

232

library: Librarian, the Huguenot Library, University College, Gower Street, London WC1E 6BT; 020 7679 5199.

- Institute of Heraldic and Genealogical Studies (IHGS): www.ihgs.ac.uk; 79–82 Northgate, Canterbury, Kent CT1 1BA.
- Jewish Genealogical Society: www.jgsgb.org.uk; Membership Secretary PO Box 2508, Maidenhead SL6 8WS; membership@gsgb.org.uk; general enquiries: enquiries@jgsgb.org.uk.
- Jewish Historical Society: 33 Seymour Place, London W1H 5AP; info@jhse.org.
- Lambeth Palace Library: Londn SE1 7JU.
- London Metropolitan Archive (LMA) (now holding most former Guildhall records and those of the former Corporation of London Record Office): www.cityoflondon.gov.uk/lma; 40 Northampton Road, Clerkenwell, London EC1R 0HB. The catalogue and a very useful series of information leaflets may be searched online. Many of the records you will need are at LMA and, as all the censuses may be searched here via Ancestry and Findmypast, as well as other records online, much of your research can be done here. NB A programme of digitising the main series of genealogical records started in 2009; the following are becoming available at Ancestry.co.uk: parish records 1530s to twentieth century (registers 1813–1906 made available August 2009); parish Poor Law documents post-1834; school admission registers to 1911. Further records will be digitised in due course, including Commissary Court wills. An index to all the main family history sources is in an 'island' labelled 'London Generations'. In the 'island' there are a series of binders arranged by borough, and then by parish according to the dedication. Thus, Tower Hamlets has a total of five catalogues covering: Board of Guardians, bishops' transcripts and Non-conformist records, two vols of parish records by dedication (starting with All Hallows', Devons Road), LCC and ILEA school-admission registers. Most of the material is on film and you help yourself. On the computer terminals you can consult the LMA online CD catalogue (also available at Guildhall and other London libraries). This has: *Dictionary of National Biography*, new index to London Consistory Court wills (a few East Enders), *Family History Resources at Guildhall and LMA*, *London Will Index 'A'–'E'* (18,000 entries, all pre-1858 courts except PCC; for East Enders this includes: London Commissary Court 1750–1858, Royal Peculiar of St Katharine's 1750–80, Consistory Court 1750–1858, of limited use

as it does not supply the parishes of the testators), *Times Index* 1906–80, *Palmers' Times Index* 1790–1905. You will need a ticket to see original material, so don't forget to bring some form of identity. To find their excellent information leaflets go to the website and click on 'collections information' and scroll down to 'information leaflets'. The catalogue and *London Generations* may also be searched online. A research service is offered.

- London Metropolitan University: www.londonmet.ac.uk, Womens' Library is at 25 Old Castle Street E1 7NT.
- Ministry of Defence Army Personnel Centre: Historic Disclosures, Mailpoint 400, Kentigern House, 65 Brown Street, Glasgow G2 8EX; 01412 242023; apc_historical_disclosures_@btconnect.com.
- Museum in Docklands: No. 1 Warehouse, West India Quay, London E14 4AL; fcormack@museumoflondon.org.uk.
- Museum of Immigration: 19 Princelet Street, London E1 6QH; 020 7247 5352.
- Museum of Jewish Life: The Sternberg Centre, 80 East End Road, London N3 2SY; enquiries@jewishmuseum.org.uk.
- Newham Archives and Local Studies Library: www.newham.gov. uk/EntertainmentAndLeisure/; 3 The Grove, Stratford, London E15 1EL; archiveslocalstudies@newham.gov.uk.
- Parliamentary Archives: www.parliament.uk/publications/arch; Houses of Parliament SW1A OPW.
- Police History Society: 64 Nore Marsh Road, Wootton Bassett, Wiltshire SN4 8BH; steve.bridge@ukgateway.net.
- Principal Registry of the Family Division (for wills and divorces): Decree Absolute Section or Probate Division, First Avenue House, 42–9 High Holborn WC1V 6NP; 020 7936 7000.
- Quaker Family History Society: www.qfhs.co.uk. Journal *Quaker Connections*. See also Friends House.
- Royal London Hospital Archive Centre: 9 Prescot Street, London E1 8PR; jonathan.evans@bartsandthelondon.nhs.uk.
- Salvation Army International Heritage Centre: www2.salvation army.org.uk; William Booth College, Denmark Hill SE5 8BQ; 020 7326 7800; heritage@salvationarmy.org.uk. Personal researchers by appointment Tuesday, Wednesday and Thursday.
- Thames Police Museum: Wapping Police Station, Wapping High Street, Wapping, London E1W 2NE. Write enclosing a stamped self-addressed envelope.

- The National Archives (TNA): www.nationarchives.gov.uk; Ruskin Avenue, Kew, London TW9 4DU; 020 8876 3444. Closed Mondays, open until 7 pm Tuesday and Thursday. TNA hold government records from the eleventh century. There are huge sources at Kew to be tapped, notably service and tax records, some of which are available online, as noted in the text. There is an excellent book shop with a good collection of works on family history. Amanda Bevan's *Tracing your Ancestors in the National Archives* (TNA, 2006) covers virtually everything that may be of use to you. The catalogue may be searched online. Probably more useful, at least at the outset of your research, are the online research guides. Before you go to Kew, download the appropriate research guide (as indicated in the text) from the website, click on records, then in-depth research guides. You can research Ancestry there. You need a reader's ticket to consult original records so make sure you have some ID. The catalogue is not easy to use, but the staff are friendly and helpful.
- Tower Hamlets Local History Library and Archives: www.ideast-ore.co.uk; 277 Bancroft Road, London E1 4DQ; 020 7364 1290; localhistory@towerhamlets.gov.uk. See website for opening times. Best for local knowledge and advice; a wonderful card index of deeds and other miscellanea, newspapers and photographs. THLHLA records are catalogued online at Access to Archives (A2A). See Appendix 5 for summary list of holdings and Appendix 3 for lists of Nonconformist chapel registers.
- Tower Hamlets Register Office: Bromley Public Hall, Bow Road, London E3 3AA; 020 7364 7880 .
- United Synagogue, Beth Din: 735 High Road, North Finchley, London N12 0US.
- Watermen's and Lightermen's Company: www.watermenshall.org; Watermen's Hall, 16–18 St Mary-at-Hill, London EC3 8EF; 020 7283 2373.
- Westminster Diocesan Archives (WDA): 16A Abingdon Road, Kensington W8 6AF.
- Whitechapel Bell Foundry: www.whitechapelbellfoundry.co.uk; 32/4 Whitechapel Road, London E1 1DY; 020 7247 2599.

INDEX

References to illustrations are given in italic.